# Famous Wisconsin Mystics

### Interviews with Practitioners of the Intuitive and Psychic Arts

*Hannah Heidi Levy*

## Hannah Heidi Levy

### Badger Books Inc.
### Oregon, WI

ISBN 1-878569-91-0

Badger Books Inc.
P.O. Box 192
Oregon, WI 53575
Toll-free phone: (800) 928-2372
Fax: (608) 835-3638
Email: books@badgerbooks.com
Web site: www.badgerbooks.com

THIS BOOK IS DEDICATED TO

My mother
JOY CONSTANCE CLARK HASSLINGER GRIMM
Who has a touch of Irish magic,

And to my father
KURT GRIMM
Who loved great music.
He was a scientific thinker.

# Contents

## Resources

# Acknowledgments

I wish to thank the many people who were involved in *Famous Wisconsin Mystics* and who made it possible for me to continue in this project with their encouragement, advice, understanding, interest, and succinct editing. This has not been a one-person journey.

Also, Craig S. Bell for his invaluable editing, advice, and writing the Foreword; publisher Marv Balousek and his staff at Badger Books, Inc.; authors Marshall Cook, Michael Norman, and Jerry Apps for their kind endorsements; friend Mary Juckem for reminding me to take a break and join her on a walk; friends R. Steeno for k.b. and G.R. for being a soul buddy for decades, and A.S. for encouragement; my son Michael Clark for his valuable opinions on writing; my son E. Nicholas for his intrepid sense of adventure; my co-workers at the VA Hospital in Madison, Wisconsin, for tolerating my bouts of eccentricity in writing this book; and the mystical people interviewed in these pages for their interest in this project.

# Foreword

*Famous Wisconsin Mystics* is more than simply a practical tool for readers seeking to become acquainted with successful Wisconsin practitioners, and the methods they use, in the pursuit of what Ms. Levy terms the intuitive and psychic arts — the arts employed to detect hidden factors in an individual's life, including past and future events. Furthermore, the book's content is interesting and stimulating even to those, like myself, who reside far beyond the borders of the Badger State. Anyone with an interest or just a curiosity about the intuitive and psychic arts will find this to be a revealing and captivating work.

In my view, it is also a unique work, for after conducting research and interviews the author does not succumb to imposing her take on the topics discussed. She merely formulates a series of astute questions, to then step aside and let the experts do the talking. One of the interesting things they reveal is who they are, their temperament. They are not eccentrics or con artists. They come across as very rational people who have come to see firsthand that there is much more to life than what meets the eye, or that which can be explained by pure reason. Beyond which they reveal themselves to possess wisdom, integrity, and compassion, and notably in light of their abilities, humility. They are also a tolerant group: tolerant of the skeptic and of those who simply view the world through a different lense.

As one would expect, theirs is a mystical worldview. Events are not isolated nor the product of mere chance, or probability. Every thing and every occurrence is interwoven in one grand tapestry, and all is infused with the Divine. As Ms. Levy points out, in their recognition of the interconnection between the myriad facets of our world they are no longer at strong odds with science. Scientists have increasingly come to perceive that even subatomic events result in far reaching albeit subtle changes in the whole fabric of reality.

The methods these practitioners of the mystical arts employ to connect with the unseen ground of reality, seeking specific insights, are varied and surprisingly numerous. One may rely on palm reading, while for another it is the reading of tarot cards. A third illustrates that graphology, the study of handwriting, can reveal more than most of us could have imagined. The recent and relatively high-tech use of aura photography that is employed by some, borders on a scientific technique for ascertaining esoteric information. Of course, there is also the use of photographs or objects, such as a piece of jewelry, to pick up vibrations that stimulate spontaneous insights of specific information. Or for some practitioners, simply tuning into the subject sitting before them may provide the same result. Some are experts in numerology, while for others it is astrology, which has been facilitated in recent years by some excellent computer programs. Native Americans employ the shamanism that has long been a tradition for their people. Dowsing, as well as hypnotherapy and past life regression are other methods. And the list goes on. The bottom line is that when employed by the right individuals all these methods provide verifiable results, results which may astound us.

For me the recognition that is reinforced by these numerous and varied means of accessing the unknown is one that relates to the powerful and unfathomable depth of creation, and of our individual lives. If so many different methods can be successfully employed to tap the vast reservoir of Supreme Consciousness, which records and lies hidden beneath and within all phenomena, that serves to vitalize It, and bring It within the periphery of our vision. Vision normally restricted by the press of mundane considerations is induced to attempt to peer within the deep, dark, and mysterious forest of creation, rather than just focus on the few trees before us that we must navigate around.

In no small measure the success of this book is the product of the questions asked, which are not just relative to the mystical arts practiced by the interviewees. For instance, they are asked how major world events such as 9-11 affect them, and about their interpretation of that tragic day's significance, the latter evoking some insightful and unexpected responses. In response to the question of how they relate to the skeptic, we find that they recommend possessing a healthy skepticism. Unlike those who suffer from what scientist Dr. Gary Schwartz terms skeptimania - not accepting any data that contrasts with a preconceived mind set - the skeptic's demand for hard evidence is viewed as desirable, and one which they themselves possess. Thus it is not surprising that their responses to inquiries about psychic hot lines evince disapproval and wariness. Refreshingly, Ms. Levy also solicits their take on children who are gifted, or curious about the mystical arts. Their feedback on that subject is equally inspiring. We find that a common thread among them is the desire to help people, and helping them to find what one terms "their true path." Are dreams significant? They can be a valuable resource. What about religion and spirituality? As a rule the dogma of religion is not their bag, but spirituality is their core.

They are also asked about the significance of coincidence and synchronicity, a topic about which I have an abiding interest. Unfortunately, even among this relatively enlightened group there is still some confusion between the two terms. They embrace synchronicity, which is revealed to be a significant factor for some of them in the paths they have taken. But some make the same mistake as others in the general population, by interpreting coincidence to signifying apparently related events between which there is no real connection. Those might say that there is no such thing as coincidence. What they intend to convey is the same as those who state that all coincidences are meaningful, which is that there are no accidents. In fact, by definition coincidences are meaningful. One definition of coincidence is "a surprising concurrence of events, perceived as meaningfully related, with no apparent causal connection." Carl Jung defined synchronicity as a meaningful coincidence that does not conform to the laws of cause and effect. Essentially, he just restated the definition of coincidence. They are one and the same.

Perhaps the reason Jung coined the term synchronicity, to identify those coincidences that he could convincingly illustrate were meaningful, was that in his time as a scientist he could not very well assert that all coincidences were meaningful. But he could provide hard evidence that at least some of them were, and label them synchronicities. All bonafide coincidences are meaningful, and can be valuable tools for gaining a greater awareness of our appropriate roles in life.

Not withstanding such occasional minor misunderstandings about my pet coincidences, the wisdom of the interviewees is impressive, provocative, and profitable for us to contemplate. This is one of those books where when you arrive at the final page you'll be disappointed the pages don't continue. But still, perhaps the pages of your life will begin to benefit from what it offers.

**— Craig S. Bell**

(Craig S. Bell is the author of *Comprehending Coincidence — Synchronicity and Personal Transformation.*)

# Prologue

It is the end of December 2001. Writing a book is definitely not on my list of things to do. I have a difficult time with lists anyway and am more adept at procrastination and tangential conversation—just throw a colorful word at me and we'll go on a journey to God Knows Where. Best friends extend me great patience. So how did this book, consisting of interviews with 27 individuals practicing mystical and psychic arts come about? Truthfully, I'm not sure I can take credit for the idea. I thought perhaps this was one of those impulsive frenzied moments, but that didn't fit. I was only minding my own business. *Suddenly and robustly,* it was as if somebody with a very good aim tossed a Wisconsin snowball at me. The idea was "just there," the title vaguely popped into place, and a sketchy outline followed along like a bouncing puppy. But I wasn't convinced. It took a series of uncanny coincidences to transform this book idea into a mission.

A couple of days after the first idea struck me, on New Year's Day, January 1, 2002; I was weeding a file drawer in my disorganized office. In an obscure file folder labeled "Miscellaneous," I ran across notes from a psychic reading done for me in 1998 or 1999 by Kathleen Schneider of Middleton, Wisconsin. In the margin of the paper I had jotted down a curious and forgotten notation proclaiming I would be "writing a book in the year 2002 with a number of people involved, but I will have the final say." At this point, I thought back to the peculiar occurrence that happened to me two days before with the thoughts popping in as they did. Okay, so maybe this notation from a few years ago was snowball number two, launched by who knows what.

I thought about the coincidence but continued to clean—still on a mundane undertaking to relieve the file drawer of excess baggage. Taking a break, I went to the kitchen to retrieve a Diet Coke. On my way back to the office, with my mind on the notes from the psychic reading, I bumped into an end table with a stack of papers on it. A lone slip of paper floated to the floor. I examined the paper, and saw that it was a receipt for an interesting book purchased in November 2001, and probably added to one of my "I'll read this later piles." I now recall how the book caught my eye as I browsed the store aisles, and I remember the clerk even commenting on the title when I checked out. Listed on the receipt was *Comprehending Coincidence* by Craig S. Bell. Now I am *really* starting to think about what I perceive to be *connections*...and counting the snowballs.

Perhaps I should read *Comprehending Coincidence* sooner, rather than later, is the thought that occurs to me. But where did I put the elusive book? I return to my office to explore uncharted territory in search of *Coincidence*. This could take hours—I'm not exaggerating. Surprisingly and instantly, however, I find the book residing beneath a *blank notebook* directly above the file drawer. The two paired up like the sun and the moon in an eclipse. It's *my* turn to fire the snowball. *Coincidence* and, of all things, a blank notebook, are staring at me! I don't need any more clues. My quest to bring *Famous Wisconsin Mystics* into existence begins.

Other than the four coincidental events that happened to me in a space of a few days, there are some underlying reasons why I am writing this book. This area of interest began when I was about six or seven years old. My mom had a strange deck of cards that were unlike her usual bridge decks. She may have forgotten about the cards by now, but they are still in the living room cabinet where the "good dishes" are stored. The odd cards had colorful and mysterious figures on them that were surrounded by curious symbols. The cards fascinated me, as they probably would many children, and I wondered what kind of card game is this! It wasn't like a children's card game such as "old maid" or "go fish" that I was familiar with, and I don't recall asking my mom about the cards. Nevertheless, the deck was alluring to me, so I made up my own game that afforded me familiarity with the pictured characters. I assigned stories to each of the cards. Then I'd pull a few out of the deck, and make up more complex stories using a combination of cards. Unknowingly, I was basically using these as Tarot cards, which in reality, is what they were…as I was to discover later….

Twice a year, my mother and my grandmother visited Mavis and Violet, two sisters who lived in the big white house up the road. They were known as the "fortune telling ladies." Their house was on a hill near a little inlet on Moose Lake where it was fun to catch frogs (and let them go) and eat the watercress that grew along the shoreline. But during part of the visit, instead of catching frogs, I'd watch the two fortune tellers skillfully throw cards and I'd listen to what they were saying—their predictions and revelations—all this coming from those cards, which were similar to the ones my mother owned.

I recall that one of the predictions for my grandmother was that she would be coming into a large sum of money within a month or two. The ladies at the table, including Violet and Mavis, were a little perplexed at this one. How exactly was that to come about? I remember my grandma saying, "Well, it would have to fall out of the sky!" Sure enough, about a month later, my grandmother received news of an unexpected inheritance of $3000, which was a large sum of money in those days. *The message came by airmail.* That was rather a revelation, and I began to look at the cards in a different light — cards that could be "connected" to things — past, present, future. This was what probably stimulated my interest in the occult (meaning "hidden"). Cards were a doorway for me.

As a child, I encountered other things "out of the ordinary," that occurred on visits to my grandparent's home. Almost every day in the summer when it was nice to be on the lake and explore the woods and the apple orchard, I spent time at their home. They lived within walking distance. The house had been part of a summer resort popular in the 1920's. The place attracted people from Chicago who came up to Wisconsin by train to stay a few days. My brother, Jack, has talked about the "gangsters" that were a part of the tourist crowd. The house had eight bedrooms on the second story, and above that was a rather creepy narrow staircase with cracking yellow plaster that was a passageway to an attic without electricity. I had repeated nightmares about the staircase.

Strange things happened in the house. For example, the glass fireplace doors had to be replaced three times because of inexplicable breakage. Sometimes the house would be empty at times during the day, and then upon return it was common for us to see the thermostat had been shoved up 20 degrees. I remember seeing a woman once with a long silky maroon red dress that appeared to be a Victorian style, standing in front of the doorway to the attic. Lauren, a friend of the family, saw an elderly man fade into the wall that lead to the hallway between the upstairs and the front porch. The incident frightened her immensely. There were bedroom doors that were snuggly shut, only to be open a few minutes later. Curtains would blow in the open windows even when the air was perfectly still. We heard footsteps on the creaking stairs that lead to the second story, and this was actually a common occurrence. My sister, Connie, feared the night and avoided the house. My brother Clark, would be inexplicably locked on the front porch by a door that could only be locked from the outside. The same very heavy door that lead to the porch, but was located in a hallway, would slam shut with out cause.

Each individual bedroom in that house had a very distinct ambience about it, so much so, that there were certain bedrooms and places I would feel okay in, and in others, I would feel absolute dread. I can still feel it now, as I write about it. These feelings would never vary from one day to the next. Always, I'd get the same feeling at the same particular places in the house. One thing I am adamantly certain about is that these were very real, strong, and unexplainable feelings or sensations I was having probably since about the age of three or four.

These paranormal occurrences, coupled with my own inclination, lead me to sense that there were other aspects of reality and different dimensions than what I learned about in school and from my everyday world. I began to search for an explanation. When I was old enough to ride a bike and travel the back roads to Oconomowoc, a small neighboring city that had a library, I started reading about mystical events and psychic experiences. Fictional and nonfiction ghost stories mixed in well with the adventurous *Doctor Dolittle* books and the *Nancy Drew* mysteries. To this day, I continue to read about the unexplainable, and recall a childhood where sometimes The Twilight Zone was a little too close.

I occasionally seek a reading from people who practice in the arts of mystery, and in many respects find these readings to be accurate. Besides the issue of accuracy, there is the component of helpfulness that I feel coming across to me in the form of suggestions or observations. For example, I might be advised to think about specific things I may have been avoiding or not looking at closely enough, or the reader may provide me with a confirmation of something that arose from my own intuition. *Famous Wisconsin Mystics* is my invitation for you to explore some of the questions that remained in my mind after many years of interest in the topic. To answer my questions, interviews recorded in the words of the practitioners, seemed to be a logical route to take. I suspect their responses may open hidden doors for you as well.

# The Interviews

# Paul Hutto

Paul Hutto has been a gifted intuitive reader for many years. He is involved in numerous events and fairs throughout Wisconsin. His clients come from several areas in the United States and around the world. Paul has been a frequent, popular, and articulate guest on Madison radio stations. He is a Certified Hypnotherapist through the National Guild of Hypnotherapy. Paul's services include private appointments and parties, lectures, workshops, and work events. He lives in Janesville, Wisconsin, with his family.

**Contact Information**
Paul Hutto
1910 Liberty Lane
Janesville, WI  53545
**Phone:** 608-758-4606
**E-mail:** *plhutto@tds.net*

**What mystical arts are you practicing today?**

A reading is a mixture. I rely on intuition, clairvoyance, clairsentience, and psychometry. For my own use, I occasionally use Tarot cards. During readings, I experience an overwhelming "knowing" or vision. Words and phrases come into my head that I know are not my own. It is language that is much more familiar to the client. It contains information that is not meant for me to have or to keep.

**Mystic defined?**

A mystic, in my view, is a person who seeks the unknown. An explorer! Some people may add the stereotype of a "dark side" to it—it's not. Mysticism is esoteric knowledge and diving into the depths. More than anything else, mysticism is a search of the unknown.

**Discuss the development of your abilities.**

Things were happening to me all through my childhood. I wanted to sleep with the light on in the room or with someone present in the room. I was raised in a strict Roman Catholic household, and much of what I saw in visions was brushed under the rug. During my late teens I was incredibly drawn to books on haunting and the unknown. In my 20's I had visions of world disasters, major plane crashes, and the Amtrak accident where people perished in the swamp. I had the vision of the Amtrak incident four days before it happened. I thought I was depressed or distressed at the time, and frankly, I feared I was going crazy. At the time, I decided to consult a woman in Madison and was able to get an idea about what was happening to me. After that, I started practicing prayer, meditation, and taking quiet time. Since then my skills have strengthened.

Meditation is *absolutely* a key. I put a lot of emphasis on ritual — prayer work, visualization of running light through charkas, aura fieldwork, listening to what I hear, and paying attention to what I see. I fine-tune my abilities by taking *time*. If I keep my ego out of it, I maintain alertness. As we mature, I believe we can become clear channels because our energies are higher and brighter. They develop similar to a child learning to walk — crawl, teeter-totter, walk, and then run.

I have so many people ask me about publications that talk about developing one's psychic capabilities—this is wishful thinking. Some people can do this; some cannot. It is a talent and a gift. Certain people are great at playing the piano. There are those who study the technical skills for years and play well, and others just sit down and play without being able to read music. Me? I can't play a note or hold a tune. Math is an intellectual high horse for some, and for others it is a difficult challenge. Everybody has unique talents and this is why we are here. Abilities and talents help people get through their lessons.

Is there such an entity as karma? I definitely believe in karma. Having ability as a medium, my communication with those on the other side is sometimes easier than with those on this side! I have to laugh about it. But what information I get from them tells me there is definitely a reason why each of us as individuals is here. Karma is deep and it sounds like a punishment, but it is not. I don't believe we can complete our lessons in one lifetime.

### Are you studying other areas?

I have strong pulls to other cultures and have been told by other psychics that I seem to be collecting things I had in previous lifetimes. Look around the room we are sitting in and notice the obvious eclectic mix.

### Yes, I see purposeful pack rat-itis.

My studies include Wicca, Shamanism, Oriental culture, Native American, and the Jewish Kabbalah. I have tried to learn some of the Hindu belief system, but it is complicated, and I don't care to get pulled into it. Ministers, business people, the lady next door, teenagers, and people from all walks of life are my clients. I want to be able to relate to everybody so I study what I can.

### Do you find there is a common thread amongst practitioners?

For the true practitioner, it is a desire to help. It's as simple as that.

### Do you have connection to a structured religion?

I am a Roman Catholic, but there are doctrines in the church that are troublesome to me. A lot of ancient original ritual is contained in the Catholic Church. People don't realize this, but ritual has great power. Some of the other churches have rituals, but they are watered-down versions. Much of the Catholic ritual is about as close to ritual magic as it can get. Do all of the priests know what's going on? I doubt it. Some just go through the motions. Many of the great readers, such as Sylvia Browne and James Van Praagh, are Catholics.

When I do a reading, I keep a part of my body crossed, usually my legs. The original Christians did the same thing by crossing their arms and putting their hands on their shoulders while praying. Native Americans have crossing rituals. We see Egyptian mummies and burials in this position. I don't know why, but it is a form of protection. Most people meditate with palms up. The right palm is a receiver of energy and the left is a transmitter. Again, this is ritualistic.

The Catholic Church pays attention to saints and angels, while many churches do not. Years ago, I had an incredible angel experience. I had moved in with my grandparents and was financially strapped and recently divorced. I own a little red Bible that was given to me in elementary school. It is always with me. Part of me was urging myself to read a quote every morning. I thought it would help in raising my energy level and outlook.

One night I hit a low point, and I said, "I want to know if there is something more than this." As I drifted off to sleep, I felt someone holding my hand. I didn't know if I was dreaming or just dozing off. I opened my eyes and there was a most beautiful woman with auburn hair and crystal blue eyes! She vanished and I freaked out. But at the same time I found an amazing calm that is impossible to describe. At that point, I knew everything was going to be okay—really okay. I woke up the next day and was actually excited. I opened up the red Bible and the verse that popped out was "In times of need and trouble, I will send thee angels. I will take thy right hand and comfort thee." The hair on the back of my arms and neck just stood up.

I know the angels are out there and I know they come when they are needed. I'll probably never have another experience like that again. It doesn't matter; I've got my proof. It was a very quick experience.

### What is your view on the skeptic?

I've dealt with skeptics in different ways. Sometimes I tread lightly and joke a little. For the strongly skeptical, I have been compelled to throw specific information their way. It is not my intention to come across as brash or harsh. If they are not accepting, that's okay. They are not intended to be at this point of acceptance. I am not here to condone or judge. It's not worth putting a lot of energy into condemnation by a skeptic. Most people know there are things going on in their lives. Often times they are searching for help, but they don't know what kind of help. I have never worked with anybody that I haven't been able to do a reading for. I had an interesting reading with a woman once and everything seemed "backwards." Later I found out that she suffers from bipolar disorder. We were definitely at one of the poles.

### Do people put up walls?

Yes, that happens when the client is afraid to hear what I have to say. The person thinks about gloom and doom, but the only information that I get coming through is whatever that person is supposed to hear or know. I have no control over that. Skeptics are probably people who need help the most. I will never turn them away.

### Is there anything unique about practicing in Wisconsin?

Oh, yes! Definitely, Wisconsin is a Mecca hot spot for this. I have not seen as many psychics, healers, and intuitive practitioners as there are in Wisconsin. It just blows my mind. Illinois and Minnesota are concentrated too. I love working around Madison. Out of all the cities, it has the most diversity. In Milwaukee, the people are a little more reserved. The Green Bay folks really like to invite me into their homes, and that's great. The South and the Southwest, even Sedona, Arizona, are not as intense.

### Do world events affect your abilities?

The events have no effect on my abilities. There are certain times of the month or of the year that are predominant. Currently, I am seeing April, parts of July and the end of February coming up in people's readings. September and October were key months for many people. I had a feeling there would be something happening in the east, but that was all (referring to September 11, 2001). Many times, I will check with an astrologer on this. There are events happening astrologically that will affect large groups of people as a whole.

### When you are out and about, do you have an on-off switch?

Yes, I have a switch. The only time it will kick in is if I or someone else is in danger. If I did not have control of this, I'd burn out by the time I got home. In my younger years, I didn't know how to turn off the light. Time and practice helped me shut down.

### Are dreams significant?

Dreams are how I really started. Clairaudience entered into my teenage years, and in my 20's dreams were my first channel. They were not normal images or symbols. I was having dreams of world events, and within a few days, the event would come about. Now I'm back into dreams with more symbolism.

### How do messages come to you — voices, feelings, visual symbols?

I call it Paul's mishmash. In other words, all apply. It has happened to me that before a person has the chance to ask a question, I will have already blurted out the answer. Usually what I hear is literal with out much symbolism. I had a reading a couple of days ago where a woman's husband was stuck with a layoff at work, and I kept getting the color green and a place near here where her husband would be working. Instead of the color green that I was seeing, I was also feeling that the name was "Green," and that turned out to be the case. This made sense to her.

**Do you have a belief in reincarnation?**

I don't know if I want to come back here or not, but I'll probably be saying I missed a few things the last time around. I can't dismiss that we come back. I have experienced too many communications and messages to deny it. I have felt it around people; I've seen it around people. A client may come to me and say, "I was born in Milton, Wisconsin, but for some ungodly reason I can't get Japan or China out of my head." What's that all about? A friend of mine said that no matter how much we question, our brain is not able to process the immense amount of information that is available.

On some level, I think we are all part of God, or whatever name you wish to give a Creator. I like to think that God threw part of himself into a bucket, and many small drops spewed out. We are those drops and fragments that keep developing. There are people who are so wise, that one knows they have lived many lifetimes. On the other hand, quite a few new kids on the block don't have a clue.

**Are there any specific readings you'd like to discuss?**

I just love this one. A client from Milwaukee came to me and a lot of facts and figures were popping into my head. For her it was exciting. Sometimes I get into emotional things, but for her it was facts and figures, data. I said to her, "You have a little boy on the other side who wants in. He wants you to be his mother. He's picked you." I dropped it, but the image of the boy would not leave me alone. I said to her, "This kid really wants in."

The woman became upset with me and said, "I am not having any more kids. There are just no more."

I said to her, "It looks to me like you don't have a choice." The woman was not belligerent, but she was certainly not pleased with the prospect of having a baby. I became upset and my feelings were hurt, but I let it pass.

She came to see me a year and a half later, and in her arms was a beautiful baby boy. The first thing she said to me was, "Paul, am I done? Please tell me I'm done!"

Children pick their parents, financial situations, countries, and so on that will suit them best to the task of why they are entering this life again. Kids pick one parent over the other. It's okay to have favorites.

In another case, I had an upset 19-year-old woman come in for a reading. I saw the image of a barefoot man standing next to her. He was telling me that he liked to go fishing. I found out this man did not wear shoes unless he had to go into a store or public place that required it. I don't get many images of bare feet, and I almost questioned myself about it, but the meaning was clear to the client.

I have seen possibilities of car wrecks within one to two weeks. I told one of my clients to be on the lookout for a red pickup truck coming from the right side at dusk. Usually when I hear information like this, the guides don't give me a time frame, so I look at it as up to three months. The client called me up two weeks after the reading and said he was so glad he listened. A red pickup truck from out of nowhere blew right through a stop sign. He said that had he not been on alert, the car would have been sliced in half. I have had many readings like that.

### Have you worked on any police or investigative cases?

I have not done much of that. Families approach me if they have a missing person they're trying to find. A woman at one of the psychic fairs asked about a missing relative. I visualized a man with a tank top tee shirt and tattoos. He was holding a beer in one hand and I knew what brand of cigarettes he smoked. He either had an association with the railroad or he lived near the railroad and his name began with an "R." Immediately the woman knew the man's name was Roger. I told her that he had the information she was looking for, but that he probably did not commit any crime. If any law enforcement people approach me, I would be more than happy to assist them at any time.

### What do your family or friends think about your abilities?

Occasionally I have friends who will say to me they've had unexplainable things happen to them, and I don't dispute that, but like I said, not everyone can play the piano. I truly and strongly believe that every individual can have a spiritual path, but not every path has to do with predicting a person's future or future events. My family and friends are supportive of what I do, and my children love it.

### What are your views on charging for services?

I charge a fee because it takes my time and it takes time from my family. I don't do this work to make a lot of money, although I wish I could do this full time and make a living because this is actually my passion. My view is that there must be an exchange. I'm doing work for somebody. We are all here to learn, and we should all offer our hand to those who are a step down and help pull them up. If more people behaved this way, it would be a much better world.

### What do you think about television hotline ads regarding readings?

Most are telemarketers. A few are actually very good psychics and work for these lines, but earn low wages. Others do this because they are experimental readers, dabbling in Tarot cards, for example. I encourage people to check out the local readers. Most of them will do a twenty-minute or more reading for far less than you would pay any outfit that advertises on TV. Not only that, your reading will be more accurate. The choice would be around $20 for twenty minutes from a local reader or $20 for five minutes from one of the TV ads. Obviously, it does not take a lot of mental effort to figure this one out. A true practitioner will direct you to appropriate sources if he or she cannot help find the information you are looking for.

### What advice do you have for people seeking readings or spiritual experiences?

Beware of the ripoff. If a person asks for extra money, back off. In fact, ask for your money back at that point. Refuse to pay and then report the disreputable person. If the reader says, "I can get you special herbs for $100, or I can say special prayers for you for $200," then just get out of there immediately. Remember that when you see a reputable reader, that person will not be able to tell you everything. Nobody is 100%. I have been told that I range somewhere in the upper 80-90% range.

With mediums especially, a client may not understand all the information. If that person then goes to a psychic, he or she might hear something different, simply because this is information the client needs to know more about.

If a person hears anything negative, or gloom and doom, the one important thing to keep in mind is that we all have free will, and can change things that may be coming at us from around the corner. Nothing is written in stone. I told a friend of mine that a man would be passing away within the next couple of weeks. I did not know who this man was, but I did know this was not avoidable. Her father died a week later. Afterwards, she called and told me, that had she not been warned, she could not have handled the death as well as she did. Sometimes gloom and doom is just good information.

Ask the psychic if he or she is someone who is going to tell you all, or are they one who is going to hold back. See someone who will tell you everything. Some readers withhold because they are unsure of information. It is better for the psychic to say something like, "I'm really not sure about this, but I'll spit it out anyhow. This is what I'm feeling and this might be important."

The only dumb question is one that hasn't been asked. People are often hesitant, and then call me later with delayed questions. Always ask — not just with me, but also in everyday life.

### Do you have any worries about your endeavors?

Oh, sure I do. I ask myself if I was able to convey enough information, or maybe I wasn't good enough at channeling. Did I get enough rest? Can I read well for people who attend psychic fairs? My wife tells me I have to get over that. But I can tell you that the messengers and spirits have not let me down. I remember a time when I was quite ill and really wiped out. My clients did not receive the phone message stating that I wanted to cancel, so they arrived for their appointments as scheduled. I had just returned from the emergency room with antibiotics to medicate a miserable infection.

Five minutes into the sessions, I was feeling great and was able to do a few hours of readings. As soon as the sessions were over and the clients walked out the door, I felt horrible again. If these people were meant to cancel, somehow they would have gotten the message. I believe that the spirits or messengers provide me with strength to get through. In this particular case, the clients told me that the readings were among the best they have ever experienced. Sometimes I think I have doubts or fears because it keeps my ego in check.

### What do you think about coincidence and synchronicity?
Everything has a meaning and there are coincidences in a sense, but usually life is a pretty good road map. There are not many distractions. At times, people wander off on a dirt gravel road, but our goals normally stay on the highway if we just pay attention. However, we have free will, and consequently can screw things up very easily.

### Do you have any advice to those with children who might have abilities?
Encourage and listen. Don't think that things they say are frivolous fantasy. They may want to engage in this, but don't push it on them. Kids are intuitive, especially when you encourage them to share their dreams. Listen to what they say. Sometimes they have advice to give to *you*. Especially pay attention to things that are repeated. Spirit or angel, or whatever you care to call this energy brings messages through various means. For example, you may get into your car in the morning, turn on the radio and the first thing that you hear is an ad for tires. The ad stands out in your mind for some reason. You arrive at work and Joe is telling Bob that he just bought new tires for the car. This might be a clue that you may soon have problems with your tires or something related. Pay attention to subtle hints. Pay attention to your children.

### Do you have any final messages for us?
A message I want to convey is that of psychic protection. I am a stickler on that. I have seen too much happen in light versus dark. When a person starts moving more towards the light side, the dark side does not care for that. It isn't always noticeable, such as windows shaking. Again, *subtle* things happen — financial problems, things breaking down. The dark

side sends "inconveniences" when a person starts dabbling and heading toward the light. Emotional, friendship, and relationship problems crop up for us. These are distractions, so I tell people to protect, and I share my techniques for meditation with them. Helpful books are valuable. Be alert and on guard. When I began working with my talents, I found that when I didn't take care of myself, annoying and worrisome things would happen. The purpose of this was to distract me and keep me from reaching my goals. I knew it and I strongly felt it.

Take time and believe in yourself. As I speak with you, I am being told that people have too many doubts and fears and they ignore their inner personal strengths. If you look at my clients, you might say they have the perfect life—beautiful and handsome, nice clothes, great cars. They are unhappy with themselves. They don't like what they see. We pick the perfect vehicle for us to get through life. We pick the best situations to learn what we have to learn. We pick the perfect bodies to get us through this. God doesn't make junk. We are all Cadillacs and Ferraris traveling our personal road trip.

The universe truly hears our thoughts. Thought has energy. We are atomic beings. If broken down to the very atom, we are electrical. Our thoughts are responses that travel in the universe. The universe must respond to it. So if we think negatively, we're going to get negative back. If we think we will always have gloom and doom in our lives, we always will. If we act as if life is a glorious place and we will have money to burn, we probably will. "Be careful what you wish for" really does apply in a metaphysical situation. Even though life is not easy, we pick the best situations for what we need to do in this life. Once again, we all drive that personal Cadillac whether it's a lemon or a diamond.

# Kathleen Schneider

Kathleen Schneider has been a practicing psychic and spiritual consultant since 1979. Her gifts of clairvoyance and clairsentience are natural abilities that have been with her from earliest recollections. Kathleen has studied with the Association for Research and Enlightenment (Edgar Cayce), Spiritual Frontiers Fellowship Inc. (Harold Sherman), New Frontier Center, and at UW-Milwaukee (Transpersonal Parapsychology). She was affiliated with Madison Holistic Counseling Service for six years as a co-counselor and received an award from the American Association for Parapsychology. Kathleen's work has included consultations with law enforcement agencies, and she has been featured in radio and television programming as well as magazine and newspaper articles. She uses photos, original samples of handwriting, business documents, and personal jewelry among other things, as tools in her reading.

### Contact Information
Kathleen Schneider
2413 Parmenter Street #150
The Pines Office Center
Middleton, WI 53562-0513

**Mailing address:**
P.O. Box 620513
Middleton, WI 53562-0513
**Phone:** 608-836-1935
(office)

**What mystical arts are you practicing today?**

The work I do involves clairvoyance, clairaudience, and clairsentience. As a life consultant, spiritual counselor, psychic, and psychic medium, I provide intuitive information regarding questions and other matters. Psychometry is often a tool that I use. This involves holding an item, such as a piece of jewelry or a photo and utilizing energy radiating from that point. Dream interpretation, past life essences, and channeling can be a part of a session. I have assisted in finding missing persons, pets, and various objects.

I was "called" in a manner of speaking. "Call" is a complicated phenomenon. It is a direction in life given by a higher power such as God, Buddha, or Spirit. Higher powers call us to accomplish certain things in this life. For example, my daughter-in-law Margaret has a beautiful voice. I like to sing, but I don't have a voice like an angel. In fact, I sing in the shower late at night. When I hear her sing, I know this is a gift given for a purpose. Margaret is a music teacher. My life's purpose is to be of service to other people. Spirit guides us in many different directions. The guidance is internal and it gives us a sense of what we do and accomplish. Sometimes the path is strong and direct, sometimes gradual, and at other times, Spirit is quiet. We meditate and pray for doors of direction, but it is up to us whether to open the doors and travel those routes or not.

Spirit also guides us through other people, which is where I come in to help. Insight, clarity, hope, comfort and a better understanding of us is the objective. Ministers and pastors are not the only people who do ministry. We all have gifts. It is not limited to a few. I find that psychic spiritual counseling can help accelerate personal change and growth. People come into sessions feeling lost, conflicted, drained, unhappy, frustrated, and worried. They seek a place to feel safe and not judged. Healing, moving through grief issues, and help in finding alternative approaches often bring people into the comfort of daylight once again.

**Discuss the development of your abilities.**

I am what is termed a naturally developed psychic, and therefore it wasn't a matter of my sitting down one sunny day and saying this is what I plan to do. I believe it was inherited. Some of the family speculate that other members, through time, were psychically gifted, but none of us knows for sure. My mother's mother seems to have had the gift. I did not understand it when I was younger, although the interest was always present. I was raised in a very traditional religious setting and these things were certainly discouraged rather than encouraged. As a child, I was emotionally sensitive and I sensed things about other people. I did not have a way to analyze this truly; I just knew what I felt and experienced.

At times, I felt presences in our house. I lived in the Fox River Valley and my parents had a small resort there. The property and the land the house was built on reportedly had a fort there at one point in history. Every spring we found Indian artifacts that would come to the surface. Psychic phenomena happened in that house. Recently I paid a visit to the place; actually, I was compelled to go there. Everything appeared so different. I had not been in the house since my two sons returned from the service in Saudi Arabia. The owner invited me in, and my excitement was boundless. I noticed the wonderful improvements in the house. So many things my mother had wanted for the house but did not have, such as an upstairs bathroom and an open stairway. It was joyful for me, not sad. Something in the house was healed. When we were growing up it felt unhappy and unsettled. The owner commented to me, "This is a happy house." She and I talked about the psychic phenomena in the house that her family had been experiencing.

My parents died in 1975 and 1976. Dad was a strong presence in life and he is still a strong presence. My point in telling you this is that there is a reason why I went to the home, and the reason was not just for me, but also perhaps for the lady of the house.

So many things occurred of a psychic nature. When my mom and dad went out on a Friday night for fish dinner, I would race up the steps; no, I would *fly* up the steps and lock myself in the upstairs bedroom. Sometimes my sister Sandra and I would lock ourselves in the bathroom with comic books and paper dolls. We did not tell our parents about things that were happening in the house. One night we locked ourselves in the guest bedroom and we suddenly felt bumping that seemed to come from beneath the bed. We were adults at the time, and I can remember both of us looking underneath the bed — Sandra on one side and me on the other — only to be staring at each other, with nothing in between. To this day, I believe this strange kind of phenomena is coming from those on the other side who are trying to get our attention.

Early on, I had a great deal of these kinds of things happening, especially when I moved to Madison in the early 1970's — a lot of wall rapping behind the bed. Doors opened by themselves, lights went on and off without any control from me. I would leave the apartment and then return to find cupboards open and lights on. An apartment on the east side of Madison was probably the most haunted or "active" places I have lived. I could *lock* the patio door and a short time later, I would see the door wide open.

It could have been the land the apartment was built on or the actual apartment itself. I don't know. I did not live there a long time. When we moved, I mentioned this to the management. They told me that a woman and her child lived there previously. The woman was a prostitute and there had been much trauma in the apartment.

Our family experienced tremendous grief in losing two parents within a year. My sister Sandra suggested we see the psychic Myrtle Haywood. Myrtle was the first professional I felt comfortable with enough to stick my toe in the water regarding my psychic experiences. She suggested books to read and invited me to lectures and conferences. Myrtle was encouraging but given my strict religious upbringing, I was in conflict. It took a long time to work through this, and it took me years before I would accept any monetary payment for my skills. I did not plan this path in life; I followed it, focused, and worked with it. Is it real? I struggled with it as anyone else might do. The work is challenging, rewarding, and energizing.

### What is your answer to the skeptic?

I consistently say I applaud people who possess a degree of skepticism. They are not hanging on to every word and they think for themselves. They make their own choices and decisions. I own a piece of skeptic pie, and I am a little of "show me and then I'll believe it." Overall, I find critical skeptics a bit challenging to deal with, especially the very hard core. For them, it is more about attacking rather than inquiring and I end up feeling kind of hammered. This does not feel positive or productive and I ask myself what is it we are trying to do here? Every individual has beliefs and I respect that, and I would hope others give me the same. I am a soul walking this path too. God knows I don't walk on water.

I was at an event many years ago, and the "Amazing Randi," all-time skeptic, attended it. I know he truly believes in what he is doing or he would not be doing it. However, I think there is an awful lot of ego entering into his work. Maybe a part of him is fearful of the unknown. He seems to debunk out of fear. I feel sympathy for him. However, he caused a lot of *unjustified* pain in many good people such as Uri Geller. It is sad. He is missing a lot of richness that can come through spiritual and mystical practice.

### Do you hear any criticisms about this kind of work?

Energy exists that does not walk in the light. We all need to be aware of that. To ignore this would be folly, and leaving oneself wide open. People or energies existing in other realms can trick and fool others along the way. It is important to remain vigilant and keep our eyes turned toward the light that I believe is God or Spirit. Perhaps through turmoil or misguided beliefs or pain there are those who look to blame others for things that are not going well in their lives. I have been a target, and it is not pleasant. No matter how much I attempt to understand where they are coming from, I am as human as the next person is. My intent is to never cause harm or misguide anyone.

When I am in session and something comes through that does not adhere to universal law or spiritual principles as I understand them, I will challenge this in my thoughts. I have done this countless times and I will say to myself "If you do not walk in the light, I demand in the name of the higher power that you be gone." I ask myself, "Where is this coming from?"

Am I personally frustrated or angry about something? Do I have something that is lurching forward into this session?

**Is there anything unique about practicing in Wisconsin?**
I have met many people who practice in other areas of the country, and my impressions vary from state to state, region, and even city. However...there is *something* about Wisconsin, and specifically the Madison area. It is enormously progressive and in most cases, open-minded. The area provides me a real sense of freedom. I do not feel restricted or think that I must practice discretely. Metaphysical type classes have been taught at Edgewood College in Madison, the University of Wisconsin, and other respected schools throughout the United States. In addition, research is ongoing in some of these places. At one time in my life, I was thinking of moving to California, but while I was visiting California, I knew without knowing how to explain it, that I was meant to practice in Madison, Wisconsin. It was to be here.

**Have you worked on any police or investigative cases?**
Yes, definitely, but I am not free to talk about much of this. I am currently involved in cases that are still open. One case I assisted the Sheriff's department with is the Gary and Ruth Homberg murder case years ago. Gary Homberg was convicted of murdering his wife. No body was found. Many families contact me about missing people. The most painful is missing children. I recently helped a woman find her older daughter. A great deal of what was channeled to me was helpful to the mother.
Thank God the girl is living.

**Do world events affect your abilities?**
September 11, 2001. Yes, it did affect my ability to work, but it also heightened my sensitivity. I was concerned about my clients in New York City. I felt panic-stricken and compelled to make phone calls immediately. One woman answered the phone and I said, "This is Kathleen." The woman was excited and said she was unable to get any calls out and nobody had been able to call except me! This happened twice in that whole mess. I told her that I absolutely had to know she was all right. At that

point, I became the designee to contact her parents and others who had been trying unsuccessfully to get a call through. Another client of mine worked across the street from the World Trade Center, but shortly before September 11, she had changed her work hours or she would have been in the building on a coffee break at the time of the tragedy.

One woman called me who had had plans to travel to India. My immediate response was to advise not to go. We waited a few days, and I had the same intense response. Another person called me who was quite distraught about a dream she had prior to the event. Her anxiety was authentic and I felt her dream was also. There was panic in her voice. She said, "What do you do when you have dreams like this?" Practitioners are always asking what to do with information that comes from a clairvoyant dream. If it is reported to a law enforcement agency as information coming through in this manner, then we are going to have our homes surrounded and people asking how we knew this. Then how are we going to prove that it came through extrasensory means? It's a Catch 22.

**What is your opinion about so-called psychic hot lines?**
This is a hot button issue for a lot of us. I think there are some sincere people working on these lines who do not have other ways of pursuing this, but I would not encourage anybody to use these lines for this kind of very specific and personal guidance. My strong word of advice on this is to research things very carefully. Get recommendations from family, friends, and coworkers who have experienced a reader more than one time. Certainly, people who are having an anxiety attack or other crisis seem to call these lines in the middle of the night. I have heard stories through the years of people running up astronomical phone bills. Any anxiety they called up to have relieved was only replaced or compounded a thousand times by a $1500 phone bill, even a $3000 bill in some cases. It is truly very sad.

**Is there power in prayer?**
Yes, wholeheartedly prayer is powerful. Anybody who has read books by Larry Dossey, M.D. will agree with this. Wishes often show up as manifestations. Thoughts are things. Also, be

careful of what you say. "What a pain in the neck" may actually *become* a literal pain in the neck. I cannot tell you how many times I have been reminded to watch what I say. I believe in praying for others as well, not only for yourself.

### How do messages come through to you — voices, feelings, symbols?

I do not hear anything talking to me outside of myself. I believe everyone has spirit guides who are angels, saints, and archangels. Master teachers are primarily guardian angels. Other guides can be, and oftentimes are, people who have lived like you and me and are now on the other side as guides. From my experience in practice, the client has not necessarily experienced the guide in his or her life here in this existence. Therefore, mom, or uncle, or dear friend is not the guide coming through. Guides seem to appear because of a specific purpose rather than a connection that we may have had with them in this realm.

During a session, your group of guides and my guides collaborate. Thought, inspiration, hope, comfort, protection, and love come through to me. I strongly believe I am not creating those thoughts. People ask me how I know this. I cannot know 100% of the time that these are not my own thoughts. Nevertheless, I can give you this example — when we are part way through a session and a client presents me with a question, my natural analytical mind will say to me the "response" should be selection "Z." Then, as I still and quiet my mind and am open to receive, so many times what comes through is either 100% different from what I thought, which was "response Z," and sometimes it is *significantly* different. That tells me it is not coming from my own psyche, because it would match up to what I wanted, and it does not. If clients only knew how many times, I am saying to myself, "Well, I'll be darned; I thought it was going to be answer 'Z.'"

Things are not entrenched in stone. A reader may overlook something or analyze incorrectly, over analyze, or not analyze completely. Because we are human too, we are at certain risk levels. Occasionally some of my own beliefs will spill over into a reading, but I try hard not to let that happen. Clairvoyance also means mental imagery, and I receive enormous amounts of that in each person's reading. This takes two forms for me. One is symbols, like dreaming when I am wide awake. The other is more literal and it feels like I am there watching an event unfold. Usually I think of this as possible future, but it may be past or present.

I see landscapes, and interiors and exteriors of buildings. I have gotten so many specifics on the interiors of buildings that I started this little joke by saying I think I am innately nosey! I love to look around at the décor and really see huge amounts of detail.

In fact, I was reading for a woman and she noted that I could not have possibly known the detail I was telling her. Because the house was in the Parade of Homes, there were things in the home that were of incredibly unique design. I ended up receiving tickets to the event so I could check it out for myself.

Mental pictures can provide affirmation and confirmation. I cannot stress the powers of additional clarity and guidance that come with this. Some of my clients claim the imagery I provided gave them absolute answers. I sense times, but time is one of the most challenging things for anyone. In some cases, I am right on, at other times, I am so off, and now and then, free will and free choice changes things. A woman in Janesville was selling a supper club, and I felt strongly that the club would sell, but it took five years. That is probably the longest I have heard it taking beyond my original estimate. She said she was not emotionally ready to let go of the property and move back to her home state.

I feel other people's emotions and I physically feel things in my own body. In one instance, I was in a session with a client and I felt a horrific pain near the top of my thigh. I asked her about the pain in her leg and she immediately said she didn't have a pain in her leg. I panicked and thought what in the world is wrong with *my* leg. As it turns out, she had seriously injured that leg a year ago, and even though the leg healed physically, there were still emotional and legal issues surrounding this injury. Perhaps I received this feeling so that it would open the door to make it easier for her to connect in this reading.

I have received images that look like x-ray films and they seem to indicate areas of the body that have experienced things in the past. Three-dimensional pictures have appeared to me also. Once I detected a client I was seeing was missing a lung. I was asking myself if I should say something. As it turns out, he had a lung surgically removed many years ago. If Spirit had started me out with this, I think I would have shut down. My abilities have come knocking at the door in steps. They just "entered" when the times were right. The spirits started me out gently with this "x-ray" reading.

I do not have a medical background and I make no claims to that. If things come up in a reading, I advise people to seek out the appropriate provider whether it be traditional, holistic, or both. My work is not about diagnosing or prescribing. For example, I had a woman in my office for a reading and during that session, I was picking up that there were cardiac problems. We talked about this and I recommended she see her physician. She sensed that the insight, guidance, or channeling that came through had credence. The woman made an appointment and got into the clinic very quickly. Immediately she was referred to a cardiologist and an angioplasty was done the same day! This one terrific incident has stuck with me. The thing is she trusted her *own* senses. She made a choice and she took action. That is really what this about. However, through her own admission, she said she might not have taken this action had it not come through in the session that we had together. She came to me for a reason and at the right time.

### What are your thoughts on reincarnation?

I have a strong belief in this. There is continuity. Past lives surface in sessions and it helps people to understand things like phobias, allergies, relationship issues, and certain situations with the physical body. Why would this be the only time we are here?

Souls have channeled for years coming through for my clients and my own family. I have had *many specific* confirmations that life continues. A friend recommended a book titled *Witness from Beyond* by A.D. Matteson (a Ruth Taylor book). I began to read it and felt enormous relief as I made my way through the book. It confirmed much of what those on the other side had already been telling me.

People come for sessions when they are grieving intensely. Certainly, they are in tremendous pain and looking for very specific confirmation, but sometimes clients receive information that is not sought. It is a mistake to dismiss this. I believe in these cases that the person has additional healing and grief work to do, for whatever reason.

Our pets also pass over. I have seen countless kitties, dogs, horses, and birds, and even a pet cow. I haven't seen any bugs. A mental picture comes through, and suddenly a dog or cat comes running forward! The other day I asked a woman, who is Alfie? She was teary eyed and said it was her pet.

### If a person reincarnates, how can we still speak to that person in another realm?

I have not run into that. Maybe once or twice in my practice have I ever felt that someone has incarnated again. I believe however that the imprint of the Soul exists whether we are here or there. I am able to link, especially if holding a writing sample or photo, regardless of the location. If you moved to New York, an imprint of you would still linger here. It is a collective consciousness. Remember that time in our world is a blink of an eye compared to the spirit world. We invented the measurement of time. There are various schools of thought on this, and it is a very interesting question.

### What is mystic defined?

The word "mystic" suggests mystery. To me it is not a mystery.

### How do your family and your friends view your abilities?

People hold different beliefs, thoughts, feelings, and comfort levels. I think in my family, as in most families, there are a variety of ideas about it. Some are more accepting and some less. Unresolved religious issues might play a part. Overall, because they know me and love me, they make effort to accept what I do, whether they believe or agree or not, it is an integral part of me. My daughter Tamara has grown up with this from day one and she is blatantly psychic in her own right. I felt this from the time she was about 5 years old. As for my friends, all of my friends accept and respect my work.

### Do you believe in manifestation from psychic work?

Yes, I believe people can manifest things. Affirmations, mental imagery, and positive thoughts are all projected outward and most importantly, they are energies. I believe we attract to us that which matches up to our thoughts and imageries. I have seen it far too many times to discount it. Very recently, an answer to my prayers literally manifested, and it was a tremendous blessing. It involved *years* of challenge. My own faith was shaken and at stake. I asked why things that I thought were important had not happened. The office I was renting was disappearing because of a road project. I had been looking for a new office for approximately four years and nothing worked out—there were frustrations and things falling apart. Through a number of amazing "coincidences," I was able to find the new office I am presently occupying. The Department of Transportation was required to pay compensation due to the road project consuming my former office. This has provided much financial and psychological relief to a person who is close to me. I began the prayer process before I knew this building was actually going to be demolished. The thing is, if I had moved when I thought it was the thing to do, I would not have moved into the great office where I am located now, and  there would be no compensation. Everything had to come full circle with all the spiritual and emotional things happening during this time. Everything is connected, and it is truly amazing.

Years ago, life was more than demanding as a single mom. One day I was ill and did not have money to go to Walgreen's and buy antihistamine. Sitting at the table and feeling despair, I thought to myself that I needed $50, which went much further than it does now. I stood up and did something very "unspiritual" by pounding my hand on the counter top and saying, "If manifesting is real, then prove it to me!" The phone rang. I groaned and thought, who can that be. I did not feel like talking, but I answered the phone anyhow. A gentleman who lived a distance away was calling for an appointment for a reading. He stated he was coming to town and wanted to discuss some things that were going on in his life at the time. So I met him in a quiet restaurant. I was not charging a set fee at that time and I received whatever it was people were going to give me. After the channeling that I did, he handed me a perfectly folded bill. I turned it over and it was a $50 bill. Trust me. I believed after that. I was astonished. I went directly to Walgreen's.

**Do you have any final messages for us?**

Seek with an open mind and keep a healthy guard in place. Anything is possible.

# Kenneth Nelson

Kenneth E. Nelson is an expert graphologist (handwriting analyst) and numerologist. He developed his profession in graphology after studying with industrial and criminology experts in the Netherlands, India, Germany, and New York. Ken has been called upon by the courts, the legal profession, industries, and individuals for his graphology services. Presentation list includes the State of Wisconsin, Price Waterhouse Inc., Johnson Wax, Milwaukee School Board, Teacher's Convention of Wisconsin, Ameritech, American Dental Association (Milwaukee), McDonald Corporation, Milwaukee Police Department, many high schools, colleges, universities, churches, businesses and other organizations. He taught handwriting analysis at Alverno College and the La Farge Institute. Ken is a popular radio and TV guest. He is listed in the *Who's Who of Graphology.* Handwriting analysis and numerology are used in personal counseling and decision-making. An individual session with Ken lasts about 3 ½ -4 hours and covers numerology and graphology readings. The sessions are taped for the benefit of his clients.

**Contact Information**
Kenneth E. Nelson
3606 W. Haven Court
Mequon, WI 53092
**Phone:** 262-242-1889

**What arts do you practice today?**

The tools I use are graphology, which is handwriting analysis and numerology. I also use acrophonology, which is the science of the alphabet, and gnothology, the higher esoteric and spirituality of the God-force. Marvelous and fascinating histories show us that letters and numbers have meaning. We have thrust letters, hinge letters, ending letters, and the combinations of letters such as *er, st, ch, mm, oo.* All of these things talk at once and verify each other.

Several companies have hired me to analyze for job placement and personnel selection. They are interested in my reports. In handwriting, we look for such traits as honesty, loyalties, productivity, who's a leader and who's a worker, not that the two are mutually exclusive. Attorneys have called on me to analyze for such things as forgeries and embezzlements. There's just no end to it.

I owned and operated a successful business for twenty-one years as a wholesale florist. It was an eight day a week job with daily shipments coming in from all over the world. When I sold my business in 1976, my current profession was laid at my feet and it started to talk to me. So I thought, well being a Virgo, I'll make another profession out of it, and I did! I belong to AAHA (American Association of Handwriting Analysts), Handwriting Analysts International where I served on the Board of Directors, GLOW (Graphology League of Wisconsin) and COGS (Council of Graphilogical Societies). In my work, I basically use numerology and graphology 50-50. Individually, we deal with goal setting, personalities, introversion, extroversion, will powers, organizational abilities, base line of life, how things are handled on a daily basis, and how they are handled metaphysically and intuitively.

**What about handwriting changes? By the way, don't look at that notebook sitting next to me.**

Even the Wiz of Oz couldn't keep that darn curtain closed. Handwriting changes go along with some of the emotions. Handwriting can change day to day, month to month, and year to year. It is quite interesting when we get into the forgeries and misrepresentations. What if somebody just prints? Printing—well, we get you both ways. In printing, we still deal with pressure of the writing tool, the spaces between lines, words, and letters; margins, horizontal and vertical expansion, and…it just goes on and on and the variations are endless. Graphologists look at upper zone, middle zone, and lower zone. The upper zone represents the "b, l, h, and k" for example. This is the area of the intellect, philosophy, and spirituality, and it tells me just what you are thinking and how high you go. The higher areas are where the answers can be found. They reach into the area of spirituality. Some folks have very little upper zone and this can be interpreted as a lesser power of thinking, or a deficiency in philosophy or spirituality.

The middle zone is the here and now, and is the baseline of life as we live it. This is an indication of how one handles things on a daily basis. The lower zone is the area of the subconscious mind and is the place where everything starts—I want, I need, I desire, I allow. It looks for instant gratification in a me-me situation. The ego comes along and this is the first policeman. Now you must ask yourself, if I want this and I do that, how does this fare in the eyes of the family, how does it fit into society, and how am I handling it. The upper zone is the second policeman. If I want this and I do that, how does it appear in the eyes of God or the spiritual aspect and Universe? We are always looking for balance in people.

Intuition is a tremendously big part of things. Letters in a name tell about the depth of intuition. Some people have psychic abilities to one degree or another. The "9" in this person's birthday tells me about the soft spot she has [Ken reads a number from client Samantha's birth date]. She comes along and people say, "Samantha will do it." *Instantly* she knows all about people, and yet there is a strong "speak softly and carry a big stick" quality she bears. Sometimes when Samantha is intro-

duced to people she comes on like gangbusters and scares the
hell out of them, but then they get to know her and think this is
a fun lady! She has what we call universal understanding. She
has universal sympathy as well. People look at her and say, "I've
got somebody with whom I can share my troubles, somebody
who understands and listens to me." But always, the intuition
is in play with Samantha.

**What is your view on the skeptic?**
Funny you should ask. I just conducted a group session.
One gentleman said, "I don't believe any of this. It's hogwash."
After I gave my dissertation and managed to pick on him, at the
end of the session I asked what he was thinking now. He said,
"You made a believer out of me, and in only one session." We
are what we write. There is no such thing as handwriting; this is
*mind* writing. What is in the hidden heart comes out on paper.
I have about seven high schools that have me working post prom
parties. My work is both entertaining and informative for these
young people. I can see immediately—hey what happened
here—you could be a little closer to dad—you have a cut off
and a whiplash the way you write this particular letter of the
alphabet. Mother, father, and relationship situations jump right
out at me.

**How did you get into this and develop the talent?**
The topic fascinated me. Detectives in the Charles Lindbergh
kidnapping case used handwriting analysis of the ransom note.
The note was analyzed here in Milwaukee. That fact always
stuck with me.
After I sold my business, my wife said she wanted to attend
some classes on Tuesday nights, which of course was my bowling night. She doesn't drive, so I decided that I'd get a substitute
bowler for five or six weeks and take her to the classes. Well,
one night I was wandering down a hallway and I happened to
drop in on a class taught by two clairvoyants. I stood at the
doorway and one of them spotted me and said, "Get a load of
the aura on that guy. Come on in, we've got some work to do."
I'm thinking to myself, holy cats what did I wander into? They
told me I was a "third ranked student of Pythagoras (Greek

Philosopher 560-480 BCE; father of modern geometry and numerology)." I stood there scratching my head wondering who in the world this Pythagoras guy was. I think I was hooked right off the bat because I've always loved numbers and math. My next stop was the library to look up Pythagoras and his history.

**Did you give up bowling? Ms. Curiosity had to ask.**

Yes! I never took the ball out of the trunk of my car again. But nobody gets to touch the golf clubs.

The history of numbers is intricate and exciting. One of my clients was a highly ranked member of the priesthood. After I finished talking about his chart, he paced back and forth in my office, stopped, looked me in the eye and said, "I have had every kind of analysis you can imagine, but the numerology and the handwriting are by far the most accurate, fastest, and most beautiful of all. The numbers explain everything."

**Have you worked on police or investigative cases?**

Oh yes, many. We look for people who are perpetrators of illegal things such as forgery. As an analytical group, our association worked on the Jeffery Dahmer serial killer case. We could see that this man was absolutely brilliant. In handwriting and numerology there are positives and negatives. Individuals choose the positive or the negative or even the destructive. If a person deals with negatives long or strong enough, that person will slide down hill into destructive. Tremendous things occur with master numbers in numerology (11, 22, 33, 44 and so on), and it has to do with inner knowing.

Jeffery Dahmer's handwriting was extremely tell-tale about who he was. In his personal pronoun "I" and other parts of his writing we could tell that he had absolutely no connection with mother or father — zero. He was strictly a loner. Everything was centered on his own thinking and his own philosophies and his own alter. He had no connection with the God-force. His "o's" and "a's" had big gaps underneath the letters. Everything would drop out of them. It was a sign of dishonesty and cover-ups. Some of the extra lead strokes and loops in ending strokes would indicate his ability not only to influence his own thinking, but that of other people too. The writing indicated he had an ability to persuade people. Some of the little spaces did not connect and there were five or six different gaps in the formation of the letters indicating he had no connection with other people—no continuity in relationships. He belonged to no one but himself. Mr. Dahmer had his share of "shark's teeth" which are little hooks and barbs in the writing. This is often seen in serial killers.

When dealing with honesty versus dishonesty, the graphologist must use astute discernment and know what he is talking about. I don't make a blanket statement or direct accusations, but I say, "There is questionable honesty here." I analyze sixteen traits before I can make a detailed comment on this. I have the original letter Mr. Dahmer wrote to Judge William Gardner. The letter came after Mr. Dahmer was incarcerated. He spoke of remorse. Believe it or not, the Judge actually reduced the sentence because of this plea. It was interesting that the letter was *printed*. Sometimes printing indicates a lack of truthful expression, or that we are withholding things, or possibly there is a cover-up. What people hold in or bottle up comes out in their weakest link. Anger and belligerence shows up in writing.

**Tell me about this chart and book. Did you memorize the book?**

One book I refer to is called *Tattle Tale T's*. It is a book on the small letter "t" crossing. This is 230 pages of crossing the small letter "t." Yes, I have this memorized because I am required to know about it. The book is specifically about the letter "t" but *every* letter is as detailed.

The large chart I developed is a landscape of a person's numerology. It takes 3 ½-4 hours to interpret it with a client. I use the birth certificate name, married name, and the vowel and consonant energies. The vowels show us what you desire in life and what intuitional qualities you possess. How you see yourself from the inside out comes up in the personality section. The consonants show us how you see yourself with no demands resting on you. The sum total of letters and numbers tells us about how you express yourself to society. My client [Ken shows me a chart] is on an "8" life path meaning she understands business and finance very well. The two pentacles in her chart show materialistic gain for the rest of her life. As you may have guessed, she is an attorney and in addition, runs a second successful business.

A chart can show us what directions you are traveling, and to what degree. Missing numbers tell a person about what needs to be learned in life and what kicks you in the heel every step of the way. This person is missing 2's [he shows me the lawyer's chart again] meaning she needs to work on patience, tact, diplomacy, partnerships and duality—those need second and third efforts in this case. The letter transits on a chart show what happens for her from day to day. The handwriting enters to show us quantity and to what degree.

### What do you think about reincarnation?

We look at people in the cycle of nine (base numerology uses numbers 1-9), but can see they come up with master numbers as well, and this is indication of the old Soul. They have been around many times, whether it was here or Russia or Japan or lying in the streets of India. We are all where we need to be at the moment, however.

### Mystic defined?

Everyone goes through growth and evolvement and everyone has some of the psychic abilities, but individuals use them differently. Various people have 7's, 11's, 22's, 55's, etc., and they don't have any gaps in the writing — meaning they haven't tapped into the ability yet. Somewhere along the line, the guy from above boots you in the behind and kicks the lights on. Look at our universe and our planets. The knowledge is phenomenal. Pythagoras was working with mathematics that we use in science today. He gave us geometry, the Pythagoras Theory of right angled triangles, even phonics, and the development of music theory. Every time we turn around we apply more knowledge he has given us. He was teacher to Plato and Socrates and a master of numbers and numerology. Was he a mystic? He offered us priceless gifts...you decide.

**Are there coincidences?**

Life is a synchronicity of events. We are at the right place at the right time either to learn something or to teach something. That is the simplicity of this. So are there coincidences? Perhaps, but they are connected events and connected for a reason even though that reason may not be immediately evident.

**Do world events have ties to numerology and graphology?**

September 11, 2001, is what numerologists call a universal day and it affected the world. The day itself was a 5 [9+ (1+1) + 2+ 0+ 0+ 1 = 14; 1+ 4=5]. The numbers 13, 14, 16, and 19 are malevolent numbers. They are not necessarily evil, but they represent additional events to be dealt with in life. The 14, which is reduced to 1+4=5, as a malevolent number, goes on a "to have and to hold and to let go" principle. People in the World Trade Center, the Pentagon, and the planes, had their lives plucked away from them. We have to say, "So this was taken from us," shift our eyes above and say, "Whatever was taken is replaced by something else, so what is in store for us?" This is a question for the world. Is the "replacement" a battle against terrorism? Time will tell.

On the graphology end of things, most of our world leaders have "d" and "e" slants over to the far right. Extent and conductivity of emotional expression are measured in the degree of the "e" slant. The "basket cases" are into the "e" slants. Hitler and Mussolini were "e" slants. On the other hand, we have those who write with the back slants. They jump in the hole and pull the hole over themselves—isolationism. It could also mean stern individuality. But before a graphologist can say anything is a trait or a characteristic in handwriting, he must find that action in at least five or six different places in the script — different letters, diverse formations, and varying pressures with the writing instrument. People who write straight up and down accept nothing at face value. They evaluate and re-evaluate and then re-evaluate the evaluated!

**What are your views on structured religion?**

Look at personalities of people. Some say meditation is the

first thing they do in the morning, and they logically ask, "Why go to church? We have a direct connection." These are the folks who have more spirituality in their little fingers than most people have in their whole bodies. The church is a necessary formality and learning tool for those who need lessons in prayer and how to act and react. Many people with master numbers (11, 22, 33, and so on) retreat to a field and do their own thing—the direct connection. Meditation serves the same purpose to the same end.

### Is there power in prayer?

Prayer can be compared to thought. If I project positives, I will receive positives. The reverse is true also. A young man working for me was totally negative. He said such things as, "If there's a cold germ in the air, I'll find it." Sure enough, the next day he'd come in with a cold. It is embedded and programmed, but we have a choice of positives, negatives and the destructive.

### How do intuitions come through to you?

Everybody is different. Dreams, *déjà vu,* hunches, precognitions, impressions, gut feelings, audios, and visuals or combinations are common. I have a "1" intuitive plane of expression in my chart, and the "1" means things come through at lightning speed — bang — there's the idea! I see not only the tree, but the root system and the positive and negative branches.

This chart [back to the lawyer's chart] has a "4" intuitive plane of expression, but she's missing 4's. She must learn how to reorganize and regroup. The symbol associated with 4 is the square. Square retains things and bottles them up. What is held inside, surfaces in the weakest link. This makes her a candidate for psychosomatic complaints. She might experience sore throats and ulcers. Her best teacher is to meet the challenges head on every day. The missing 4 indicates she seeks an escape route. These are big lessons for her. So you see, just from the complexities of the number 4 that guide my intuition, I observe the tree, the roots, and the branches.

### Do you have any messages or advice for us?

Everything is explained through the universal language of

numbers, including the knowledge found in things like astrology and tarot reading. We take numbers for granted. Get up in the morning and set the hair dryer on 3 and then hop in the car and watch the numbers on the speedometer and wave adieu to the numbers in your address.

Stop at the bank to withdraw $50 and on the way home fill the car up with 10 gallons of gas. What is time but a system of measurement? Acres, inches, meters, micrograms, area codes, zip codes, phone books—see it *never* ends!

Pay attention to handwriting. One of my clients had a bad situation with her father and there was a cutoff at age 7. We looked at the handwriting and there were early cutoffs in the lower loops on the "g's" and "y's." This has affected her relationships with men all through her life. Even though her father has passed on, she can write him a letter and get the garbage out. "I have all these hooks in my handwriting, Dad, but I want to improve." Step one is to forgive self. Step two is to love self. Step three is to forgive others *if you want to do that.* Step four is to finally release him. "Not only do I release you and send you on your way, Dad, but I have gotten rid of this." Her handwriting will change. This is called graphotherapy and we work on changing handwriting into positives.

Graphotherapy can get a jump on potential problems. It is a wonderful tool. If we catch kids right off the bat, from kindergarten on up, even if it is drawing instead of writing, we can analyze things so parents have awareness and know what to expect. It helps.

The knowledge is phenomenal and it's there for all of us. It is undemanding, and multifaceted.

# Jean Reddemann

Jean's Native American name is Wasaki Emani Wi, meaning Strong Walking Woman. Jean is a seer actively using her psychic and healing abilities. She is on the staff of the retreat team of the Wisconsin Breast Cancer Recovery Foundation and is part of a team that conducts retreats for women from a residential alcohol and drug treatment facility. Jean's company, "Journey's Way" specializes in retreats for corporations and businesses throughout the country. She was honored by Wisconsin Public Television as one of 20 people who has influenced the health of Wisconsin women. Jean is recognized in the United States and other countries for her work as an artist specializing in Native American beaded and leather jewelry. In addition to retreats, Jean conducts private spiritual consultations, classes, and workshops.

## Contact Information

Jean Reddemann
12440 MacAlister Way
Unit 201
New Berlin, WI 53151

**Phone:** 414-529-5282
**E-mail:** *jeanreddemann@aol.com*

**What mystical arts are you practicing today?**

I use the traditional Native system, energy healing, and shamanism. I am also known as a seer. My communication with spirits assists people in their journey to make decisions, assessments, and clarify some of their struggles. I am open, but this is the direction the Creator has taken me, and this is *my* journey. Women's Medicine is once again practiced in the United States because this is the time when we must compile the Soul ways of all women. Look at what has happened in this country since 1995. Before that time if someone said to you, "I know a great acupuncturist, the average person would have said, "Oh...ah...really...?" If in 1995 you complained of a terrible headache, most people would say here, take a Tylenol. Today many people would say, "Let me do a little energy or pressure point work on you." All of these ancient medicines of the women have returned.

The years 1997, 1998, and 1999 were the years for women especially. Women were reshaping and redefining what they wanted in their lives. That's when women quit their jobs, quit their relationships, relocated, quit their religious practices, and developed more spiritual pursuits. It was the time of transition. We saw a resurfacing of ancient arts — a reconnection with soul memories.

Soul memories are now reopening and utilizing holistic ways of Mother Earth. I honor other methods totally, but I must stay with what I am trained in, perfect that knowledge, and use it. All methods are needed to bring the circle of healing. It is not merely healing in reference to the body, to the mind, or to the spirit, but it is in reference to healing all things. This is the time we are meant to heal the water and the earth and all things that sustain life. We each have an important job to do and each medicine has become important.

The Red Man is the caretaker of the earth, the Yellow Man is caretaker of the water, the White Man is caretaker of the air, and the Black Man is caretaker of the fires.

We failed because we did not work together as one people supporting each other's journey. We were told that when Women's Medicine returned to Mother Earth, we could shift and heal that. Women have medicine that is spiritually driven.

We do not have that separateness. We need to sustain that circle for future generations. We are in that time now where we each contribute wisdom. None of us has the whole wisdom.

**Discuss the development of your abilities.**

I was born with the gift of seeing, communication, and healing. Fortunately, I was able to connect through my entire lifetime with incredible elders, starting with my own grandmother. In Native American culture, it is acceptable from day one to have knowledge and ability for spirit communication. I also have training in South American shamanism, Oriental, and Western medicine. Deep spiritual training however happens one on one in our culture. It is not found in books for us. Books give us supplemental things, but in training someone, you are there to know that the person hears you, understands it, and lives it. A mentor is a serious responsibility. If I give you certain keys or gifts to open doors, I must make sure you are using this correctly, because there are also ways to hurt people.

Part of the circle is to have knowledge of other ways. I see it now, even in the medical profession. They really want what is termed alternative (complementary) medicine. I laugh at the term "alternative" because it is really the ancient medicine of women. Modern medicine is small in scope when compared to how long medicine has been practiced on Mother Earth. The practitioners of today's medicine have gifts, but they are not the *only* gifts.

**Do you find there is a common thread among practitioners?**

Those that are truly immersed in healing in any practice and are truly successful, come from a spiritual foundation. The body, mind, and spirit are totally connected in order to assist in any level of healing—be it heal the earth, heal the people—it doesn't matter—any level of healing. Learn how your body has to move, where it has to move, what it has to do, and always keep an open mind. We need the left-brain to gain the knowledge. There are certain things that you need to learn and store, but when that is fragmented out, and you are only coming from one place or another, it does not connect. The circle is not whole.

### What is your view on the skeptic?

Everyone is exactly where he or she needs to be at this time, and that is to be honored. There is no right or wrong, no blame or shame. The skeptic today may be one of the healers of tomorrow. I cannot judge them or put a barrier there.

### What advice do you have for people seeking readings or spiritual experiences?

It is very important to use discernment. I specifically mean trust your heart and trust your instincts. Spirits guide us to exactly where we need to be. Some of our greatest teachers are those that show us what *not* to do, through their behaviors, through their examples, and through their results. If we lived in a perfect world, if we lived in perfect balance, perhaps there would not be these challenges. Notorious people throughout history and even modern day terrorists bring lessons with them.

Many of my clients come to me and ask, why am I here, and do I have spirits with me. Yes! Everyone has spirit. No one comes into this life alone. Moreover, it is that communication that you must develop to trust yourself and your instincts. Listen when the spirit communicates with you. A small example is, you are driving down the road, and in your mind comes the immediate thought to turn left, but in fact, your intention is to drive five miles straight down the road. So you travel three more miles and discover the bridge is out. Now you are saying, "I should have turned left." Well who do you think sent you the message? It is just that simple. We need to listen, identify, create, and acknowledge communication. Next time, turn left and say thank you!

### Is there anything unique about practicing in Wisconsin?

Yes, Wisconsin is unique. I travel all over the world working with indigenous people and others, but there is something very sacred and special about Wisconsin. We have beautifully defined seasons. We have the rivers. Mother Superior surrounds us in the north; Lake Michigan surrounds us in the east, and the Mississippi in the west. The greatest waters and all the rivers that flow within surround us. We have the four legged — the deer, moose, wolves, coyotes, bear — and we have the eagle. In the north, we have wooded ancient lands including the Apostle Islands. Madeline Island is the Women's Medicine Island. She is Wisconsin and is located in Lake Superior.

Wisconsin is an incredible powerfully sacred place. The archeologists keep discovering — I love that word "discovering," although we have known it all along — more and more sacred sites. An ancient medicine wheel was discovered in Wisconsin and it is believed to be the oldest medicine wheel on the continent. That is no surprise. Wisconsin is one of the only places where we can find all four of the sacreds — the sage, cedar, tobacco, and sweet grass. The cancer medicine, the stroke medicine, the heart medicine, the diabetes medicine — it is all there. You just have to know the Earth. It is amazing to me that so much of Wisconsin is undisturbed.

### Do world events affect your abilities?

No. I am blessed because I think the spirits shelter me from much. I am conscious of world events, but I do not read newspapers or watch television news. When I need to know something, I find out. Someone will come to me or call me or there will be an interruption. The only world event that totally affected my ability was when I had two sons in Desert Storm. My heart hurt so badly and I was in my fear. Fear blocks spiritual energy. I just sat in front of the TV crying. I couldn't eat. I couldn't sleep. I couldn't work. That event truly affected me, because my heart was there and my children were there. I cannot begin to imagine the pain of mothers of the world who live with this. I am so grateful that I can be a woman who can be in alignment with Spirit and not live in fear on a daily basis.

For many years, I was told that a time would come when there would be a mass exodus of highly evolved spiritual beings to bring forward and herald in the period of a thousand years of world peace. At least 2.5 thousand people in this country die every day—car accidents, illness, things like that. This doesn't affect the collective consciousness. Nevertheless, on September 11, 2001, a horrendous act elevated the consciousness of the world. People who perished gave us an incredible gift to open our eyes and our minds to stop the abuse, the violence, the terror, and the struggle. Unfortunately, as humans we have to see that big outward symbol. It would be easy to say this was a horrible disaster — and it was — but let's look at the gift.

When we look at Adolph Hitler, we know his behavior was not of loving kindness or consciousness. What I look at is how he influenced the world. While in Washington D.C., I visited the Holocaust Museum. I was standing in front of a display of hair, and a young Dutch woman was viewing the display, too. She spoke broken English and asked me what the hair meant to me personally. I said that in my culture our hair is the only thing we own. The rest belongs to the Creator. Our only gift to give is our hair. That's what was taken from these people — their identity, their power, their gifts. I have spoken with Holocaust survivors, their children, and their grandchildren and they tell me this piece of history, atrocious as it was, caused a shift that resulted in strong bonds, strong commitments, courage, and strength for them that would not have been there otherwise. These are sustained and continue to survive.

### Do you have connection to a structured religion?

I have been taught there is one God and that he gave us all the same teachings. What we do with them depends on the culture and the controlling society. I've met with Australian Aborigines, South and Central Americans, African tribal women and Buddhist monks. So many of their spiritual practices are ours, even some of the ceremonial words are similar. Spirituality and religion are related, but one is a way of being and one is a business. Religion is the business and it is a safe structure for some people. Of course, true spiritual essence can be utilized effectively within the confines of religion. Some folks go to church faithfully. But are they *experiencing* it?

I was recently on a plane and sitting next to a young woman who asked me what I did for a living. I replied that I am a spiritual teacher and counselor. She asked me what I meant by "spiritual" and then she said, "I will save you. I am a born-again Christian, and I am here to save you." I listened, and at the end, I thanked her for the kindness and said I appreciated her prayers and guidance. I also complimented her on living her religion. What she had been told was that someone like me needed to be saved. She asked me what I thought about the idea of born-again. I responded that personally I felt if they had gotten it right the first time, they wouldn't have to be born again. She understood, and she was right where she needed to be. So religion is right where it needs to be, but I am seeing change. Religion is becoming spiritual in the true sense. I am seeing religious people seek people like me and we communicate. Catholic nuns find me—that would not have happened ten years ago.

**When you are out and about do you have an on-off switch?**

The Creator brings to me exactly who needs to be with me no matter where it is. Do I invade someone's sacred space? I can read them and know what they are thinking and I can scan them, but I don't do that. I will not invade someone's space. Who would want to do that? When someone comes to me and says, "I am opening myself to you," that is permission. When I venture out, it can be difficult and chaotic, so I do not permit myself to be an open vessel. I would go crazy. At times, information arrives that is crucial and urgent, however. For example, my husband and I were driving and we passed an oncoming car. I immediately grabbed my husband's arm and said that man is going to have a heart attack. We turned our car around to follow the man. His car slowed down because he had taken his foot off the accelerator, and then the car slid into the ditch. We called for help at that point. So sometimes I am shown information for a very important reason, but I don't seek information when I am out and about.

When I share information with clients, it belongs to them. I disconnect from it and I am done. Even names pass by me. I told a friend of mine that I thought I was being disrespectful and she commented that I don't identify people by names, but by spirit. I think I'd go crazy if I had to remember all those names.

**Are there any specific readings about which you would like to talk?**

The Creator brings me some of the most incredible people; it leaves me awe-struck. Some of my work is in Washington,

D.C. The political energy is chaotic and tumultuous. Despite all, I have worked with some very spiritual women to rebalance and harmonize. One of my clients works for the World Bank. Because of her position, the World Bank is now seeking the advice and opinions of the indigenous people and spiritual leaders to see what is in alignment with their culture, and with the journey of their continent, rather than just going in with bull-dozers.

I never reveal confidentiality. That is not my information to give. Reading for a prominent politician is no greater than reading for the little grandmother on the reservation.

### Have you worked on police or investigative cases?

Yes, however I do not seek this kind of work. It is not my specialty. Often, when this comes about for me, it has something to do with investigations into occult activity. I have had instances of entering people's homes to cleanse the home of negativity. Violence has been present in the home and it has left a "residue." Work involving violence is very hard for me. I have worked with certain murders that may have been ritualistic. I do not like the work.

### What are your views on charging for services?

I had a lot of difficulty with charging. Being Traditional, we were raised that one doesn't charge for medicine because it is not owned. When I went to the hill to pray about this dilemma, I was told that I had to give up my career and follow the spiritual path. Leaving the hill, I was apprehensive and I said to Auntie, "I have a mortgage; I have children."

Auntie said, "Our people always took care of the spiritual people. We provided their home and their food and clothing. Today we use money to take care of people. If they come to you and want to pay your mortgage and bills, take it. But if they don't come with money, take what is valuable to them."

Even though I was given permission, it was still uncomfortable. A woman came to me one day and requested a reading in the "traditional native way." I thought to myself, oh my God, you are the answer to my prayers. I said, "I have waited so long. Please sit." I then wrote out my list of bills and their due dates.

The woman said to me, "That's not what I meant." However, I reminded her, this is what she asked for. She left the room and came back later with money. It was a humorous situation. I must live in today's world, and money is the exchange...the mortgage company agrees.

**What do you think about television ads that coax people into calling for readings?**

Again, pay attention to discernment. It is pitiful that this is a system making it difficult for spiritually gifted people. I know a very talented woman who worked for one of the lines. She was given a script, and told to keep clients on the line as long as possible. The woman told the business that she could not do that. I've heard from others that they are in it exclusively for the money—period.

I called a line to check it out, since people occasionally question me about this.

A woman answered the phone who could barely speak English and kids were in the background making all sorts of noise. She was asking and telling me things that were totally bogus and bizarre. It was sad, really. These lines prey on individuals who live in fear, are insecure, and are in crisis. People are vulnerable and will be hurt. Some people use the lines for fun and entertainment...all I can say is beware and know what you are doing.

**Is there power in prayer?**

When we put forth spiritual intent and energy, it is very powerful—it aligns, balances, and creates a vital vibration that is universal. We are in our peace and our presence. Be very clear about your thoughts because you will create or manifest them. If you have a bad thought—which we all do because we are human—shift it right away! Words have power too, so be careful what you say. Consciously focus on prayer. It is vital.

**What is your definition of mystic or mysticism?**

We are all mystics. We have the opportunity to develop into the highest spiritual essence. Someone who is a mystic utilizes this essence. If you are physically in a mystical place, you are picking up on the power of that place because it is a connected-ness of body, mind, and spirit that allows us through the door. Everyone and every place have that potential.

### How do messages come through to you — voices, images, feelings?

The best way to describe this is that there are no bells, whistles, or drama; messages present themselves. When my grandmother's spirit comes to me, I definitely smell lilacs. I don't have to light a candle, concentrate, ohm, or pray. It's just there. When I am working with certain spirits, certain smells or tastes are at hand for me.

### Do you have any advice for those with children who are curious?

Totally honor their curiosity. Enter into what they are telling you. Don't put up a barrier. If a child tells you he or she just talked to the imaginary friend, say, "What did your friend look like and what did you talk about?" Children are so close to Spirit. Learn from them. They are here to teach us.

### What do you think about coincidence and synchronicity?

We have no accidents, just incredible opportunities to grow and learn. Coincidences are the Creator saying, "Take note, watch this, we are giving you this message!" When the Aunties told me I had to go out and teach, I got a phone call. It was a friend calling about Cedar Valley Center, and she suggested I do a retreat there. Two hours later, I received another phone call that was the same message coming from another person. Four hours later — same thing happened again. My husband and I visited Cedar Valley and I booked a year worth of retreats. When Spirit speaks, we get out of our own way and listen. You have to watch everything.

One day on the hill, I was praying so hard and I recognized I was off in my left-brain, and this was not working. "Creator," I said, "Teach me how to pray." A huge colorful fly landed on my thumb and I watched that fly. First, it faced west and stood there, then faced east and stood there, and then it turned north. I said, "Thank you." Then I faced all the directions and prayed.

Now I know I have to *be* the circle, not merely skirt the fringes when I pray. The Creator brought the fly. We need to be aware of every thing around us. It comes when the thunder rumbles. Very few times, will direct messages come to you from a human; it is rare. Watch for subtlety.

### Do you have a belief in reincarnation?

The soul never dies. The physical body is the most limiting part of who we are. Our soul or spirit is who we *really* are. I hear a lot about karma, karma, karma. The philosophy that we keep coming back until we get it right because we did not accomplish this in a past life, is not true. Get that out of the way; it impedes you. We choose to come back. We are not forced. Life is a gift, we are the gift, and everyone we connect with is by divine plan. Own your journey and honor what you are meant to experience.

### Is there a Dark Side?

Balance exists; light and dark exist in all things. Darkness is real. It comes in many forms — the light and the dark, the good and the evil. That is balance. Are there evil people? Yes, and that gets back to the idea there are people who come into this lifetime to walk a "journey of evil" because that was their purpose in this lifetime. It affects everyone and everything. We need to be conscious of dark forces and dark entities. We must not engage in that, give it energy, or fear it. I have a client, an African woman, who established a relationship with a man who is a voodoo priest, although she did not know it at the time. She chose not to continue the relationship when she recognized where his journey was headed. He cast some voodoo power or magic on her, and she started having physical and emotional problems—couldn't eat, couldn't sleep, her body was having great difficulties. When I met with her, we did a cleansing and removed that power. I strongly reinforced in her that she did not own it. Do not give it energy; do not give it power. Send it off. Your power and your spiritual essence are stronger. People manipulate using darkness. It is fast and easy. They believe it is empowering them, but they don't realize it is taking over them. They don't own it; it owns them. I do not recommend this.

**Do you have any words for the hardcore, scientific minded?**

They cannot deny the miracles in their own lives. When a person acknowledges the miracles in his or her own life, that person knows there is a higher energy, a higher source. Where the hardcore scientific people have difficulty is that many of them are told to pigeon hole knowledge, and in this kind of arena that can't be done. If they are empowered to recognize the small miracles, they can breathe and accept, and not be required to define. Sometimes people have to shut down their emotional and spiritual side to function from this incredibly high intellect. Does that mean they are not spiritual? Absolutely not! Of course they are spiritual. Does that mean they are not comfortable with recognizing it? Yes, sometimes it really does. Does that mean they cannot develop a spiritual side? Of course they can, and do. In addition, the wonderful part is they can recognize developing the spiritual side does not compromise the intellect! In fact, it may complement it!

**Do you have any final messages for us?**

One of the things that I teach, and I am my own best student, is when we tell the Creator what we want, we have to get out of our own way to receive it. I gave up my career, and essentially, I've gotten out of my own way. Do I try to regulate where I'm going? No, and it is virtually amazing where this takes me! Years ago, I would have said I'm not leaving this country. Now I travel throughout the world doing my teachings and workshops and creating circles of women. Five years ago if you had asked me about doing a TV series, I would have said no way. Yet today my TV series was elected best cultural programming of the year on the local Milwaukee Public TV channel. I simply (or not so simply) got out of my own way. I am in the process of writing a book on guiding women along the spiritual journey. My video and tape series is coming out this year. I never would have sought any of this. My commitment to the Creator takes me where I need to be and lets me fulfill my purpose in life. Get out of your own way and you'll be amazed at where life will take you!

# Paula Novatnak

Paula Novotnak has been an astrologer for 30 years and has a rewarding and full time practice in Madison, Wisconsin. Paula conducts classes in astrology and in creative writing, and is developing a book related to the writing process that she has created and taught for many years. She has developed and presented beautiful and creative slide shows on the topic of astrology. Paula studied astrology in Madison, Wisconsin; Berkley, California, and in San Francisco. She is sought after as a lecturer, mentor, teacher, and consultant in the complex field of astrology.

### Contact Information
Paula Novotnak
408 South Baldwin Street
Madison, WI 53703
**Phone:** 608-243-8343

**What mystical arts do you practice today?**

I specialize in astrology consultations for individuals and couples, taking a psychological and spiritual approach. I also teach astrology. In reading, we usually start out with a birth chart interpretation. The natal chart shows the planetary positions at the moment of a person's birth. The date, time, and place of birth are used to calculate and depict the birth chart. In a natal chart, we talk about major lifetime themes and issues as well as particular gifts, challenges, tendencies, interstice, characteristics and strengths that may be emphasized over the course of a person's life. We can explore areas of identity, career, relationships, and family.

I also do update readings using particular techniques called transits and progressions. Astrological energy patterns in relation to the birth chart reflect an individual's transitions and life situation. Astrology can help us gain perspective, direction, and meaning. Couples sessions involve chart comparisons using the natal charts of the individuals, and a composite chart that symbolizes the relationship itself. Relationship readings provide understanding and appreciation of the dynamics and themes of a relationship.

Another part of my practice involves teaching. In my beginning astrology classes, I teach the overall system, the fundamental principles, and meanings. Intermediate level classes build on this foundation. Students learn how to prioritize and make sense of the mountain of information in a chart. They learn skills and techniques for interpretation. Special topics classes, like the Saturn Return class, or classes focusing on various issues such as midlife crisis, use astrology to provide language and perspective to enhance awareness. In all my classes, students have their charts and we apply the materials to them so that it's personally relevant and meaningful.

I like using photographs and slides in my classes to illustrate astrological principles. As a poet, I've enjoyed writing narration to accompany the beautiful images. I combine all this in slide presentations at conferences, in lectures and workshops, and in the community.

My spiritual practice includes meditation, guided imagery,

and mindfulness. These have influenced the classes I teach in astrology and in writing.

### How did you develop your talents in the field of astrology?

In the early 1970's when I was in my twenties, I was searching. Nothing in my early environment introduced me to astrology. I was living in central Michigan, going to graduate school, and was drawn to, and began snooping in metaphysical bookstores in Ann Arbor. I studied and began to use numerology, which lead me into Tarot. I wanted to know more about the astrological references on the Tarot cards, and this is how I entered the field of astrology. Initially, I was confused and overwhelmed, but astrology made sense to me.

The first book on astrology I read was Dane Rudhyar's *The Pulse of Life,* which correlated meanings of astrological signs with nature. This approach was a catalyst in my process. I struggled with astrology and the connections for quite awhile as I read and absorbed many books on astrology. After I actually calculated my first chart, which involves applying a very complex system and complicated math (before the days of computers and astrology software), a door, popped open for me and I experienced a breakthrough. It was like an avalanche. Something shifted and I knew I had entered my life's work. I've had several teachers in Madison and the San Francisco Bay Area, and I began teaching astrology in 1984. It has been a long haul and a tremendous learning experience, in which I've found support, love, and connection.

### Have you studied other arts in conjunction with astrology?

Numerology and Tarot are metaphysical arts that have strengthened my understanding of astrology. In California, I studied the Enneagram System with Helen Palmer. The system originated in the Sufi tradition, and it was practiced as a sacred art, hidden within the walls of the mystery schools and monasteries. It was brought to the West in the 20th century. It doesn't interface directly with astrology, but the Enneagram, with its nine personality types, has helped me to understand people. I also work in the creative arts, predominantly writing, but also drawing, collage making, photography, and slide show production.

### Explain a little about the nature of astrology.

Astrology can be used in a reductive sense. I'm sure you've heard, "Oh you are a Pisces or you are a Taurus," but those ways are degenerative from the original intent. I regard astrology as an Earth-based cosmology. It is a map of the solar system viewed from our perspective. How we relate to that perspective is significant. The natal chart is nature, but it is also the Tropical Zodiac. Our foundation is based on the seasons and the connections of the signs within the seasons. Astrology is an ancient art and science that probably originated during the Paleolithic or Stone Age. Engravings on bone and antler show records of the lunar cycles, and the depictions drew connections between celestial and earthly events.

Historically, astrology has been used to determine things such as the best time to plant to the destiny of kings. During the 20th century, Western astrology paralleled developments in psychology, and in doing so, it became more focused on understanding the individual person. Astrology is also used to observe large-scale astrological cycles in relation to world events. The individual's natal chart describes a set of potentials and possibilities. Choices made, and awareness of the choices, aid in determining how the chart manifests itself. Astrology is a model of the whole, in which all opposites co-exist: light and dark, activity and rest, work and play, the individual and the collective, etc. The task is to integrate the complexity of the planets in the chart, their sign and house placements, and the relationships to each other.

### Is there a common thread in those who practice astrology and other mystical arts?

Astrology glows with a common language, along with commonly understood skills, techniques, and information. The practitioner, as in other mystical practices, launches his or her own perspective. This depends on things such as the alchemy between the people, and the emphasis of the astrologer. Within the field, there are areas of specialization. For example, financial astrologers use the art to follow stock market trends. Counseling astrologers take a therapeutic approach. Other astrologers use it to predict. Different schools and traditions, such as Vedic astrology are gaining wider use in the West.

Another common thread found in these practices is that a certain match must exist between what the client is seeking, and what the astrologer, or other practitioner, is offering. The astrologer has an obligation to know the material well, to study, and practice, and obtain feedback on the charts. It is *essential.* A business sense is indispensable too, because it is a risky venture. Astrology is growing rapidly as people get a realistic view of the ancient art. Much of my work is intuitive. I have practiced such a long time and have studied endlessly. Connections occur that are "just there." Knowledge and intense study reinforce my intuition.

### How do you teach your classes?

I usually work with groups of six, although I occasionally teach larger classes and workshops. Small groups afford me a level of trust and closeness that develops quickly and easily. Students can apply the materials to their own charts and lives to any degree. In teaching, I use words, images, visual aids, and handouts. We apply all this to our personal charts, and sometimes the charts of the famous and infamous. I encourage questions, discussions, sharing, and respect. We have a lot of fun!

### What messages are actually within the chart?

The whole chart is the whole person, and it has relevance and meaning for the entire lifetime. It can reveal lifetime themes, Soul choices, direction, strengths and weaknesses, what comes easily and what's difficult, and our gifts and talents. Some parts are very compatible and other parts are less so. The chart shows both need and capability. For example, the chart may show a strong need for security and at the same time show our ability to fill this need. The astrologer's language and perspective are important. I feel that it does no good to denounce insecurity and say it is bad and needs to be eliminated. Insecurity can be a gateway to letting go of a need to control. In this case, we don't want to "fix" insecurity by getting rid of it. The question then becomes how we can tolerate the uncomfortable feelings of insecurity.

Astrologers must be aware of their biases when working with clients. What signs do you have a prejudice or bias against and how can you recognize this? It is important to be open to clients without imposing an agenda. Nothing in the chart speaks of good or bad—it just is. Information gleaned from astrological techniques can be remarkably precise, but does not necessarily indicate what will or will not happen, or what one should or should not do. The client has the power of choice.

### What is your answer to the skeptic?

I say, "Try it; you'll like it!" Positive coverage and intelligent discussion of astrology in the media are lacking. Widespread misunderstanding and prejudice regarding astrology has caused it to become denigrated, trivialized, and dismissed. Unfairly, it is considered unscientific, flaky, and hokey. This came about because in the 1920's, newspaper Sun Sign columns began to appear. The intention was to make astrology accessible to the public and "democratize" it. If you knew what your birthday was, you could read something about yourself in a Sun Sign column.

Unfortunately, the *reduction* of astrology into Sun Signs had a negative impact, and contributed to the misuse of astrology. The Zodiac, or Sun Sign in one's chart is important, but it is only one part of this complex pattern. The newspaper columns are written for millions of people so it is impossible to get anything personally relevant. To make it worse, some of the columns are not even written by astrologers anymore! Many professionals in the field and astrological organizations want to clear misunderstandings and renew a respect for the art and science. The more this happens, the less skepticism will prevail.

### With the complexity of it all, do you ever do readings outside of the office?

I do readings at conferences, psychic fairs, and at Mimosa Bookstore in Madison. Laptop computers have made this much easier to do, and I can be Mobile Astrologer Will Travel. On the computer, I enter the birth information, the software calculates it in about 30 seconds, and then we proceed with the reading and analyze the chart. If someone does not know or have available their birth time, I can still run a chart that contains a lot of information. I enjoy doing readings this way, and do phone consultations for long distance clients. Technology, if used correctly, is an asset to astrology.

### Is there anything unique about practicing in Wisconsin?

It seems that a greater percentage of people living on the coasts utilize astrology, and there is a larger community of peers—people practicing or seriously interested in astrology. For me, the biggest contrast is with San Francisco. I experience the Midwest as having greater stability and a slower pace, which can contribute to depth and thoughtfulness. In Wisconsin, there is a growing understanding and use of astrology. Wisconsin itself is so beautiful, and scores of curious, open-minded people live here. I love living here and I love working with the people.

### How are world events and astrology connected?

Astrology is useful in understanding what is happening in the world. For example, we are presently entering a 2000-year phase of a 26,000-year cycle. We commonly know the phase as the Age of Aquarius, and it reflects qualities of the sign, such as instantaneous global communication, the development of electronic technology, and the importance of information. Aquarians seek freedom, egalitarianism, respect for differences, and community building.

Our transition from one major age into another indicates we are on a *threshold*, and will experience a tremendous amount of turbulence as we are transitioning. Several large-scale astrological processes are reflected in the intensity and backlash of the times. Consequently, we are experiencing intense clashes of belief, religion, ideology, challenges to established institutions, and an intensification of violence, or "old" forms of response to conflict.

Astrology is a repository of wisdom that can help the change process. The study of astrology is esoteric and down-to-earth, inspirational, and practical. My interpretations and work involves supporting recognition of a paradigm shift that will affect institutions, beliefs, and how we live our lives. This involves a shift from linear and hierarchical to a holistic model that invites integration of the complexities. Our 20th century growth, signaled by significant astrological events, includes the ability to destroy the planet through weapons of mass destruction or through elimination of eco-systems, cultures, and species. In astrology, questions arise, but there are keys; and it is *fascinating* to look at history and current events through the lens of astrology. It helps us to align ourselves to the most positive aspects of a *collective* process.

### Do you have a belief in a structured religion?

I am not a member of a structured religion at present, although I believe religious institutions can be important and meaningful. I do not accept that any one religion is the absolute truth, and I don't believe that a Universal Force, which one might call God would align with any one particular religious cause.

### Do you have a belief in reincarnation?

Yes. It is hard to say it is a "belief" because to me it is merely what makes sense. I encountered this concept in my late teens and it has *always* given me an intuitive feeling of truth. Considering this view, it makes sense to me that we choose our charts, as we choose our families, and the place and time in which to incarnate to further our spiritual evolution. There is a link to destiny or fate, yet it includes Soul choice.

Sometimes when reading a chart, I don't specifically use the word "reincarnation," but instead I will say in a manner of words, "this is where you come from." Reincarnation does not have scores of "should" and "dictate" facets. Because I feel we are co-creators, I want to help an individual feel more empowered and connected to the Universe. Karmic aspects may be present in a chart. This is not good or bad, again, it just *is*. I understand karma to be simply that certain actions bring certain results.

The north node and the south node in the chart speak to reincarnation. Traditionally the south node links to influences in this lifetime that come through from other lifetimes. By contrast, the north node is what we are drawn to and working on in our life today. If I bring my orientation into a session, I let people know I am referring to reincarnation. I don't impose this, because I want to respect the individual's spiritual and religious beliefs.

Personally, I relate to the south node and I take a non-linear perspective on this. In other words, I don't refer to a chronological sequence in the lifetimes, but more of a timeless presence. On that level, all of our existence and all of our lifetimes are available to coexist in the present. We have access to qualities, characteristics, and perspectives that come easily to us and might be connected to other lifetimes.

**When you are out and about are your abilities in action?**

Yes and no. What I have internalized about astrology is there, but on a back burner. The system can provide me with insight, connection, information, and awareness. It is a useful perspective for me to have. I don't mean it in a sense that I am out there wondering what people's charts look like. I have an aversion to the question, "What's your sign." It sounds so hokey these days. I keep boundaries between my work and the rest of my life. I consciously create "sacred space" in which to conduct my consultations. After a client session, I purposefully tend to forget most of what was said and shared. In this regard, I am in a somewhat "altered" state of consciousness, and this enables me to let it go.

**What have a few of your clients said about their experiences in a session?**

I receive consistent feedback that the readings are meaningful, relevant, and helpful. Most of my clients come through word of mouth. Many return to me and refer others. A young man recently told me after the session that the work really helped improve his self-esteem. Some people say the session puts a lot into words what is difficult to articulate, or they find a feeling of validity and renewed sense of wonder.

**Have you helped in any police or investigative cases?**

I refuse this kind of work because I'm not trained in it and I don't have much interest in doing it, although I have been asked on occasion.

### What is your view on charging for services?

Initially, when I was first learning, I didn't charge for my services. Now my livelihood and much of my family's support depends on my practice. It is difficult for me when I have to raise my prices, but as the cost of living goes up, I have to face this decision periodically.

### How do your family and friends view your abilities?

My immediate family is tremendously supportive and views my work with respect. In my extended family, some understand and accept my work more than others accept. Some have used my services as a consulting astrologer or as a teacher. There is a general atmosphere of tolerance as to whether they "get it" or not, and I don't run into any put-downs or dismissals of my work. With my friends and family members, I can engage in discussions that include an astrological perspective.

### Do people ever show up with a wall between you and them?

A few clients come in with an attitude or agenda that is intent on challenging astrology — a "prove it to me" stance. This is hard, and fortunately, it does not happen often. It is not my intention to prove or convince anybody of anything. I'll work with the person, but it really is not where the best work happens. Usually if a person is serious about making an appointment and paying for services, they have an open-minded attitude.

### Mystic defined?

Mysticism is a way to see through the veil. It sees through the mists between the physical dimensions and those that are subtle and operate with different, faster frequencies. The mystical arts include astrology. It is very mysterious and intertwined with something greater; literally, astrology uses a map of the macrocosm to affect the microcosm, more commonly known as you and me. Mystical arts have been known as occult arts, meaning "hidden" or "secret." Some of the secrets hidden in mystery schools, are coming out into the open and are more accessible to people. Practitioners are gaining credibility. Science and technology are tapping into this tool also.

### What would you caution people about when going for an astrology reading?

Ask questions when calling an astrologer to get a sense of who that person is. If you have something that you definitely want to get out of a reading, bring this up at the time of the initial phone call. You may be looking for something that the astrologer can't provide. Because I take a psychological and spiritual approach, I would refer someone seeking predictions or business forecasts to someone else. It is a good idea to ask how long the astrologer has been practicing. Does he or she have any references? Follow your gut response and intuition. If you are coming back for another reading, let the astrologer know if there are certain things you want to focus on or get from the consultation.

A client needs to be aware of his or her own vulnerabilities. At a session, be aware of power issues, of giving away your power by thinking that because the practitioner has access to some metaphysical realm, he or she knows what is best for you. You are in charge of your life.

### Is there a Dark Side in any of this?

Generally, I defend and affirm the dark. I don't equate darkness with evil and ignorance. The dark contains mystery. It supports rest, relaxation, and healing. It can be a time of dormancy and gestation. When I see something in a chart, I think this person could really have some challenges in a particular area, and I wonder how he or she will relate to this. When I look at the rest of the chart, I can get an idea of how a person might attend to the hurdle. However, the chart does not tell me anything about their level of understanding, compassion, or integrity.

Things are a matter of perspective. The planet Pluto associates with Scorpio. Some people think of this as bad and dangerous, and to be avoided. The original meaning for Pluto was "riches." Pluto is about depth, and might be scary because of buried trauma and things like that. Ultimately, we go deeper and find an immense richness that I would associate with getting to the core or to the truth. That process can be transforming and healing. Like everything else, astrology can be used for good or evil. Hitler apparently used astrology. On a smaller scale, unfortunately, people can use it to create a mystique about themselves to have power or influence over people.

**Do you have any advice for those with children interested in astrology?**

Support them. Maybe go with them to an astrologer with whom you are familiar. If a child truly has an interest in astrology, it might be worthwhile to go to more than one to compare the ways they work. Go to a library or bookstore to look at astrology books. Children read their horoscope, and questions come up that are beyond a superficial Sun Sign blurb in the newspaper. Encourage children's curiosity and help them to be discerning. It's okay to disagree with things they may hear, see, or read, and they need to know that.

**What is your opinion about coincidence?**

Coincidence means things coincide — connect the dots. We are not always fully aware of the connections. How and why things coincide can be mysterious. What is wonderful and magical is that "in-the-moment glimpse" of some connection to a larger context that we previously had not been aware of consciously. Astrology is one way of putting the larger context into perspective.

**What do you think about a connection between astrology and science?**

Astrology is not necessarily disconnected from physics. A few years ago, I attended a conference where a physicist gave a wonderful presentation about the relationship of astrology and physics. In the context of new physics and working with matter and energy, astrology makes sense. At a time when astrology was integrated with astronomy, they were parts of the same science and art. Nevertheless, over time, science began to view the

Universe as a machine, and this denied the spiritual aspects and connections. Astrology was relegated to a "psuedo-science" at best, but things are definitely beginning to change.

### What is your mission with astrology?

My deepest, most fundamental intention is to further love and peace. Astrology has the strong potential to deepen respect and renew purpose while connecting us with large-scale collective and evolutionary events. Part of my mission is to "revision" astrology. I want to reclaim things that have been stereotyped, misinterpreted, and misrepresented. In my research, I looked at Paleolithic and matrifocal Neolithic eras. Recent evidence indicates the existence of peaceful and flourishing civilizations, thus the conclusion that violence and war are *not* endemic to our life and human nature. I have applied these findings to astrology. For example, the animal symbol for the sign of Aires is the ram. The ram, with its tendency to run forward and butt its head against something, has been associated with the battering ram, even with Rambo-like aggression, and therefore selfish disregard for others. Some people with strong Aires energy may act in this way; however, we need to be cautious, because there are other expressions of these energies, such as assertiveness, that we are obliged to consider.

Originally, the spiral of the ram's horns was considered symbolic. Spiraling and uncoiling energy is the symbolic significance. Essentially, Aires is about fresh possibilities, creating the momentum in life, and intuition that acts in the moment. Aires is related to the planet Mars, which was a god of vegetation. Much later, in Greek mythology, Mars was the god of war.

Going back to uncover these earlier layers of meaning can expand how we use astrology as a tool to cultivate wisdom, love, compassion, and peace. Experiences — pleasure and pain, happiness and sorrow, rage and celebration, the bitter and the sweet—are a slice of a larger process of retrieval and envisioning what is crucial during these turbulent times.

# Sylvia Bright-Green

Sylvia Bright-Green is a spiritual intuitive, clairvoyant, healer, and counselor. She acts as a bridge between the physical and spiritual world to bring insight and descriptive information about past life and present life relationships. Her interests lie in spiritual mediumship, intuitive health reading, Reiki, remote or non-local viewing, and photograph reading. She also facilitates spirit circles with group settings to aid in spiritual communication. Sylvia works with individuals and with groups of people at various events. She lives in Sheboygan Falls and has been active in paranormal work for many years.

### Contact information
Sylvia Bright-Green
103 Evans Court, Apt. D
Sheboygan Falls, WI  53085
**Phone:**  920-467-9829
**E-mail:** *ladyhawk@taoworks.org*

**What mystical arts do you practice today?**

I practice as a medical intuitive, spiritual medium, and clairvoyant. I also do remote viewing and photograph reading of
people and dogs. I normally sense whoever is alive or deceased
in your energy and describe the personality of that entity. If a
person is deceased, I ask the sitter or client, if he or she wants to
talk to that entity. A person who has passed over retains the
personality and individuality that was present in this life. It's
interesting. They can be comical or facetious, and if they used a
lot of expletives in their language, that will come through too.
Sometimes they come in with a scent, and the client recognizes
this. The spirit projects an image that I describe to the client. If
the entity had a hangup in life about obesity or thinness, for
example, I won't be able to see certain parts of that psychic image.

Remote viewing comes in handy. I can be sitting at home in
my house and often I can describe a place the client is living in
or had lived in previously. I've helped people find lost objects.
If a spirit is in the house, I can detect it and proceed with sending it to the light, "ghost-busting" per se. Through spirits, I've
helped find deeds, wills, and lost objects. If a person is afraid to
have a reading, I look at the emotional heart like a valentine
and see love or hate situations that are stored there. Envisioning inner parts of the client, I detect areas that have separated at
various ages due to emotional incidents.

If a person tells me he or she can't remember childhood or
any part of childhood, that tells me there is a lot of soul loss and
the person might benefit from soul retrieval. . If there is pain in
life, these parts of fear, anger, and sadness hide within a person,
causing physiological and psychological problems. Retrieving
lost soul is a simple process.

**When did you develop these abilities?**

I became aware of these abilities in the 1970's. I had a bleed-
ing ulcer and four children by then. The physician said I needed
to learn to meditate to heal the ulcer. So I began quieting myself. The first day I tried this, I found myself in a jungle scene
where I was shown how to heal a baby. I decided this was just

my imagination. The next day I tried the meditation again and found myself in an old farmhouse with a couple who were fighting, and a 12-year-old girl had been injured. I was worried about all these events, and I called the doctor. He thought I was having "mild schizophrenic moments" and gave me Valium. A short time later, I ended up hospitalized to be weaned off the Valium. Another doctor eventually said I was having visions, and I should go to the library to get books on Edgar Cayce and Ruth Montgomery. The books opened the metaphysical door for me. Years later, I learned the initial visions were glimpses into past lives of mine.

Prior to this discovery, it took me four years of practicing meditation and learning it properly. At first, I listened to music and then went to using a mantra. Now, going into meditation is automatic for me, just by using the intent to do so. I do a clearing of the energy and I do a prayer of protection. Before I do readings at a fair, I pull light around me and call for angels and guides to assist me. I use a ritual to do this.

### Is there a common thread among those who practice mystical arts?

I believe so. It's learning to read, sense, and feel the energy around others. Originally, I thought we were all different. I started doing readings at fairs and discovered that among readers, nothing is sacred. It's interesting how one psychic can see your whole life, and then a different psychic can tell you the same thing many months later. I think the common thread is a "knowing" of what's going on with people around them. We pick up on thoughts, emotions, and people we've interacted with that are all in your energy.

### What are your comments for the skeptic?

In the beginning, I avoided the skeptic. Other readers told me skeptics could close me down and make it difficult to read for them. Now when someone does this, I simply tell that person who is in his or her energy field, describe the entity, and the problem is solved. For example, I recall a teenager who was helping at a facility where a psychic fair was being held. I told the boy there was a woman standing behind him with curly hair, glasses, height is 5'3" and weight is 135 pounds." He said that was his grandmother, but he was unconvinced. When a person says that could be many people, I then go into specific personality. Then I might hear that I've narrowed it down to two people. If this is the case, I tell the person something that I couldn't possibly have known.

Before I do any readings, I ask that Spirit only send me people who need my assistance. I am here for a purpose, and that's not to play games. I am here to help and sometimes find answers for people.

### Have you heard any criticism about your type of work?

I've heard such things as this is the "work of the devil." Truly, it's not. Evil is the dark side of humankind, and it is an energy. I have a friend who wanted to set me up with a male friend of hers. In a phone conversation, I told this man that I'd be honest and tell him that I am a psychic. He stated, "Well, I'll be honest with you and tell you I'm a Sunday school teacher. The scriptures tell me psychics are from the devil."

Then I said, "Didn't Jesus say to the multitude of people before him when they asked how he performed miracles, 'All that I do, you can do and more'? What do you say to that?" We agreed not to get into a religious debate, but I reinforced that I am a spiritual person who's not fond of being preached at. I am familiar with the Bible, and as a mixed up teenager, looking for me, I read it more than once. If I need to find something in the Bible, I can find it quickly.

### Is there anything unique about practicing in Wisconsin?

I believe Wisconsin is a bit on the conservative side. When I "came out of the closet" in 1995 in a Dutch Reform community there was a newspaper article written about my journey into parapsychology. I thought I'd have crosses burning on my lawn and my children would have it rough in school. As it turned out, I received an extraordinary number of positive letters and phone calls. Now the door is open for many who practice mysticism. We have fairs all over the state, and I've read for people from all walks of life. Numbers are growing in Wisconsin.

**Do world events affect your readings?**

They do not affect my abilities. On September 11, I personally, as a human, felt extremely sad. Many people sent blessings and white light to the people and the cities that were directly involved. I believe there is a higher purpose for all of us personally, and for whatever happens in the world as a whole.

**Do you subscribe to a structured religion or take a universal approach?**

I studied many religions, and then decided I am who I am. I respect all religions and offer to read for anyone who is open-minded, no matter what the religious practice is. Helping people is part of love, and that's where I'm coming from. I have fourteen brothers and sisters in a variety of religions, including a brother who is a Jehovah's Witness. I studied with that faith for three years, so I know where they are coming from, but it truly is not me. I don't debate religion with anyone. I usually inform those who knock on my door that I do psychic work. The visits to my door are infrequent now. Some are fearful of this, but that's where they are at, and I respect them.

**When you are out and about are your abilities on hold or on and off like a light switch?**

I can and do turn my abilities on and off. There is a spiritual law that says do not trespass on another person. However, there are times when I am in a public place and just focused on what I am doing, when a stranger passes me and I'll feel like I've been bombarded with a blast of emotional or thought energy. Then I ask myself whether I should say something to this person or not. What I end up doing is walking up to this stranger and saying something like, "When you walked past me, I noticed you are in turmoil over a decision, and I have a message to give to you if you want it." Usually the person takes the message, and walks away without questioning me on how or why I do this. Understand I only do this if I am compelled to do so. This can happen when I am busy in my own house and I receive a message for someone I've done a reading on previously.

**Do you think dreams have significance?**

Yes, they can be significant. I have been working with a woman for three years. In the beginning, she was calling me frequently every day. She was quite depressed, but is now doing well, and I rarely hear from her. I had a dream where I saw her in a bar scene with two men. The bar stools were covered in red upholstery, and there were wooden tables to the right of the entryway. I described the men in the bar very well, and my friend happened to know one of them. When I told her about the dream she told me she was not familiar with the bar.

Two weeks later, the woman went for a job interview to work for a lawn care company and she was to meet the owner at a bar-restaurant during the lunch hour. When she walked into the bar, she immediately recognized this as the bar in the dream description. Her new boss was standing at the bar talking to an old friend of hers. I believe this dream was tied to obtaining new employment for this woman. Dreams have information, and we should pay attention.

**Are there any specific incidents that you would like to talk about?**

Finding lost objects and reading photos are things I love to do. I helped a woman from Janesville who was going on a trip to Thailand. She misplaced her passport and had to find it within a week. She contacted me and asked about its location. I told her I'd have to meditate on it and call her back. In meditation, I determined it was in a suitcase. She said she searched every suitcase she owned and there was no passport. I then became more specific and said it was in a case within a case. Well, you can imagine how confusing this was becoming. The woman said she didn't know if she could rely on that since she had thoroughly searched everywhere. I told her that was the only information coming to me.

Within a few days, I got a phone call. The woman said she was about to make the trip to Chicago to get a new passport quickly, but something happened. She had two make-up cases, a large one and a small. She opened up the small case which was inside of the larger case and there was the passport — a case within a case — simple as that.

In another situation, I read for a 29-year-old man and I saw an old woman standing behind him. She seemed to be Native American. I think she is what is known as the "wise woman." The young man said that when he looks in the mirror he senses there is a woman behind him. His wife senses an old woman, too, and it is frightening. I told him that the woman's message to him was that he was off track and not following what his heart's desire was, and that he had to get back to that soon.

The young man called me back in that same week and said that he wanted to get back into music very badly, but he was so overwhelmed with work that he did not have the opportunity. Then "out of the blue" a phone call came from a former high school friend who remembered that the young man was a guitar player and was writing songs in high school. The guitarist from the caller's band left and he was wondering if this young man would fill in for the Bratwurst Festival in Sheboygan. Now that's an open door.

### What strikes you as the strangest ability?

The weirdest is when people ask me to do a body scan, and sometimes I find that a spirit is attached. Attachments seem to be deceased loved ones that the living person was very "attached" to in life. Teenage girls playing with Ouija boards are candidates for trouble if they are receptive. One such girl contacted me because she was having trouble with a bedroom door opening and closing, lights going on and off, and things on a dresser being rearranged. This was freaking her out. Girls visit me in batches of three because they are frightened and don't want to be alone. They'll say they have a health issue or that they think there is a ghost in the house. I *always* ask if they have been playing with a Ouija board. In this particular case, the answer was yes, so then we have some "detachment" work to do. It turned out that the attached spirit was that of a 17 year-old boy the girls knew had committed suicide. They were attempting to reach his spirit using a Ouija board.

### Have you worked on any police or investigative cases?

No, not much. I was able to help a woman with a hit and run case involving her son by describing what happened in the accident and providing a description of the driver's car. I couldn't make out the license plate, however. I tend to see through the eyes of the deceased. This accident happened late at night when the boy was walking.

### What are your views on charging for services?

I keep my fees low because my purpose is to help others. My fees have been the same for twelve years despite increased rates at psychic fairs and other readers' fees. If someone is at a fair and says he or she can't afford a reading, I barter or do the reading for free. Acts of kindness repay me in one way, or another.

### What do you think about psychic hot lines on television?

There are some legitimate psychics and there are phonies. I know people who have worked on these lines, but they were being scammed, too, because of the pressure to keep people on the line for longer periods. People have to be careful about psychic hot lines. I would not recommend contact with these lines. There are so many fairs around the state where legitimate readings happen that people don't need the hot lines.

### Do you believe there is power in prayer?

Definitely, there is a lot of power in prayer. I believe that what you create with your thinking is what you receive. If you believe that you deserve something or you want something in your life, a sort of "mystical marriage" is formed between your heart, your solar plexus, and what it is you desire. Then you have to let go of the thought, because to hang on to it, and obsess over it, will not promote the manifestation of it. We create all day long with thoughts and emotions that flash through us, good or bad. We can create that fast. Notice the subtle things. For example, I was at a Christmas party and there was a gift exchange. A friend of mine received a box of chocolate-covered turtles—a prize I coveted. When I returned home, there was a gift waiting at my door that had been dropped off by a friend—chocolate-covered turtles. I also create parking places that way and stopping the rain when I want to get out of the car. I know it sounds hokey, but well, it works!

**What are your thoughts on reincarnation?**

I believe in it. When I look into my past lives, I have found that I had similar afflictions from one life to the next. It's interesting. I was at a spiritual conference in Milwaukee a few years ago listening to a lecture on symbols. An elderly woman came up to me and put her hand on my left shoulder. She said, "You have a left side wound from a previous life and today your shoulder feels sore and is knotted up." I told her that in a past life regression, I had been shot in a bank robbery. At times when I have had bronchitis, chest x-rays showed a small calcification in my lung, which the doctor described as "pencil or bullet hole-sized." Yes, I think reincarnation has credibility.

The state of mind that you are in when you exit Earth is what will be on the other side. If you leave in a positive state of mind and expect to find a heaven or glorious place, that's probably what you'll find. In contrast, if you are looking at life on Earth as living in a hellish place and there's nothing beyond that but more of the same, then that is what you'll find. It's all a matter of where you are in your spiritual beliefs.

**How do messages come through to you — symbols, voices, smells?**

Voices, smells, flashes are strong for me. Psychic flashes and visions are especially useful in finding objects and reading photos. Such an incident happened when a friend who had hidden a Christmas gift for her husband forgot where she put it. She called me to ask, and I said I'd meditate on it, and call her back. The following day, I was watching a movie on the TV and an image flashed before me. I immediately called the friend back and I said it looks like it's in some kind of shoebox with a handle on it, or a purse with a handle. The woman was frustrated because she had looked in boxes and purses with no sighting of the lost gift. The daughter came home and heard about the fiasco and what I had envisioned, and said, "That's it, you put it in the safety deposit box — a 'shoebox' with a handle on it." When I get flashes, I run right to the phone!

### What's your definition of mystic?

A mystic is someone who is open-minded in the spiritual realm. What is out there does not frighten them. They accept it for what it is.

### Do you have any cautions for people who seek a reader?

Be careful. I have heard of people who do a reading and they are very good, but then they go further to say you have a "block" on you, and that to do a ritual, and set you free, will cost hundreds of dollars for candles, crystal, and so on. All this does is "free" you of your money. I have had clients come to me for help with these complaints, and I tell them the so-called block isn't necessarily there unless they believe it is. I think this is awful; it bothers me, and gives honest readers a bad name.

### Do you think there is a Dark Side?

The only dark side that I feel exists is the dark side of the human. Maybe it should be called the negative side of the ego. A young fellow calls me on occasion and tells me that his sister writes to the notorious Charles Manson in a California prison. He says that his sister is sick. I say to him that she is at where she wants to be, and all you can do is allow yourself to know this.

I see some young people these days wearing freaky clothes, earrings all over the place, rainbow-colored spiked hair, and so on. I have met these people, and many have gentle Souls. They dress bizarrely to make a statement, but contrary to that, they say, "This is not who I am, and if this is all you see, I feel sorry for you." I feel there is no good or bad, there just *is*. Related to this, I believe everything is energy. How we use that energy is a determining factor. We can use it for good or bad, black or white, or any shade in between.

### Do you have any messages for us?

We should be grateful for what we have in our lives, and not what we think we need in our lives. There is ultimately and always a message. Say thank you many times a day, even if it as simple as someone opening a door for you. In 1995, I had a very difficult time after my husband passed away. We had only been living in our new place in Rhinelander for a week. I had no family or friends in the area. I had no job. One day I said, "This is it God, you sent me here, now take care of me." That's exactly what happened and income started coming my way. I moved back to Sheboygan Falls fourteen months later. I felt like Dorothy clicking her heels and coming back home. When I arrived, I had a car insurance payment due. Coincidently, I happened to open the newspaper and found an ad looking for psychics to work at a fair in the area. I was able to do that, and earned precisely the amount I needed for the insurance payment. I know it sounds strange, but it is an example of being in control for myself. It's also an example of things having meaning and connection.

I have learned to accept that whatever and whoever comes into your life is a gift. Look at each person as a gift and know that if you did not see him or her again, that you may have lost something of value. We hurry about too much and we lack appreciation. The number one comment I hear from people involved in a relationship is that there is a lack of communication or that passion is gone. Stop the negative nitpicking. Communication and passion are gone only if we allow them to be. Don't let personal agendas get in the way of learning and growing.

# Gary Dischler

Gary Dischler is an intuitive practitioner using tools of clairvoyance, clairsentience, astrology, and numerology. His practice is spiritually based. Gary also uses channeling to help people. He is a teacher in many walks of life. Gary travels extensively and studies other cultures to enhance his abilities and understandings. He continuously learns and searches for questions and answers that guide him on his soul path. Gary lives in Middleton, Wisconsin.

**Contact Information**
Gary Dischler
7012 Fortune Drive
Middleton, WI 53562
**Phone:** 608-320-0662

**What mystical arts are you practicing today?**

I do readings using clairvoyance, clairsentience, and astrology, numerology, and clear channeling. I have also become aware of the Masters and Guides who are assisting the Earth. In the 1990s, I went public with this. I am not necessarily who I was trained to be by society. I found that if a person gave me a birthday or certain bits of information, I was able to connect that to information that pertained to that person's experience in this lifetime. The snippets of information I received made sense and there were relationships to particular words, places, or events. Most of the information I receive is likely to be channeled from the other person's Guides.

I have learned to keep good boundaries. For example, a man came to one of the fairs where I was working, looked directly at me when he entered the room, and waited until I finished with my client. He then sat down and told me of some experiences he'd had which began in the 1970's. The information he gave me was far beyond the realm of my experiences. He seemed eccentric, maybe even psychotic, or neurotic. He said to me, "The beings told me you would be here." Strange as that incident was, I try to keep an open mind and still maintain the boundaries. I learn from anyone with whom I work.

I have worked in the area of past life regression. This comes through clearly for me. When I talk about past lives to clients, they will say such things as "Yes I am drawn to that area of the world and I have books about that country." Past lives can be a fascination and perhaps serve some purpose for personal healing in the present time. I believe we are really an accumulation of everything we have ever experienced, whether it is in this lifetime or another.

I have been drawn to specific areas in Europe. My heritage is German-Czech-Bavarian. When visiting Prague, I was familiar with some of the streets and mystical sites. While touring the homeland of my ancestors, on the Czech-German border, I managed to get lost and subsequently discovered a building that turned out to be an old brewery constructed by Alois Brickl who was my mother's grandfather, born in 1864. Talk about synchronicity! I think I felt almost every cell in my body when I saw that. Ever since I was a child, I have had a fascination with

Spain, specifically the culture and the language. When I visited the country, there were places that had familiarity to me. Another fascination I've had is with various sites in Russia, and Lake Baikal, which is in southeastern Siberia. I have seen myself as an old woman living in that area. The lake appears to me in mediation and I actually had the opportunity to visit in 1999. These experiences seem significant to my past lives, and I treasure them.

### How did you develop these abilities?

When I was a young child, I knew things, and could sense things. However, if I spoke my truth it would get me into trouble. With parents, brothers, and sisters, I knew where the conflicts were without anybody saying a word. I also had a sixth sense about the weather—rainstorms, blizzards, windstorms. On the farm where I grew up, I was the Pied Piper of cats and other animals. However, for many years, I denied what I knew so as not to cause family trouble. My Catholic tradition certainly was more left-brained and did not allow these things to surface. Even so, the Catholic Church really does have a great deal of mysticism about it if we look closely at its roots.

In 1973 at the age of 22, I was having difficulty sleeping, and I sensed a Great Being around me who said, "You have studied it before; go back and study it again." It was the *Book of Revelation*, the final book of the Bible. What that was about in 1973, I'm not sure, but I developed a fascination with *Revelation*, and perhaps I was being guided to awaken more to my life's purpose. This experience prompted me to learn more about decoding this wonderful book, not that it can be directly decoded in our language. The study of symbolism in the book is what is of interest to me. To this day, I feel we are in the 18th or 19th chapter in the book. I'm *not* saying the world is about ready to destruct, however we are literally ending one period or cycle of the Earth at this time. I believe the last book in the Bible is an indication of this transition.

### How do messages or intuitive things come through to you — voices, feelings, symbols?

Clear knowing is mainly the way for me. Clairsentience and

clairvoyance assist me, and this is meant to be for the client. I can sense symbols around people. I don't see them clairvoyantly in this case, but it is a simple "knowing." Sometimes I pick up colors, as in an aura field. If I don't see them directly, I still know they are there. I believe colors have significance, and that people are born under one of the Seven Rays. Each one of us is influenced by any one of the Seven Rays in perhaps five or six areas of life. The Seven Rays refer to energies and work through certain charkas. They are essential to our make up as a being.

**Do you have other areas of interest in mysticism?**

I'm interested in the path of the Kabbalah. There are some mystics, even of the Christian tradition, who studied the Kabbalah in depth. One was St. Francis. I am specifically interested in my own personal growth, and study the teachings of many writers, mystics, and Masters in the area of transpersonal psychology. I also study the *Keys of Enoch* which is an esoteric text written in 1973. I am of the opinion that each one of us is guided by a presence around us; some would call it a soul. When the soul reaches a certain level of growth, I believe we have the ability to become conscious of our connection with our own Soul. There are tests in life however. Some areas become easier, and others cause consternation. Tests determine our level or proficiency as a step to the next level.

**Is there a common thread among those who practice mystical arts?**

The common thread probably has to do with a level of our own growth. When the time is right for something, spiritual lessons naturally unfold for us. It is a level of our soul beckoning to our personality. It seems that humanity evolves in this manner, and practicing a mystical art is what may open up as a person's purpose in life. Authentic healers, such as Chopra or Kubler-Ross are examples of people who have worked in the sixth or seventh initiation of their lives. Not everyone is deemed a Mother Teresa or a Princess Diana. Those who are successful at their art are at another level of initiation that other people may not necessarily understand.

**Do you have an answer for the skeptic?**

Skepticism is a good thing. Many people, including me, in their quest for knowledge, learn how to stand in our own power without giving our power to anyone else. John Edward and Oprah Winfrey come to mind. A skeptic will learn to manifest his or her own dream without giving personal power to others. It is also good to look at scientific realms. In the future, I see the paths of mysticism and science agreeing on things, and becoming aware that they have traveled different paths to get to the same endpoint. What could be considered admirable about the skeptic is that this person does not give his or her individual authority to another person. On the other hand, skeptics need to be cautious of ego battles.

Sometimes it is better if neither the mystical nor the scientific is proven. For example, the Hindu saints contend that nothing needs to be proven because the being within the body is the only one whose truth is important. What's important is *what* is known. I would be reluctant to get into a "prove it" exchange with anyone — again, battle of the egos. I think people should look introspectively as to why they need to be right.

**Is there anything unique about practicing in Wisconsin?**

Well, no doubt about it. Our northern European influence tends to be strong in the left-brain, and maybe not quite so open to the right brain things that are happening globally today. Reluctance to look at some of the intuitivism and the healings seems to be part of our local culture and contained in a shell. On the other hand, there might be a purpose to that also. When the root of science brings this home, some would say in the area of quantum physics, there could be many people who say, "Oh that's the way it works!" A global Renaissance could arise. Coastal areas, such as California, the Pacific Northwest, and areas of Canada around Toronto, Vancouver, and Montreal tend to be more open. Different countries tune into different energies. Aborigines of Australia and Native Americans are opening doors for people to walk through. Perhaps the world is in turmoil to raise our consciousness. Wisconsin tends to hold back; however, in Madison there are groups who are more active in mysticism, the healing arts, and ideas around New Age Philosophy.

**Do world events affect your abilities?**

Yes, they affect abilities negatively and positively. Since about September 1, 2001 it felt like my hands were burning and this sensation went all the way back to my elbows. After September 11, 2001, it all went away. Global events have a large impact on various people who have sensitivities to particular things. I believe there are people who can physically feel and see the terror in the eyes of people living in Afghanistan, for example. We need to be very careful about how we portray countries or cultures as enemies. We can grow to be an enemy to ourselves. If humanity is part of a greater soul, what purpose does disharmony have?

Recently, I returned from a trip to China. During that trip, I sensed a new awareness in that ancient land. People seemed to have a spirit of cooperation and universal goodwill, which left many members of our tour group in awe.

**Do you have a belief in a structured religion?**

As a child, I had a belief in a structured religion. It was a tight container, and by the mid 1970s, I found this system was not for me anymore. At first, I was angry and judgmental, but through the 1980s, I could see that most religious traditions were aiming toward a common goal of manifesting and aspiring to the highest state of integrity. Nevertheless, I am always grateful for my structured traditional religious training because it allowed me to grow into the person I am today.

**When you are out and about are your abilities in action or put on hold?**

I think people have to have good boundaries and surround themselves with divine protection. In certain areas, you can be open and safe, and you will intuitively know this.

There is a time and place to share information. I am reserved, and the on-off switch is determined by what's going on around me globally and locally.

### Are dreams significant?

Yes, dreams have significance to the person who has the dream. Document and work with the symbolism in dreams, and they will teach you about yourself. I'm not sure that another person can accurately interpret a dream for any particular individual. I think the dream is given to that person for his or her own decoding. Perhaps general things apply, such as a house representing a person's body, and so on. The idiosyncrasies are significant to that specific person. If I saw myself as a football player in a dream, I would be wondering if I am trying to shield myself. Am I overprotecting myself? Am I vulnerable in some ways? Many questions pop up in interpretation. Our soul may be the teacher in some types of dreams.

### Are there any specific readings you wish to discuss?

Recently, a woman who had been to several readers said to me that none of what she heard was applying to her life. She was beginning to think readers were fakes. I suggested to her we see what would come through in a session and maybe we could pull it all together to make sense. The messages given to me indicated she was concerned with diet, yoga, and had a quest for the metaphysical. In addition, I told her she would be going on to medical or veterinary school, and in fact she was in the process of applying. This information fit her perfectly and she was amazed. She was then able to apply some of the other information given to her in the readings.

I had a client in state government who came to me before "Y2K" (year 2000) with a question about possible areas that were being neglected by the Legislature. What came through were *many* areas of computerization that really were in need of protection. It was interesting for her to experience this, and she made notations about these areas in the State government that needed work.

I'm not really interested in telling people about relationships or trying to guess lottery numbers. This all seems so insignificant in the scheme of things. Sometimes I can give a date, and the message will come through as to this thing or another thing will work out by April 30th or whatever. Occasionally the person will call back and ask me how I knew that. I tell them that I personally didn't know, but this is just what came through for them.

### Have you worked on police of investigative cases?

Occasionally, I have had that opportunity. A woman came to me wanting to know where her son was. After centering myself and going within, I could see her son as east of Highway 41 somewhere around Lake Michigan. She thought this unlikely, but he was in fact, in an area just north of Milwaukee. She was kind enough to let me know that she was able to find him living in the area we had discussed. He had chosen to "drop out" and wanted it to appear that he had disappeared.

### What are your views on charging for services?

All spiritual knowledge is best given freely, but I realize that the way our society is structured, we need to live, eat, drive a car, and have an income. Legitimate practitioners should have the privilege of charging reasonably for their services.

### What is your opinion on the psychic hot lines advertised on TV?

All of us have innate psychic ability that unfolds when we are ready. Ability is unlocked in various ways such as through synchronistic or developmental experiences, or through meditative and spiritual study. Some people access psychic ability by using "artificial" means. Liken it to opening a glass jar. You can take the lid off slowly with little resistance, or you can just break into the jar. Authentic healers have naturally unfolded into their Soul's work. I am skeptical about the authenticity and methods of most workers on the psychic hot lines.

### How does this work affect your other job or relationships with friends and your family?

Some people are skeptical, or they view it as witchcraft. Some may have fundamentalist views and are afraid of this sort of thing. They see it, from a fear factor, as something diabolical. This is all good indication that these individuals are not yet ready to hear about an unfamiliar spirituality. I respect people, regardless of their beliefs.

I come from a family who were somewhat accustomed to mysticism and this was accepted some of the time. I had an aunt who predicted the death of her young niece. My grandmother revealed prophetic dreams that were on target about future events. Of her eight brothers and sisters, four were open to these occurrences. Maybe there are genetic components as well as age components determining what's going on with the person's soul at any given point.

### Is there power in prayer?

Yes! Every thought we generate has power. Prayer comes in several forms, including emotion, devotion, and invocation. If all people would just stop for a minute and call on the cosmic mind for world peace and divine guidance, the whole planet would just light up. Prayer in meditation contains power. Anything that we put energy into will create something. Being aware of one's conscious thoughts is important. We are the master of our own ship. Interestingly, scientists will likely teach us the same concept that thoughts create reality.

### What is your definition of mysticism?

Mysticism is examining the mysteries of the unknown. It parallels the mysteries of science in another plane. Mysticism is found in all Spiritual traditions and is brought forth through mediation and spiritual practices.

### Do you have any advice for those seeking a reader or a healer?

Ask yourself if you are comfortable with that person. What is your gut feeling? This reader may or may not have things to offer you. Use caution if things don't feel right mentally or physically. How do you feel when you are in that reader's space or energy, and how does the reader appear to feel? If people are looking for a reader or a healer, it is important to ask others about the practitioner's track record. There are extraordinary readers and healers who don't necessarily come with a billboard announcing their gift.

**Do you have advice for those with children who are showing abilities?**

Children are remarkable and they are changing the world. Many wise "old souls" are incarnating now. They come from great cultures of the past and they have gone through preparation to be here at this point in Earth's time. These children should be encouraged, and we need to listen to them. It would be wise for parents who notice "unusual" abilities in their children, to handle some situations as just one more experience. Many children born since 1987 can tap into multiple dimensions that are unfamiliar to many older people. These children are a gateway. They will undoubtedly change the world.

**What is your view on coincidence or synchronicity?**

I think more of synchronicity than I do of coincidence. I believe there is a difference between the two. A synchronistic event is one that provides us with one more tool or one more action of the universe for us to look at and say, "Oh now I'm being shown something that connects to something else. How do I put it all together?" This is a personal process of growth. A coincidence might not have the same degree of significance.

**Do you have any final messages for us?**

One of the laws of the universe is the Law of Allowing. This has to be acknowledged and honored. If a person asks a question, then they are ready to know. As Jesus put it, "Ask and you shall receive." We have free will to unfold in our own time. My goal is to do the work of the soul when I clearly know what that is and when my paths are open. My wish would be that all humanity would recognize itself as one and realize that we are the gods of our own creation. Many times I think we have forgotten this. We co-create with Universal Forces.

It is important to keep an open mind to all possibilities. This book and others can give great hope and help document a change that is occurring globally. The knowledge opening up to the world today was once esoteric, and may have been harbored by individuals in times past, or it may have been stowed in a Greek monastery, or a Buddhist sanctuary. Now, however, a worldwide awakening to this wisdom and knowledge will lead to changes.

# Cherie St. Cyr

Cherie St. Cyr is a Tarot card reader and has a busy practice in Madison, Wisconsin where she does many private consultations. She also consults by telephone and is available for social events. Cherie is an artist and massage therapist as well as a professional psychic. When she first moved to Madison twenty-one years ago, she said, "I don't care about the weather; I care about the 'astral weather,' which is superb in Madison." Her survival strategy is to "bag out" to warmer climates during February. Currently, she is exploring her life's work, which she enigmatically describes in two phases: art equals healing and healing equals art. Cherie is a frequent guest on radio shows and answers phone-in questions. She acknowledges the "interconnectedness of all beings, and how people grow as a tribe." Her tribe is largely centered in and around the neighborhood of East Wilson Street in Madison, where she is described as a pillar of the community.

<u>Contact Information</u>
Cherie St. Cyr
Madison, WI
**Phone:** 608-257-6697

### What mystical arts do you practice today?

I am a Tarot card reader, and I also practice dowsing, which primarily involves the use of a pendulum. My favorite Tarot deck is the Rider-Waite. In 1972, I was living with several people who worked with cards. From 1974 to 1981, I began working very seriously with the Rider-Waite deck. I moved from Colorado to Madison in 1981 and have read cards professionally for twenty years, but have really been in it for about thirty years. During my radio shows people call in with questions, so I do some work in that format too. I've been on the radio now for over a year and like it very much.

### How did you fine-tune the ability?

If you're psychic and you don't have a spiritual practice, you are in a pickle! I have a spiritual practice. In my opinion, intuition is a spiritual gift that keeps needing refinement. My work is in the course of a true lineage by studying through Paul Foster Case and Rachel Pollack. I've used other Tarot decks, but I have a high level of attunement with the Rider-Waite deck, which really is part of the lineage I speak about. Other decks don't engage me. The various new decks have an "idea" but they don't have roots like the Rider-Waite. Lineage can be traced and it gives us a rich and deep history.

I am obviously a person who really believes in the powerful benefits of having that family tree — having a teacher and knowing who your teachers were ten back — hanging with some heavy hitters instead of some airy-fairy who says I can make pretty pictures so I'll make a tarot deck. There is no study in that and no grounding, no path to it, no core. Even in the Rider-Waite, there are some problems. The person I studied with, Paul Foster Case (now deceased), was in a study group with Allistar Crowley. Paul was angry with Edgar Waite because he changed some of the classic images. The shape of the Emperor's leg and the card number of the Lovers, for example, were changed. He went on a tirade because of the interference with this ancient esoteric knowledge. Changing this was considered a serious matter. Then Allistar Crowley changed it too, and in one of his autobiographies, he said he intentionally changed it so people would not get it.

### Is there a common thread among those who practice mystical arts?

I don't really know many readers. Personally, I have an astrologer and I have a trans-channeler for the teacher Michael. Those people who read for me, I would say, have an intense inner life, a practice, and both of them are extremely old souls. They have been here many times. This helps in synthesizing wisdom. I would think that some of these characteristics would be the common thread. Counseling is another aspect. People who come to me reveal their deep needs, longings, and wants. With that in front of me, I frequently become a counselor and I often ask, "Are you seeing a therapist?" In that respect, a common thread would also involve sorting out things that might need attention from a different resource.

### Is there any specific advice that you have for people who are consulting a card reader?

Yes, keep in mind that the more specific your questions are for the cards, the more specific the answers will be. The best of the best psychics are right eighty percent of the time and they are frequently wrong about dates. Validate everything for yourself, and if it doesn't ring true to you, then throw it out the window! It's hogwash. *You* are the one who has to say whether this makes it real or not. Why would someone have a card reading to find out "if I don't change anything, this is what I get." A card reading means *here is your avenue to work on.* For example, the question, "Is this the right man for me?" comes up often. If the cards say absolutely not, what do you do? I ask clients all the time, "Are you going to dump him if I say no?" In the case of saying no, this is not the man, the resolution might be to enrich and enliven the relationship, and to move it in the direction that you want it to go. Therefore, the much more interesting question is: "What do I do to deepen this relationship?" Nothing is written in stone. Be very careful of what you ask.

It is *extremely* rare that I would do a card reading for myself. I'm invested too much in my own personal reading, so it would be better to go to a neutral party. For example, if you come to me and ask about some relationship, I can be entirely neutral, mainly because I don't care what the answer is. The answer is what it is. Part of a good reading is in the *talking*, which often leads to a person gaining some insight, I hope. There is a door or a road of Divine transmission that opens in the speaking that I cannot obtain if I read for myself.

### What is your answer to the skeptic?

The skeptic…well, sometimes I let them play and sometimes I don't. If the skeptic asks something like what's my favorite color, I say take a hike. I don't want someone to ask me things they already know. Sometimes a radio caller will ask about the gender of an expected baby, and usually the caller does not know the answer prior to asking that question. In this case, I will use my pendulum and will check on the due date too. In general, if the skeptic is not a jerk, I try to work with that person.

### What are some of the criticisms that you hear?

People might say the Bible frowns upon use of the Tarot cards. No such statement is in the Bible in any form. The notion actually came about in the early Dark Ages around the late 1200s when the Church began killing witches (mostly women). They were burning libraries, but in their own cellars, they had powerful esoteric texts — and they still do. The Papal Libraries house some of the finest collections of esoteric writings in the world. At that moment in history, the Church was trying to suppress knowledge and so the officials led people to believe this kind of work was bad and was "of the devil."

Why is the serpent hated and feared? It is beloved of the goddess in cosmology studies. The Church took iconography of the goddess; the tree and the serpent were biggies, and they incorporated the serpent as the devil into the whole creation myth. For 4000 years, we have hated the serpent because it was beloved of the goddess. My point is that there has been contortion and perversion of ancient esoteric teachings throughout history. People who believe Tarot reading is "of the devil" don't come to me, or any other reader. Who would pay a fee to say to me, "You are of the devil."

### Is there anything unique about practicing in Wisconsin?

I am from New Orleans. Flavor and level of acceptance there is very big. New Orleans is a Scorpio city, but besides connected with sex and death, as Scorpio is, the sign is a protector, and governor of what is unseen and mysterious. Tarot work is much more blatantly accepted there. Germans, Poles, Norwegians, and conservative people who often say this is hogwash settled in Wisconsin. Most of my clients are women. Women are more open to this. Interestingly, on the radio I find men are frequent callers. I do six to ten readings per week on the air. My Tarot is very strong right now, but as a massage therapist and an artist, I stay quite busy also.

### Do world events affect your abilities?

The first day of my radio show was an election day for a president, and I knew people would be asking. I used the pendulum and was correct, and generally, I would say I am extremely sensitive. However, I don't read the newspaper or watch the news on TV. I don't read magazines except for those related to my field of art. I don't listen to talk radio and I don't see many movies. It was a decision I made quite a few years ago. I'm still processing what I saw on TV when I was five — the good, the bad, and the ugly. I just can't go there. So yes, world events affect me, but probably not similar to the way they affect people who watch CNN.

### Do you believe in a structured religion?

I take a universal approach and I am a Sufi. We don't exactly call it a religion; we call it a path. We honor prophets from all the world's religions. Originally, this was a branch of Islam, but it went in quite a different direction.

**When you are out and about, are your abilities on hold, or are they in action?**

Sometimes I can read people perfectly from a half a block away and sometimes not. My intuition is cooking more if I'm giving someone a massage. For example, I was doing massage on a client's left hamstring and I told him he had a car problem that involved the brake lining on the left side. He informed me that he had just taken the car in to have the brakes replaced. So there it was—a car problem was showing up on the left side of his body. This doesn't happen every time with people. I think it may depend on how close the person is to me on a spiritual level.

**Do dreams have significance?**

I don't work much with dreams. I think they can have meaning, but it depends on how willing you are to work with them. A dream can be valuable or it can be insignificant. A world of knowledge can be gained from symbols in a dream, but again, it depends on what you do with it.

**Do you have any specific reading that you would like to discuss?**

When I'm reading, the words just come through to me and then I usually forget them instantly, but I will tell you about one interesting incident. I did a reading for a woman who came to me with a particular question and I told her that she was obviously with her "soul mate." I said that she was, with certainty, supposed to be with this person for the rest of the incarnation. Then I said the problem is that "soul mate" is a pain in the behind. She said, "Oh my God, it is so incredible to look at life through this very unusual filter." Here's this woman who is beautiful and successful and has children and she is with a person that is the most difficult and challenging part of her life. That is what she has to live with. Ties are intense. He is the soul mate.

It would be wise for people to understand that a soul mate is not always a good thing to have or desire. It can go either way. This person could be challenging to your soul and consequently you may not experience growth. Somehow, people relate soul mate to the positive, but this is *not* always the case. Finding a soul mate can sometimes make things worse instead of better, and then you're in it whether you want to be or not! A friend of mine once said, "it's not a soul mate; it's a cell mate."

If there is one thing I could say about my entire Tarot practice is that people are desperately and incredibly lonely. They are looking all the time. People repeatedly ask me the question, "When will I find that special soul mate?" I've seen people all across the board — beautiful, ugly, good finances, bad finances, successful, not successful — it doesn't matter. The question is the same. It is a curious time we are in right now. Society and families seem be coming apart at the seams. I see an inability for people to commit and work through things. Is it karma some people are with soul mates and others are alone?

**Have you worked on any police or investigative cases?**

No. When I am asked, I send people elsewhere to others who have an interest and experience in this. I could do map work, however, since I work with a pendulum.

**What is your view on charging for services?**

For years, I did not charge, and people often said that I should charge. That is really part of the difference between an amateur and a professional. I am a professional in what I do. It is good to have karmic exchange and it puts a value on things. If I am just giving and giving, karmic debt is created and it puts a "string" on me. Charging for services makes this energy clean and of significance. I do 1-2 readings a day and 1-2 massages a day and make a living.

**What do you think of the psychic hot lines advertised on television?**

There are hundreds of people working these lines. I have a friend in Indiana who is a very in-tune psychic who does this work, and genuinely helps people, but the person calling in has no idea with whom they will be speaking. The other disturbing part is that people will run up a $400 or more phone bill. That's sad and unnecessary and causes hardship.

### Is there power in prayer?

There are studies that say people who are prayed for heal better than people who aren't. I think positive attitude alone has power. I do affirmations and Feng shui, which deals with intentions, is highly intuitive and has an intense spiritual side to it. What is your intention? You can hang the little crystals up, paint the door red, initiate the Feng shui with its intentions, use sacred words, and do the prayers. With all of this, the power is magnified astronomically. There are sacred sounds and words that have been tapped into for thousands of years. The words and sounds are also the core prayers of my Sufi practice. It's in the roots of Feng shui also. They work with two mantras, and I would call that prayer. Just the sound opens things — it does something.

### Do you have a belief in reincarnation?

I don't particularly have a *belief.* I have a direct experience in my body. My earliest memory of this phenomenon occurred to me when I was about six or seven years old. I had a flash of a group of little old women with bandannas looking at me and frowning as I lay on the ground and I kept thinking a car would hit me and I would die. I had this flash about three to four times per year from the age of seven to the age of thirty-five. Then I had a session with my teacher who is the channeled entity Michael. He said to me, "Oh, that's just your last life-time. You were in Dresden in the war. Your mother warned you not to play on the roof, but you disobeyed her, fell off the roof, and died." Then my teacher said, "Here's how to heal that." He gave me the solution, I did it, and the flashes never reoccurred, but I have always been terrified of heights and I still have that imprint.

Tarot is a spiritual path and is enmeshed in esoteric teachings that say we are one with God, and that all souls are one. We see this in the Fool card of the Tarot deck. For the Fool, there is a casting out. He steps off the cliff, then the Fool becomes the Magician, and he becomes the High Priestess, and then the Empress, and the Emperor all down through the twenty-one phases. At the end, he comes back to the World, and after this, there is a reunion and a reincarnation.

The Gurus of India talk about reincarnation like this, and my teacher Michael talks about it the same way. This is accepted as to how reincarnation works. We're all together, we're cast out, we're in this body and that body. That's why I think the Tarot works well. It guides us in this path. When it was developed, Tarot was shielded because of the Dark Ages, with its persecution and suppression of information. The Tarot was the best description that esoteric authority relied on to explain the mechanism of reincarnation. Some things such as the Ouija board were given to darkness, but the Tarot was always protected and sacred. It has a very high level of truth.

### How do intuitions or messages come through to you?

I am clairaudient. Really, varieties of things happen. For example, something like the "Star reversed" card will come up and I'll ask the woman if her boyfriend has an alcohol problem, so that the next time Star reversed comes up, I can ask if there is an alcohol problem showing in this situation or not. Certain things will take on their own meaning based on empirical characteristics — it happens once, so then I ask, and it is true again, and again, and again.

### How often do people come to you?

I don't recommend people come in on a frequent basis. I don't want them asking the same questions. With a session, you get answers that need to be processed over time, and this is important to realize. Time and patience is a factor. I like to do birthday readings and sometimes those people come back at the half year. I have had clients that have been with me sixteen years. I do a special reading within five days of the birthday, and those outcomes are always interesting.

For example, one of my clients was in love with an incredible man, but he became profoundly depressed and they broke off the relationship. Within a seven-week period, they decided to get back together and went on a trip around the world for a year and a half. She had a reading done after the breakup of the relationship and remarkably the King of Cups came up indicating there would be a reunion. Well, it certainly didn't seem like it at the time, but in fact it did happen. There is a card for every

7.5-week position. The King of Cups reversed is an indication of major depression. It was interesting to see the whole thing turn around in that seven-week period.

**What is your definition of a mystic?**
A mystic is someone who is attuned to the unseen world. The mystic has personal intuition finely honed and can trust it to speak his or her truth. This coincides with a spiritual practice. There are dark forces. I don't see much evil, but you must be careful when you go for channeling. If someone is channeling for a person who has died in pain and confusion, and the person who has passed on comes back as a channeled entity, what are you going to say? Buy canned tuna? You must always validate and check out things. Good information can come from an Ouija board too, but you must be very specific about what you ask for. What is the quality of light you put around yourself? Beware of entities who may take over. I've seen that and it's scary.

**What do your family and friends think about your work?**
They are used to my eccentricities, and they are accepting and friendly toward my work and me. Now I am doing Feng shui and this fits in perfectly with my artwork and spirituality, as well as intuition, as I mentioned earlier.

**What advice do you have for those with children who may show psychic abilities?**
Children can be very intuitive. I've taught use of a pendulum in elementary schools and over half of the kids can do it. They love it, but some of them are scared. On occasion, I have met an extremely old soul in an eleven-year-old body, for example. I could work with that person for days. It is difficult if you are in a highly Christian modality and all of this is "of the devil." In Germany, dowsing is considered a reputable scientific method. There is no mysticism about it. It is just science there. Dowsing has been used for lay lines, detecting water, what kinds of vitamins and minerals we need and many other things. Nobody in Germany is accusing anybody of being a devil or anything close. It has been in the culture so long. I've seen old

German lithographs of dowsing. Some people even dowsed to find out where pictures should be hung.

### Do you have any final advice or messages for us?

Remember that the best psychics are right eighty percent of the time and you have to validate everything. Things are not written in stone, so please use judgment. There are times when putting up boundaries is a good thing to do, such as when visiting a psychic fair. The energies are flying all over the place. Don't go to a fair saying, "Tell me everything, and I'll believe anything you say." Use your mind.

When you go to a different reader, don't expect to get the same reading the last reader gave you. Always go in fresh and open. The more specific the question asked, the more specific the answer you'll get. Not every reader works like this. "Yes-No" questions do not yield a good deal of useful information. "Why did this happen to me?" is not a useful question to ask either. You could get the talk of karma from past lives, the relationship with your mother, the way you treated your ex-husband, and on and on. However, this does not really make any difference. Don't waste your time. Ask questions that make a difference.

# The Reverend Phoenix

The Reverend Phoenix is an aura photographer. The Aura Camera 6000 that she uses photographs an electromagnetic field that surrounds all living beings. The colors that show up in the photographs are said to reflect physical, emotional, and spiritual well-being. Aura photography is based on biofeedback. Phoenix has participated in lectures and various events in several states. Her photography services include an interpretation of the photographs. She also takes before and after photos if a healing is involved. Phoenix lives in Tomahawk, Wisconsin.

**Contact information**
The Reverend Phoenix
North 12014 County Road L
Tomahawk, WI 54487
**Phone:** 715-224-2334

**What mystical arts do you practice today?**

Aura photography is related to the Kirlian photography tradition, which photographs a coronal pattern around objects, living and non-living. I work in the field of aura photography and I am considered a magnetic light healer, dealing with the light of God. Several types of healers deal with light energy. I'm a little different, in that when I heal with the light, I tend to raise people's vibrations to a much higher form of light. We can record the healing with the aura camera by taking before and after photographs and see a change in that light. For example, I helped a woman who had been paralyzed by a stroke on her right side and she was unable to use the arm. When we took a before picture, her light was in the reds, oranges, and gold. Very little light surrounded the arm that had been affected by the stroke. Three days after the light healing, we took another photo and found the light to have returned and the energy was flowing again. She regained use of the arm. We can heal physically and spiritually with the light.

**What are the meanings of the various colors that show up in the photos?**

Every color tells me something different. The position of the colors, the intensity, the lightness, or darkness of a color is considered. For example, the *red* light would indicate you are connected to Mother Earth and you have a lot of power and strength showing leadership abilities. It is a physical color — go go go, survival, materialism.

The *orange* tells me that the person is intelligent and there is more analytical type thinking going on with that light. Creative and artistic people have an orange light too. Some healing energy is associated with orange light. It's like armor, a strong light with a thicker density, and negativity could bounce right off of you. With the *gold*, we see very organized people, strong personality, and strong intellect. They work well in a courier type business. They show knowledge, harmony, balance, and discipline and are organized because they've done a lot of work on themselves. They are generally happy people and have a lot of joy in their lives.

The *green* people are balanced in body, mind, and spirit. Healers and teachers carry that vibration. There will be growth and change occurring in their lives. They are connected to nature more so than the other lights. With the *blues*, we see people who are meditating or praying a lot, spiritual growth is definitely occurring in their lives. You have to earn these higher colors. They are involved with wisdom, truth, and devotion. Blue people are patient, forgiving, and calm. We determine how light or dark that blue may be. If the person is a dark blue, he or she has a lot of compassion and empathy for others. A light color blue would tell me that you are a beginner on the spiritual journey.

The *indigo* is the spiritual energy known as the third eye and it takes on a smoky gray-blue color. With indigo, people have unity and balance. It is a high vibrating healing ray. These people will experience visions, revelations, prophecies, and maybe strange dreams that are trying to guide a person in some way. The *violet* comes next, and we see magical, mystical-type people carrying this color. It shows they have the ability to absorb spiritual information and they have super-sensory abilities that come into play. We can see a transformation happening in their lives. The violet is really the highest color that can be attained. Then we know that all of the chakra are activated and open. The violet is really the blend of all the other colors I mentioned.

Finally, we see the *white* light. All the colors combined are encompassed in the white light. This light is spirituality itself. You are spiritually motivated, and more evolution that is spiritual, is in store for you. The person with white light shows enlightenment, wisdom, and drawing in pure Divine energy. We might not see the white light if the violet covers it. Our sight can only pick up certain things and so can the camera. There are different frequencies. White light can show up very boldly, but if we see an all violet person, we already know there is underlying white light; we don't have to see it.

**How did you develop this work and how long has aura photography been in existence?**

The concept for this particular camera has been around since

1891, and was developed by scientist Nicola Tesla. He called it the "thought machine." In 1975, UCLA worked with the technology and measured the aura with accuracy. In the 1990s it became more available to the public. My work kind of fell into my lap. It began through a vision that I had — known as a Christ Visitation. Saint Faustina, a nun in the Polish Catholic Church, had a diary where she recorded a vision that occurred about seventy years ago. I had an amazingly similar vision, but knew nothing of the vision of Saint Faustina. In fact, I didn't know there was such a person.

Then I had a profound dream that revealed essentially what she was talking about and believing in, all of which was highly spiritual. One thing happened after another. Prophesies occurred to me in dreams. I studied Saint Faustina's writings, and this confirmed for me that her messages would be around for quite some time. Faustina was canonized in the year 2000 for this work and the prophecies that came to her in the vision. It really has become my life's work. I am the only woman I know of who has done research on what is referred to as the supernatural shield, which was also described by Faustina.

My mother believes I am the reincarnated Saint Faustina, but well…that's just my mother. I did not know her writings at the time, but what I saw and wrote about was nearly the same word for word, as I discovered ten years later. We were identical in the teachings.

**What about aura changes — hour to hour, day to day, year to year?**

For the most part, you will stay centered with that light. There are some variations in the light every day, unless something significantly changes in your life, such as a big move, a career change, a divorce, or death. Then the aura can change and there can be a big shift. It seems like the aura takes on the energy we need to get through that. If we need different energy to come in, for instance, the red light, that physical energy to get us through, or the gold light that comes in to switch us to a new career, changes can happen. The shift can occur up to three months before you even know it. So subconsciously, we know when these big changes are going to occur.

**How does the camera work?**

The electromagnetic energy of the body is photographically recorded. A physical-chemical process takes place, and the camera records this through a mechanism similar to biofeedback. In addition, we look at chakras and the light in these areas. The chakras are associated with glands in the body. If the glands are functioning properly, the light will stay very healthy. If a gland breaks down, that light is not functioning properly in the body. We see a physical connection and a spiritual connection with this.

Light surrounding a body is considered the *natural* light and is influenced by everything a person thinks, says, and does in life. Over the heart, a different light vibrates, unlike the natural light surrounding the body. We consider the light centered on the heart to be the *supernatural* light or the spiritual light, in other words. We can see the difference between natural and supernatural. Someone may have a natural light surrounding him or her — but may have a specific light in the heart chakra that indicates a lack of belief in God or a higher spirit. I have taken *thousands* of photos for people, and there is not one single time that I've been wrong when I say, "You have a belief in God," or "You don't have a belief in God." The person will confirm my statement for me. I base my reading of spirituality, in this case, a belief in God, around what I see or don't see in the photographed area of the heart chakra. It shows immediately. It is amazing.

**If a person doesn't have a belief in God or Creator what would you be seeing?**

We would be seeing the red zone colors over the heart. God shields you in any event, because somewhere down the road, He expects you to jump on the train. Your vibration will rise. Scriptural reference depicts the light of the body, and depicts what the light means. "Hear that you will be judged by the light of the body," is rather a scary scriptural reference. If the heart chakra were a red, perhaps you would not be ready to enter into what you consider Heaven. Supposedly, we must be in the white light. In scripture, the light is withheld from the wicked. It's all a little scary.

**If someone is anxious or stressed, will that show up on the photo?**

Yes, that will show up as a little too orange or red. People are tired and stressed, and that does have an effect on the aura. On a more relaxed day, it might shift to a more balanced hue. As I said earlier, you will likely hold that light you are centered with, but a temporary red or orange shift could easily take over with stress. Anger—the aura will shift to a deep dark blood red. Under the weather, you could see a blue shift.

**What do you say about skeptics?**

Most people that see this tend to believe. If I do run into a skeptic, it seems that the person might not have the full knowledge of what this is all about, so I think it is more a state of confusion rather than skepticism. Either they choose to believe or they don't. Fear can play a part.

**Do you see different kinds of photos in areas of Wisconsin or other places that you go?**

Yes, in areas outside of the bigger cities, people tend to have brighter light. I don't know what that's all about yet, but I do tend to definitely see more spiritual people in the areas outside of the cities. But that's just a general observation, because of course I see spiritual people living in cities too. Most of my work is in a five state area around here. Wisconsin has a lot of "nice light."

**How does your family view your work?**

They are supportive. They believe in what I do, and there is a message here that it is something big. What I do touches them and they often travel with me to events.

**If people put up a wall, does this affect the photo?**

No, it does not. A person can try, but it doesn't work. The photography is kind of like a lie detector. The light doesn't lie. In fact, someone out there will research this to the extent that it makes a good lie detector. I have seen a little research that dips into this area. I personally don't study that application of the photography. We're really looking at a wall of light that shows who you are. I believe it is accurate.

### Explain the meaning of a combination of colors.

When I'm interpreting a photo for a client, I read it from left to right and explain each color to the person. There can be a number of colors appearing. My specialty is the heart rays, and that's what my observations and research are based on, so I definitely go over that carefully. People are amazed and some even start crying. I discover deep areas that are often well below the surface. Often times, what I say is confirmed by the person, or it's something that the individual has been told about himself or herself by another person. People are usually happy when they walk away.

### Does a Dark Side show up on the photo?

As there is a good side, a light side, we can also see someone who is "chained to hell," as it's called. The photo sometimes can pick up "possession" by a dark side. A pattern known as the "band of hell" comes up. What that means is that you are chained by your own doubts and your own fears, your own infirmity about yourself. These lights are on the lower vibration. If you can break those bands and move out of the doubt and the fear, you can move on to higher vibrations, definitely.

### What do you say to these "chained to hell, dark, this is not my favorite trip" people?

I pretty much give it to everybody straight, but I don't come right out and say, "Oh by the way, you are possessed." I will go into the heart chakra and see what's going on. If the person is void of God or any type of Divine higher spirit, I say so. I have to tell you, I've taken photos of people who say they are witches or warlocks, you name it, and some of these people are on "the other side." They still believe they are spiritual, yet they are void of God or a Divine spirit. There is a particular shield that comes up over the heart, and that is usually the yellow shield, the shield of the warrior. Let's say you do believe in God or a Creator, but you are angry at this power at the moment, then the yellow shield does appear. The shield is sort of like a "sore thumb" in the heavens. This shield usually means one of three things. Either you are angry with God, or you don't believe, or you're angry at someone else. Speaking of colors, this is so "black and white."

For non-believers in God, or for angry people, there is a loss of spirituality, or gift, including knowledge, with each particular missing color in that shield. So until a person comes out of that darkness, he or she is more or less stagnating in a state that does not draw spirituality and knowledge to him or her. It is an individual thing. We all have choices, but to those who believe, they receive more in the way of spirituality. With that final seventh shield over the heart, the violet shield, He will reveal all mysteries to you upon your asking. To those who hold a red shield, he gives much less. You go backwards if you don't watch out. I'm seeing about half and half when it comes to believing or not believing in God or a higher spirit.

**Can the power of prayer change the aura photo?**

Yes, definitely. I've had people come back to me even though it is months later. They travel hundreds of miles to have a photo taken with the purpose of seeing if perhaps prayer had worked for them. Originally, they start out not believing in God, and not practicing prayer. Their light is dim and of low vibration. Once they make *serious* efforts to engage in prayer, the photos change dramatically and they take on great light and improved shields over the heart. It is like God stamping his approval.

**If my aura report card reads "needs improvement," then what?**

Prayer, meditation, faith, a positive attitude will all make that aura much better. What I'm saying is self improvement and discipline has a lot to do with it. If you seek the light, it becomes stronger and more evident. Greater knowledge of spirituality will come to you.

**What if the aura is not centered over the body? Say, for example, it is behind or in front.**

If the aura is in front of you, and there's hardly any light over your face or body, it means you are looking into the future, leading the way. If it is behind you, it means you are dwelling in the past. The aura can actually just follow you around like a friendly dog — you're not in the light, your kind of "beside yourself," because of this dwelling in the past.

**Could interpretations vary by photographer or camera equipment?**

Yes, there could be variation in interpretation. My focus is on the rays over the heart. Other readers may not even know about this. I want the client to get the full reading, or full effect of what we're talking about. We are considered to be wearing the "robe of many colors" talked about in scripture. There are aura photographers who don't give readings at all. Instead, they only use a biofeedback printout, and that result only tells you what colors mean and what you're centered with. As far as I know, I'm the only one who talks about the heart ray.

**Do you base interpretations solely on the photo reading, or is intuition also involved?**

I believe I work through the Holy Spirit, and because my work is based on the supernatural light (light surrounding the heart), I tend to go on what I have been fed by the spirits or the angels in dreams and visions. I interpret by the basis of what the colors, intensities, and hues mean and where they are situated. A combination of things comes into play really.

**Where would someone interested in this type of work begin to learn?**

That's not easy to answer. It sure would have to be in you. The kind of work I do, which is Sacred Shield study, came to me in the dreams, the visions, and my writings. It is unique and esoteric when you think about it. If someone had said to me many years ago, you'll be working as an aura photographer teaching about the Sacred Shield of Light, I would have wondered *what in the world* is this person talking about. I feel that it was "given" to me in a sense. My feet were on this path because God put me on this path. I don't even know how I started, except that the vision started the whole thing, and then I followed through by faith.

**Do you have a goal or a mission in your work?**

Yes, my mission is to encourage a worldwide convergence of people accepting the Light of God supernatural rays that are protection from God himself. This is the message I spread. Faustina prophesized too, that everyone would come under this light ray, the heart ray, so that all are protected on the Day of Judgment. We should pay attention to that.

Science shows the existence of the light over the heart and Scripture refers to the body as the "lamp." According to Scripture, we have to keep the lamp lit with "oil." And that oil is faith.

# Anneliese Gabriel Hagemann

Anneliese Gabriel Hagemann has extensive experience in the art of dowsing and divination through dowsing. She was born in Lassan, Germany and immigrated to the United States in 1955, having survived World War II in Germany. From that experience, she credits her mother with giving her strength to deal with any problem the world tossed her way. Today, Anneliese and her family are worldwide travelers. She has conducted many workshops and given lectures in many countries throughout the world and has visited Russia, China, South America, and Europe. Her appearances, lectures, workshops, and workbooks entail instruction in the art of dowsing, and guidance in spiritual growth and enlightenment. Anneliese also works in individual sessions with clients. She and her daughter, Doris Hagemann, have written several workbooks to aid in her teaching. Anneliese lives with her husband, Rudolf, in Wautoma, Wisconsin, and in Mesa, Arizona, during the winter.

## Contact information

Anneliese Gabriel Hagemann
W10160 County Road C          **Phone:** 920-787-4747
Wautoma, Wisconsin  54982    **Fax:** 920-787-2006

1452 S. Ellsworth Road          **Phone:** 480-986-6720
# 1331 / 2740
Mesa, Arizona  85208

**E-mail:** *ilovedowsing@hotmail.com*
**Web site:** *http://store.yahoo.com/dowsing*

### What mystical arts do you practice today?

I practice and teach dowsing and divination. It's what I love
to do. Through dowsing, I have found many gifts, including a
journey into writing. I had been collecting information for ten
years, and my daughter Doris and I decided to put a book together called *To Our Health.* We had a lot of material in that
first book and actually, we have a third edition out now in the
Spanish, French, Portuguese, and German languages. My goal
is to reach people and teach self-healing and self-empowerment.
I provide tools to help people help themselves through my classes.
One of my tools is an emphasis on dowsing. I use a pendulum,
primarily.

Dowsing is an ancient art used prior to Biblical times. It
uses a device such as a pendulum or dowsing rods. The act of
dowsing and asking a question enables us to tune into a higher
consciousness and find responses that would not be available
through our usual senses. According to *The American Dowsers
Quarterly Digest* (Spring 1997), Albert Einstein explained, "The
dowsing rod is a simple instrument which shows the reaction of
the human nervous system to certain factors which are unknown
to us at this time."

### How did you develop your skill?

It was a long journey. When I was a child, I had many
physical illnesses that included throat and digestive problems
resulting in surgeries. I had the notion that I personally did not
fit in my life somehow. I was learning a lot, but I was always

searching for health. Fear of tomorrow was present for me. My husband and I owned a business, and in 1980, I began listening to tapes, and reading about positive things in people. My mind shifted and my thinking shifted, but my physical problems did not shift. We had a Laundromat business, and as it turned out sometimes people would spend an hour talking to me. I became a very good listener.

In 1984, a young man came into the laundromat and said to me, "You have to meet my mother-in-law." I asked him what it is she does. He said, "Something weird."

I did not know what "weird" was because I didn't know about dowsing. I was still dealing with all the health stuff—another CT scan and so on. So, I met the woman, learned the skill, and she said, "You can do it too." That's all I needed to hear. I started using dowsing in the laundry cleaning business to tell me what to use to get different stains out of various fabrics — so already I was literally in the "cleaning business." I used dowsing while listening to other people as a way to clean out what was troubling them. To add to that, my husband had a car wash business — more cleaning. My goal was to encourage people to make good changes. In the meantime, I was personally shifting and this included improvement in my physical health. I began taking classes in self-healing, hospice care, reflexology, and biokinesiology. For me, dowsing became the simplest way to tune into myself.

### How do messages come through to you — images, symbols, scents, voices?

I write down what I receive and what comes through to me. In the process of dowsing and physically writing things down, I find information. The messages are there in a clairsentient kind of way. Sometimes I have physical reactions. I frequently write poetry and that is often how things come to me. There is power in words that we sometimes take for granted. I did not have a religious upbringing, but I find messages from God in my poetry.

**What do you think is a common thread among those who practice mystical arts?**

I think they are always seeking and searching. Searching is the key. We all look for enlightenment. With dowsing, I can find the keys that hold a person down. Once you know what the problem is, you can address it, if you choose to address it. "If" is a big word, funny as that may sound. Some problems people may not want to address. We are caught up in society a lot, but the truth is really in your heart. It is a long journey of many years. Mystics know this.

**What is your definition of a mystic or mysticism?**

Life is mysterious and mysticism is the mystery. I believe we have a lot to learn, but the knowledge is there somewhere, and that's the mystery. We must be careful in mystical pursuits however. That can be another game to play. What are you going to do with the truths? Are you going to use them in an enlightened way, or in the darkness? We all have both within us.

**So you do think there is a dark side? How would you clean this mess up?**

Oh yes, there is a dark side. Hell is what we make it. If you live in anger, hate, and resentment, you have created a hell in your life. I have worked with people who have been possessed with entities and under voodoo spells, and they aren't aware of it. These people are generally from other countries. South America comes to mind.

We can overdo it though. For example, I asked for an experience, and I got more than I wanted. I met a woman who works with angels, and I asked her, "What angels are you calling in?" I overstepped my boundaries on that one. This angel of darkness, which could have been the superego from this being, delivered a message of, "Don't you dare interfere in this person's life." I asked for that experience, but it really sucked me dry. That's my issue, not hers.

My goal was to help. I was getting symbols in my mind and the first thing that came out of me was, "You like everything on a golden platter." It seemed to me that she was taking things away. I was very depleted and had to walk out of the room.

Nevertheless, I knew I had to experience this, uncomfortable as it was. I had nothing against her, and it was my lesson to learn.

Be careful about asking for things. There is everything out there—including darkness. One day, my daughter, a history teacher, called me and said she felt like she was going crazy. I asked her to give me some names of kids in her class. She gave me some names, and I indicated to her that she was picking up this crazy feeling from a particular student. However, in some way, she asked to experience it so she could be of help. Why are we so open that other people's experiences wash over to us? Experiences of sympathy, passion, empathy, fear—we're open to all of that. Fear is a big thing. In a flash, that energy can enter. Each word we write, or we speak, or we sing is an energy. Dowsing is an energy — nothing else.

### What about people we would normally see as evil?

These people, evil as we may see them, spark change. We see them in darkness, but they are just messengers. They are tools that tell us to wake up. As terrible as it sounds, wasn't Osama Bin Laden trying to set the world right in *his mind*? Think about the people burned at the stake in the Inquisition. They were striving for things too. We sometimes learn with very hard lessons and judgments made by us. Maybe there is karma involved. We forget there is a huge picture that reaches beyond our times. To escape my responsibility in what happens, I lay it on others, but I am just as responsible. It has been dark in our corner, but there is light if we look for it. Things we do in other parts of the world come back to us.

### Has there been any criticism of your work?

I really have not had people question me. The people with whom I work have an interest. They have heard about me through others, or they have taken a class. An article was written about me once, and a person said to my husband, Rudy, "I wouldn't want to be in her shoes on Judgment Day." Rudy said nothing. I think he decided the comment wasn't worth a response.

### Is there anything unique about practicing in Wisconsin?

I feel Wisconsin is really opening up. It is much more open than some of the other states are, and I have been to many. Compared to other countries however, Wisconsin is not as accepting. Germany, England, and Holland are very open, but understand that these places are attractive to people seeking spirituality. The United States is a very young civilization compared to other places in the world.

### Do world events affect your abilities?

World events don't affect my abilities. September 11, 2001, was my bluest day. I asked God, "What is this all about?" I think many people were asking the same question. The message I got was that we think this country is indestructible, but we are wrong. He said to take care of your country and start in your own back yard. Your own country has to be in balance before you can help others. What is this energy known as destruction?

There is a disconnection in this country. This is a young nation and we can compare it to a young kid who thinks he is indestructible. We won't find peace anywhere if we put glory in destruction.

### Do you subscribe to any structured religion?

Structured religion becomes stale for many people. It can turn into useless stone. Spirituality can be found in religion, but religion does not have a corner on the spirituality market. Each religion creates its own Divine Principles, but in the comparisons, it all comes back to "the One God within." So, is it fair and accurate to say one religion is superior to another and the *lack* of a religion is any less?

### When you are out and about are your abilities on hold?

Things are always in action for me. I don't enter minds, but I feel vibrations and energies—sadness or whatever is present.

### Are there any dowsing experiences you want to talk about?

Generally, people say to me that they have a new life. They have to do their own healing. I just give them information. I give them a wake up call, and sometimes I am accused of being blunt. This is what the message is, and you can take it or leave it.

I had a lady in here the other day and she talked for an hour. Finally, I said to her, "Do you want to live or die?" She told me that she had wanted to die so many times. So I asked her why she was still living. She said she was living for her father's sake. I said, "I honor you if you make a choice to live and I honor you if you make a choice to die—plain and simple." She is still living, and that was the choice.

### Do you work on any police or investigative cases?

I had an interesting call from a woman and I told her what I felt. She was asking about a relative who was missing. I said to her that he is alive, but he is in a hospital. She had apparently made other calls, and was told by others that he was dead. She called me back and said, "What do you mean he is in a hospital when other people say he is dead?" I did not want to get into a defensive argument. That's simply the information I had for her. He showed up, was alive, but was indeed in a hospital. This meant his vibrations were low, or his energy was low, and other people were possibly having a hard time picking up on them.

Looking for lost objects is not my thing, but others are doing this and have abilities in that area. We all have our different capabilities.

### What is your view on charging for services?

I had difficulty with it. I use a lot of energy, and a lot of time, and I am still an instrument. I ask, do I need to charge, and sometimes I don't charge. It is an exchange, and not necessarily a monetary transaction. What does this service mean to you? Some people pay me more than I ask for and say, "You helped me, and this is what I think it is worth." I am in business to help people clean up the mess.

### What do you think of psychic hot lines advertised on television and other places?

I don't believe in them. I think a person working those lines has to be a true connector, and this is not happening there.

**Do you think there is power in prayer?**

I pray every day. Things will come about, but they may not be what you think. Seek and you find. Knock and it is open. Ask and you receive. Everything is in the present moment. I was working with a Chinese man and he asked me why the people he was working with were not healing. I said that the consciousness was not accepting it. I asked him what he was writing using his Chinese characters. He said that he was writing, "I *will* do it." It does not matter what language the word "will" is written in—it's out there in the same vibration. He took the word out of what he was writing, and all went well after that. Words such as "will" and "try" should not be used. Stay in the present.

**Do you ever feel people put up a wall instead of looking for help?**

I can feel it, and in general, I say they are blocking. I find out at what level the person is blocking, and if they choose to unblock then we can continue, otherwise not. It is a defense mechanism. We have the truth, but we are not always ready to deal with things. That means work.

**Do you have any cautions for people who seek a reader?**

They go to find an answer. They are looking and searching. Whatever they experience is what they need to experience. They are going for a lesson that says the answers are always within you. A reader should not make anybody do anything. They should be totally detached from outcome and problem. A reader is a tool, but anything can be a tool. A book can be a tool, as can a blade of grass. If you look at a blade of grass, and in some way it gives light, use it; it is a tool.

**What is your opinion on synchronicity or coincidence?**

I feel things that happen in a form that we might call "coincidence" are things with a connection to the soul. It's all intertwined. It's all one, but sometimes we need to untangle. I ask for all kinds of experiences, and I get them — like it or not. Once I asked for a "blessing." As it turned out, I saw the face of a cat in an image and a few days later, I had a horrible back pain, like a cat scratching down my lower back. I took some medication and took three pills, and then three more pills, but the pain was still bothering me so much, my head felt numb, and I was losing my hearing. I called the company who manufactures the pills, and they said to go to a doctor. The hearing came back, and I learned to be careful of what I ask for. I had trusted in another energy and that was a mistake. It was a lesson — and that was the blessing.

**Do you have any final messages?**

I'm not out to change the world. I don't know what you or anybody else needs to learn. It is not my place to step into someone's experiences. There are, however, a few things to pay attention to as we exist every day. By loving others, you love yourself. Angels can be present in human form and they are another figure of vibration. Watch for them. Pay attention to the children, and we hope they do not shut the door. Remember, too, that shifts happen. Your life is beautiful, so live it.

# C.N. Rodgers

C.N. Rodgers is a Psychic Spiritual Counselor and Usui Reiki Master. With over 25 years of experience, Master Rodgers brings counseling and teaching to a variety of clients and students via office, phone, or live internet contact. He has an office in downtown La Crosse, Wisconsin, and continues to build a worldwide clientele through his own Web site and such Web sites as *kasamba.com, birthpatterns.com, keen.com,* and others. Students have come to him from as far away as California. He practices and teaches Reiki at all levels.

### Contact Information
C.N. Rogers
117 8th Street North
La Crosse, Wisconsin  54601
**Phone:**  608-784-9775
          888-530-9775
**E-mail:**  *contact@cnrodgers.com*
**Web pages:**  *http://www.cnrodgers.com or http://www.coryrodgers.com*

## What mystical arts are you practicing today?

I am a professional ARtuvian-Usui Reiki™ Master. I practice and teach the art. Spiritual reading and counseling, along with psychic spiritual reading are a part of my practice also. Working with Runes (stone tablets) helps to pick up additional information. Voice vibration helps me a lot because I do much work over the phone. Words, feelings, thoughts, and pictures come through to me for my clients. Reiki is energy bodywork and can coincide with intuition, but they are not the same process. In a way, I am a modern shaman.

## Discuss the development of your abilities.

From the very beginning, I was seeking spiritual answers to things. I don't remember any time that I wasn't tuned in to this. I did not know what it was, for one thing. Secondly, I came from a time when people were not talking about things that might be out of the ordinary. My mom died when I was born, and I see that it started a process for me. It was trauma. I was brought on to this planet in a dramatic traumatic way. I ended up as a spiritual person seeking a religious thing, which is not always necessarily spiritual.

## How did you fine-tune it all?

In high school, I was involved in theater and things that are physical, but eventually, I entered into a religious mode, sought information through the church, and then went on to discover Catholicism. I converted and followed a process through prayer, but I didn't work on this until I completed high school. After that, I pursued the priesthood in the United States and Canada. My religious fervor went on for 3 years. I wanted to enter a monastery, but it was just not my calling. I discovered the church really was not ready for me, so I left that and went on my merry way. In 1976, I had a near-death experience, an NDE, but that was unknown to me at the time. I am now realizing the importance of that experience, and knowing this is something I could not have imagined. It literally changed my life into working with the mind and consciousness. Today I use prayer and my relationship with the Divine, as I perceive it to be. I think it has been a *process* of trying to get somewhere, but you have to get into your body so you can experience and grow. This has to happen before you can leave the body.

### What happened with the near-death experience?

In 1976, I was living in New York City on 58th Street. There were some forces happening that caused me to make changes in my life. I went to bed as usual and I started to become aware of something crucial happening. I was in a dark place and was trying to hold on to the sides of what I think was a tunnel. There was light at the end, but all I could see was the dark and the light. Then, out of nowhere, I was given two firm words: *Stop Struggling.* Instantly, I stopped. The voice was extremely clear and it was impossible not to respond. I was in absolute bliss; I went to the full end of the tunnel and was sent back. I have heard explanations on that from people who say I was "refurbished" and given a better tilt on life. I have reason to believe certain energies moved into me that help me in what I do now. There is a term called "walk-ins" that supposedly are high-level energies that enter. In a sense, the experience awakened me. It really caught my attention beyond words, and I only started talking about it four or five years ago. I had not been in a hospital; I was just on 58th Street in New York City.

Scores of challenges in life arise and sometimes we are struggling so hard that we cannot hear the answer. This is the basis of my work today. It is my own personal work and the work I impart on others. There is a need to understand the spirituality of life. To stop struggling doesn't mean much unless you know why.

### Is there a common thread among those who practice mystical arts?

Commonly it is a quest for answers — or maybe we all had dysfunctional parents. I was told that once. Seriously, I think the thread is turmoil in life that has brought about a quest for answers to aid in personal learning. I hope that people who are doing healing are doing their own healing too. The need for healing is often the need for answers.

**Do you have an answer for the skeptic?**

I don't think I have an answer! I'm not trying to sell it. People's skepticism is understandable, because things have been distorted along the way. I cannot do anything that will not benefit the person. I encourage people to be skeptical about everything, not to block answers but to question. If someone asks, "How do I know you can do this type of work?" my answer is that you don't until you're sitting with me. It is OK to question. The word "psychic" has gotten a bad connotation, and there are those who are doing what might be considered psychic work, but they are getting a lot of information from how people are talking, looking, and standing. I don't work that way, so it is difficult to understand. The information such as whether or not you will get married seems so unimportant, but a lot of commercial psychics work in this way. I try to determine why they are working in a manner that may actually be destructive. Some people want magic answers, and there are no magic answers. We all have to do personal work to get rid of karma. Issues must be peeled off in layers. I work with the issues and the energies that help people speed things along, but not in the format of a fortune telling session.

**Is there anything unique about practicing in Wisconsin?**

When I first landed here nine years ago, nothing was happening. In New York, all the practitioners had strong practices and were building. Here in Wisconsin, I think I was the only Reiki Master in the area. The practice is still going through a period of growth. What moved out of larger cities has traveled this direction — such things as working with crystals and past lives. I am on a different safari, but it is not something new to me. Distinct genres go through their own processes in a natural order. We are spiritual beings that happen to be physical at the moment. The West and East coasts have moved into the Midwest. We were not behind, so to speak; this phenomenon was just not readily available. When I arrived nine to ten years ago, questions were beginning to surface and people were looking.

**Do world events have an effect on your abilities?**

They do in the sense that I point out to people we are seeing an energetic change that wants to happen even though the events may be tragic. It is not a mistake, even though it looks like a mistake. A significant statement is trying to come through, not from individuals, but from other forces. Right now, we are not perceptive of it, and sometimes tragedy can push us closer to understanding or it can push us the other way.

September 11, 2001 was horribly tragic, but let us reflect on how we got to this point. We had better take a look at *why* this is happening rather than shooting at each other. There seems to be a huge push to police ourselves — a circling of the wagons. The anger and the impoverishment need to be put under a microscope, but it doesn't show up like this at top governmental levels. I do not condemn what the government is doing, but what is the breeding ground for using God to show hate? No one can stop people from thinking, but certainly, we can create a different climate with setting an example one by one not to hate.

**When you are out and about, are your abilities on hold?**

Yes, they are on hold. It has shifted. I was strongly identified as a healer and a teacher in this city, but I have come to a place through learning in this quiet community of looking at who I am without my sensors open. I used to identify myself with being on full tilt all the time. Like the guy walking down the street, I have to identify who I am. My instincts would always be in the forefront, but sometimes I just want to have normal conversations with people and do fun things. Having conversations with people who are just looking for answers about serious things is something I don't want to do all of the time. I have a sense of humor and I enjoy humor. It's nice just to have a pleasant chit-chat without the switch turned on. I had to look at Cory (me) and then look at Cory again because I have other interests, too.

**Do dreams have meaning in your work?**

Dreams have a lot of meaning. I don't interpret dreams, but there can be messages that come. There is a notion that we are all the people in the dream. Some people are very dream focused and receive a lot of information. I have had dreams that are more real than others dreams but never anything like the near-death experience. I don't think we need to get "stuck" with certain interpretations. Each person has to find his or her own shelter in which to dwell. Maybe dreams can help people to look deeper — this is what I push — deeper examination.

### Are there any specific examples of your work that you would like to discuss?

My work is not scary, but sometimes a client talks about things that have not been discussed with a therapist. One client was amazed that she got to a certain level so quickly and it was safe. She had worked with medical doctors, but she was having a hard time succeeding with a therapist. So we worked on things, and the client was able to get to a more respectful place in herself and that was her goal. My work leads to people feeling powerful and respectful of themselves. In New York, I worked with AIDS patients, and in some cases, people were looking for a place to feel more comfortable with their illness and its inevitability. They were going through a transition in which they would not necessarily return to physical health.

Healing does not mean a person will be up and walking. It is important to know that we are not in the wrong place physically or emotionally. I've worked with people who truly are living in fear, especially those with AIDS. I cannot take on an illness for a person. That would not serve a purpose. However, I can be with them to face the fears. Somebody has to be leading; therefore, I have to know personally where I'm leading to and where I'm coming from.

### What is your view on charging for services?

I charge for my time. I can't charge for information or energy. They don't belong to me. Nobody wants to come to a hungry healer who lives in the streets, which is why I have to pay rent and eat. I adjust my fees to anybody's needs really, but I don't promote free services because it just becomes frivolous. People may want to experiment and not honor the intent of the service. That is fine for them, but I just can't do that. I'm not here to entertain necessarily. Sometimes people will call and I simply ask them to give a donation to the animal shelter or St.

Jude's Children's Hospital. Money is energy and many people do not understand it. In summary, I give my time and experience and I feel it is appropriate to charge for that. It is not the money that should stop people. Some people don't know how to ask, but most of us have money issues and we're all working on them.

I do this full time as people find me. My work or my non-work teaches me in my own professional life. When I am not seeing clients, I breathe and I eat. There was a time that I didn't do that; I only had a professional life. At one point, I was teaching a lot and then decided to step back to see who I was without the trappings of reiki master and healer. I had to identify the private, personal Cory.

**What is your opinion on the psychic hot lines advertised on TV?**

I have no idea what these people are all about, but one of these groups has contacted me. I think there are people on those lines who may be good, and I have no concept on how people can fake that. But there must be some that do. A well-known medium is quite popular these days on TV. My sense is, yes, he is in fact doing something, but what? I'm a little suspicious about his communication with those who have passed on, and my sense is that he might be interpreting experiences from departed souls through the individuals who knew them. I believe souls go on, and I don't think they wait around two years just to give a few messages. On the other hand, I also think some are stuck here. A spirit may be trapped, and it is usually when a trauma has been involved. I don't get into that a lot at present, but dimensional transition isn't working for them. They don't want to be stuck either.

**What cautions do you have for people getting involved in the mystical?**

My message is for anybody seeking deeper truths. I would caution people not to get involved with too many modalities. Find one that you resonate with, whether it is meditation, yoga, reiki, and so on. Don't spread yourself thin, because then you aren't helping yourself anymore. Don't get hung up calling a psychic reader every day. Sometimes people open up and look for answers, and often times they are trying to break away from religion. At that point, they will try many things — past life regression, crystals, reiki, anything out there, and then they end up doing nothing. They burn out when they realize there is no magic answer.

Personally, I love crystals, but I don't work with them except for my own purposes. When I'm working with clients, I don't combine anything with reiki. It is a hands on process *and that's it*. There is so incredibly much out there. You can be led in numerous directions and find yourself confused and "polluted." At that point, a person is "playing metaphysical" but not doing it. I observe people taking workshop after workshop in several areas, and they enjoy them but when the workshops are over, they move on. This is the "workshop junkie syndrome" and it does not lead to the deeper truth so many seek.

### What advice do you have for people seeking a reading?

Don't depend on a reader to have all the answers you seek. Own only what feels comfortable to you. Always be cautious and questioning. Don't get lost in what other people are telling you, and don't blindly accept. Start learning what you need to be telling yourself.

### Is there power in prayer?

I often focus on affirmations. This positions positive thoughts in consciousness. We should not depend on this "positioning" totally, because we need to do actual *work* on our issues too. We need to understand why we are OK, even if it does not look OK. People may be shooting at us physically or emotionally. It gets confusing, but there is still a perfectionism happening. Definitely, there is a home for affirmations, but an individual in a good mental place does not purposefully need to "do affirmations" because that person is thinking them anyhow.

There are dwellings in the mind that will sabotage the "I'm OK" feeling. We want to do some cleaning in these places. Prayer is a natural urge in people. The reason it helps is that it feels as if you are doing something. Understand that sometimes prayers are not answered in a timely way — there may be years in the making before an answer arrives. It is far better to know we are already being helped, and this is more important than to depend on a miracle that may not materialize. Always keep in mind prayer can give us the impression that we are helpless, in which case we are waiting for God to "do something," when in fact this force is already doing it. We are just not registering it.

I don't say to people, "God help you," because I know He already is. When a prayer is seemingly not answered, we think there is no Divine power involved, and this is a mistake. On the other hand, even God won't hack through a lot of briar. Miracles happen. We need to be clear to get that help by getting back to spirit, not religion. Humans can only give a human perspective to it. Soul is in good shape; it's the encasement that we have to refine and polish.

### Is there such a phenomenon as reincarnation in your beliefs?

I believe souls go through a process. This is a process of incarnations that ultimately arrive at a higher level of understanding. I also believe the spiritual being somewhere along the way decided to try a separation from God (Adam and Eve in a Biblical sense). Perhaps this was to experiment and see what it would be like not to be one with God. Symbolically, this comes out in the Bible. It feels like we are separate, but we're not really. In Hinduism, learning and karma bring each lifetime closer to the understanding of God. A time comes when we no longer need to be here. Praying to God "above" is amusing, because God is here, there, and everywhere.

### What are your thoughts on synchronicity or coincidence?

We have to be open to it even though it can be challenging sometimes. The realization of a synchronistic event is likely to happen more readily if we are open to it. Meeting the right person, finding the right book, many different things start happening. We are all interconnected continuously, but sometimes we rebel or don't know what is happening. We have a plan even though it doesn't look that way. In the near-death experience, specific and simple words were given to me in 1976. I suppose I could be somewhat annoyed that I didn't receive this message earlier, but I have to remember the patience of the Divine plan is unbelievable. There is no linear time frame as we know it.

A person undergoing a synchronistic event may not grasp what is going on when it is happening. Although there is a definite plan, we have no way of seeing this because there is a whole other agenda taking place, and that is moving through life and getting closer to spirit. I have often said to clients, "Don't worry; you've got time." It's hard to really hear this when I say it to me. When I am working with a client, however, I see a different perspective on things. Yes, you have time, and you don't have to be an amazingly clear person by tomorrow. We are accustomed to human plans; we are not good at Divine plans.

**Do you have any advice to those with children who are showing psychic capabilities?**

Yes, don't become a stage mother! Furthermore, nothing will stop them even if you put them in a cage. Listen to them. Exceptionally evolved spirits are coming here now. Don't put your children in a category that they may never live up to; they need to play baseball too. When it comes to psychic ability, you don't need to encourage; it will happen. These children may have very important messages for their parents, families, or the rest of us.

**Do you have a final message to give us?**

Everything is in perfect order, no matter how disorderly it may appear. The appearance is something we may want to keep in consideration, being careful not to be caught up in the fact that it could be an uncomfortable place. Look deeper and dissolve the issues; don't put a bandage on it. This is how I work with clients, but I've had to look at myself too. I am not sitting on a mountain. The process is very different if you've been there and then it's not so scary if you take someone to that place. I work with many "dark spaces" that are scary, and people don't want to look back at that. I have to go with them. The energy really changes and things get easier when energy is not blocked. You are never alone on the journey.

**What would you wish for the world?**

Not peace, as it is typically defined. I would wish us to discover and live in a world of accepting one another as individuals — acceptance of shapes, sizes, colors, sexual orientation, place in life, and so on. And I guess that's peace, isn't it? Understanding of each other is a small step, but it would be nice to have this when one walks down the street or lives in another culture. I'm not saying that people need to be in agreement; just acceptance.

# Vanessa Hand Beard

Vanessa Hand Beard lives in La Crosse, Wisconsin. She practices in the area of intuitive reading and mediumship. Vanessa is a creative person who works extensively with stones of many varieties. Her web site has an excellent listing and description of the stones with their historical meanings and powers. As an artist, her photography and other works have been on display locally, and she has recently worked on a major film as a makeup-special effects artist.

## Contact Information
Vanessa Hand Beard
810 South 8th Street
La Crosse, Wisconsin    54601
**Phone:** 608-796-2495
**E Mail:**  *vanessahand@yahoo.com*
             *vanessa@intuitivetimes.com*
**Web site:**  *www.intuitivetimes.com*

### What mystical arts do you practice today?

I primarily do intuitive readings. Sometimes I use Tarot cards if a person desires a card reading, but I don't need to use them to access my abilities. Cards take the pressure off the client, especially if this is a first reading. Mediumship is also in my practice. When clients come to me for the purpose of working with a medium, they usually have a specific person in mind with whom they would like to make contact. That's difficult, and I usually take some time to prepare for this.

I've had good results in contacting people, but there are times when the person who comes through is not the one sought after. Nonetheless, the messages that come through are important for the client. A major problem is that people become so focused on contacting a certain departed individual that the message intended for them is not taken as seriously or is taken as incidental.

### How did you develop your abilities?

Now I am aware that I have always had some ability, but as a child I saw this to be the norm, so it didn't stand out for me as some sort of uncommon phenomenon. It was a negative thing in my life because my mother was spooked by it. She belittled things and lacked understanding. I tucked it all away and would not tell anybody even when I knew things were about to happen. I did things automatically to prepare for what I knew was going to happen, and that's what really bothered my family and got me into trouble.

After I married and had children, the abilities seemed to grow, and gradually they became stronger after I was out of that marriage. Finally, this ability teased my interest, and I began to explore. One fall I was quite ill and had surgery. It was a sudden and traumatic illness. Again, these abilities became more pronounced.

In 1995, I was working with a teacher in Arizona because mystical pursuits were starting to be accepted, especially in certain areas of the country. The first place that I worked along with the teacher was at a Barnes and Noble bookstore. People lined up to see readers, and there I was. I was catching all that

my teacher was saying, and knowing everything she was knowing. For the life of me, I could not understand why this was so
fascinating to people. To me, it was like telling you that you
were wearing a red shirt and blue shoes. I still have a problem
with that. I was not charging, and in addition, I was doing
readings for friends and family. I've learned this is an unwise
thing to do, and I discontinued that practice.

When doing readings for friends, I often hit the target. Then
they tended to pull away and would not associate with me any
longer. Similarly, it's difficult to tell a family member when
something is going to happen and it's something they don't care
to know about. I tried to help my sister once, but it turned into
a sticky situation. It's so hard to give advice to the family and
then load psychic information on top of that. My rule of thumb
is that I don't do readings for friends, family, or people I work
with on a daily basis.

### Are you pursuing any other mystical areas?

I am always interested in the metaphysical. Some things
intrigue me, and some things don't. I read my horoscope everyday, but I don't get into astrology. Palm reading doesn't interest
me. I like exploring unusual divination. I like dowsing with a
pendulum. It really amazes me how well it works. My real
preference is in working with stones. I have a passion for stones
and a connection with Earth and stones. My former husband
said I was the easiest person to find a gift for — stones and rocks
are everywhere.

### So you were rocking with the stones. How did that all start?

When I was about five years old, I started collecting pretty
stones such as rose quartz. It was easy to find this in people's
gardens. I loaded the stones into my wagon, and off I'd go as
the door-to-door saleslady. I'd name the rock and tell my
"customers" what the rock wanted and what the rock was about
— made perfect sense to me.

Stones still speak to me. I get a feeling of what the stone
wants and what it can provide. It's an inner connection and
knowing that is difficult to explain. Each stone to me has its

own personality just like a dog or a cat. When my daughter was three years old, we were at a show and she began crying because she had to leave a large piece of malachite there. This was apparently her "friend." I guess whatever this is has jumped across into another generation.

### Just what is it with these relics of antiquity?

When I hold stones, I get messages. Some stones make me feel better. Nebula stone is the one I carry with me right now. It is a beautiful stone found in Mexico. I love the sparkly rocks, crystal points, lepidolite; there are just so many. When I go to a festival, I love matching people up with stones, depending on what they need in their lives. This is part of the intuitive process. It just seems to help.

My neighbor, an older woman, was curious and I matched her up with a stone, and she carries it with her all the time. She may not believe in it, but she thinks it is an interesting thing. My husband recently lost the stone I gave to him. He was very upset about it. When a person loses a stone, I believe that means the stone has finished its work with you. It's not meant for you right now, or perhaps another person needs to work with it. At least that's how I view it, and it helps in getting over the trauma of losing that friend.

### Is there a common thread among those who practice mystical arts?

I believe there are two schools on this. There is one common thread that runs through everyone. Certain areas don't interest me. Channeling does not interest me. I respect it and I'm sure it has significance, but I don't follow it at all. When I work with people, we generally focus on life in the here and now. Sometimes we can get into past life regression with phobias and fears, but I don't do this frequently because it can become a parlor game. The thread that I follow more would be in helping people to find their true path, and what it is they really desire in this life. At the same time, we solve roadblocks they have encountered.

**Do you have any cautions for the person seeking a reader?**

First, decide if that reader is someone with whom you want to work. Trust *your* intuition. One of the things certainly to watch out for is people who want to do work *without* your presence. For example, someone who says they will do some candle ritual for you, but you need not be there. Talk about a red flag flying in the breeze — I mean you have to do your *own* work. Any kind of reader who says don't share the information or don't tell anyone, is someone to be cautious of.

When you leave a reading, you should be feeling hopeful, focused, and armed even if the information is not wonderful. All news, good or bad, has a purpose at that time. I have not had a person leave a reading sad or upset. Even in mediumship, I try to find a positive focus. Some readers upset people. Be careful when sitting with a reader because you are opening yourself up. Use trust as your guide. You're not obligated just because you are sitting there. Tell the reader you are not comfortable with this and then leave. As a reader, I would be grateful for this rather than traveling too far into the reading.

**What is your answer to the skeptic?**

I've had a lot of practice, since that's the atmosphere I grew up in. But honestly, I respect everybody's opinion. I used to get upset because I felt I had to prove myself or convince someone. Now my feeling is that you are entitled to your opinion, but don't force it on me. I have proof for myself that this works for me and it works for the people who come to see me.

**What criticisms do you hear?**

I don't hear much. What I do hear is criticism of scam artists. I might hear reference to "not really doing anything that the person could not do for himself." I suppose it is true that you don't need an outside voice to help, but everyone that I've worked with has truly benefited from the information they get, even if they could have gotten it for themselves, technically. Sometimes you can't see the forest for the trees.

**What do you think of the psychic hot lines advertised on television?**

I'd stay away from that situation. It has become pretty obvious that those are a rip-off. I have a friend who is actually a good psychic and worked for one of these outfits because she wanted to give customers someone who is actually legitimate. She ended up talking to many people who were drunk or severely depressed or people who had a variety of medical problems. It is just not a good format. It is fraudulent and I sincerely hope people are waking up to that.

**Is there anything unique about practicing in Wisconsin?**

I find that in the Midwest, you really have to build trust with people. Midwesterners take it more to heart, and going to a reader is a big event. In Arizona, people were generally seeking the entertainment aspect. I find Wisconsin very refreshing in that people here really want to work and to help.

When I moved here, I didn't know what the environment would be like, and then I found out this kind of activity was actually against the law! No kidding — I found out there was a law sitting on the books since the Ice Age and nobody had noticed it, I guess. When I moved here, I wanted to practice openly, so I checked things out, and the city authorities said not to worry. "Just go ahead because we don't enforce the law" is what they told me. But I decided I didn't want to take that chance. I didn't want an obscure law cluttering my mind at any level. That card could be pulled at anytime if someone disapproved of what I was doing. My solution was to study the law, apply to get it changed, and speak in front of the City Council a few times. I expected opposition, but I had none! Through that experience, I felt good about practicing in Wisconsin. People won't fight me or condemn me. If they don't like me, they just don't seek me out.

**Do world events affect your abilities?**

No, they do not. I feel certain things before they happen or very shortly after. It manifests itself in the form of a headache or something physical. Sometimes I know when something is coming, but I don't know what it is. That's difficult.

**When you are out and about are your abilities on hold?**

I shield myself when I can. After my illness, I could hear conversations in my head coming from a building ¼ mile away. That was disturbing. This happened at a festival where I had a craft and jewelry booth. I went to the bathroom, which was in a different building, and I heard my husband and his friend conversing about loading things into the car. In my mind, the conversation was occurring right outside of the window next to me. I was angry that they were not in the main building protecting my belongings. When I returned to that building and described the conversation in detail, they were upset about accusations that they had not stayed in the booth. In reality, they had never left the area.

After that came the grocery shopping fiasco. I arrived home with strange items that I had no recollection of buying. My husband would pick up an item and say, "Do we really need this?" After I studied the predicament, I found out I was pulling in other shopper's thoughts in the grocery store, because most people really concentrate when they are shopping. And here's me, picking up those concentrated thoughts like pebbles on the beach. For a long time I did not go shopping because of this problem. Now I take a list and stick to it. I worked with people at Camp Wonewoc to learn a shielding technique. I had to practice by going shopping and shielding myself to the thoughts; strangely enough, it felt as if people were speaking a foreign language. It's a delicate balance.

**What is your answer to hard-as-rock science?**

I think science is becoming softer. My belief for anyone is to follow what your heart believes. I'm not going to convince you, and vice versa.

**Do you think dreams have significance?**

They are important to me. I'm doing a lot of work with myself personally right now, and I dream of houses and things in the house. In dream interpretation, the house represents oneself. Initially, when I was dealing with outside influences and family things, I had several dreams of not being able to lock the doors. So, there was that safety factor. Other times, I could find a new part of the house that doesn't even exist. Then there were all the neat things in the room. I think my dreams tell me I am on the right path. Dreams sessions that occur in the morning seem to have messages. To hold onto a dream, keep a notebook and pen, and while you are still in the position in which you awoke, try to remember as many things as you visually detected. Once you get up, it's gone. If you write down the key points, this will trigger the rest of it. It's a habit of mine to do this. Talking about a dream will help you hold it for a long time too.

### Are there any specific readings that come to mind?

Mediumship is more what stands out for me. I have been offering readings without charge over the internet or over the phone because I want to document my results. Recently, I worked with a woman in a mediumship reading, and I saw a man standing under a tree. I described him exactly. The man was the ex-husband, and after he died, he had been buried in some sort of western outfit sewn from textured fabrics. He was holding a gold necklace in his hand as if he were showing it to me. After the man passed on, his daughter asked for the gold necklace, but the current wife was unwilling to give it up. This man was trying to tell me the necklace was for his daughter.

I was trying to communicate with him more deeply and the left side of my body felt like it was burning. Apparently, his wife shot him in the left side and caused the death. That pain actually stuck with me for a couple of days. Now when I work with a person, I ask if there is any physical pain. I'm not fond of hurting for days on end. I feel those physical manifestations, and I have not been wrong.

There are messages for this side, but nobody on the other side ever has questions. I've had cases where people who have passed over will come to me just as I'm falling asleep at night. They try to get a message through, but I don't know for whom the message is intended.

**Oh, sounds like a mess to me. Glitches in Cosmos Express.**

Wait, it gets even stickier. I worked with a woman who was pregnant and whose husband had been killed. He was coming through forcefully and very adamantly about something. He kept repeating to me that the *baby is not mine.* How do you tell this to the woman? I was anxious about the whole thing and just didn't know what to say. Finally, I said, "I have to tell you what I'm hearing. He is saying the baby is not his."

She took a deep breath and said, "Oh, that's so good to hear. There is another woman who was claiming she was pregnant at the same time, and that it is his baby." So his message was referring to the other woman, and not the wife. Of course, the information made sense to my client, but I have no idea where it's coming from or what the focus is. I bring the information through, but it's not my job to interpret it. Sometimes I do radio shows here, and I am discreet. I don't want to say anything on the air that would cause an uproar or be indelicate.

**Have you worked on any police or investigative cases?**

I have been approached to look at missing child cases, but I am not comfortable with it. There are so many traumas in that, and I can't open myself up to it. As far as criminal investigations go, I would not want to expose my family to that sort of thing. If I were on my own, I probably wouldn't mind participating in this. I can't say I'm totally oblivious to it, because I have gotten information on things that have happened in this area of the state on occasion. What I do is watch the news on TV or get information somehow, and make sure they are on the right track, so to speak.

In one case, a man had supposedly committed suicide, but I knew this was not how things ended for him. A woman I knew was loosely connected, since the guy was a friend of hers. I said to her, "I want you to know it was not a suicide." She turned rather chalky and said that the police were investigating it as a murder. I was glad the police were on to that, but the woman has not spoken a word to me since then.

My latest endeavors have been in working with structures, buildings, and homes to find out about spirits that are still hanging out there. I recently worked with a family in Reeseville, Wisconsin and was able to connect with three entities. What I got was confirmed by incidents the family has experienced and felt. I make it an *absolute* rule to seek clean information by not hearing or knowing anything about a person, situation, or place before I do a reading.

In this case, I was able to connect with one person in particular who had been in much pain with headaches during his life. I asked the parents if the daughter in that room had been suffering from frequent headaches. They were shocked, and confirmed that the daughter gets headaches when she sleeps in that room. During the summer, she had been sleeping downstairs and the headaches had ceased. The man in her room apologized to them through me, and he seemed so relieved to be able to explain to someone that he hadn't been a crazy old man, as believed. He had just been in such pain, he couldn't stand it. Things really have calmed down for the family.

### How do family and friends react to your abilities?

The situation has turned around in the last four to five years. I don't have the problems of the past because they understand and accept what I do. I have very few close friends. When people get information from me they tend to stay away. But for those who do come to me and ask, I just tell them that I don't want to go there, and they are OK with that. The most amazing reaction has been the fact that my mother has completely changed her views about what I do. I was even able to get a message to her through her deceased husband, whom I barely knew. The message was something only the two of them had shared. This had a significant impact on her coping with his death, as well as helping heal our relationship.

### Is there power in prayer?

Yes, putting a thought or feeling out in the universe is powerful. I believe there is a power of manifestation. Poof! It won't appear right in front of you, but the pathways are going to open up if you are aware of them. Beware, because it works the other way too. If you dwell on how broke you are, or how upset you are, or how miserable you are, then that's where you're stuck.

What you are putting out, you are manifesting, and there is a lot to be said for that.

**What do you think about reincarnation... the ultimate recycling plan?**

Many of us have traveled through in similar circles before. I don't do much work with it, but I think it is interesting to explore. The relationships I've had in the past have been with people who are born in the spring. My daughters and I think we have been in past lives together. One of my daughters is convinced she was my mother in some previous life, and she really acted like it while she was growing up. People that you meet and instantly like or dislike could be associated with recognition of past life.

**How do things come through for you — symbols, voices, smells, images?**

Primarily my tool is clairvoyance. Sometimes symbols or letters of the alphabet are present. Very rarely do I get actual names or hear much of anything. When I see images, it's like watching remembered scenes from a movie. It feels like a memory, but I know it isn't from my own memory.

**What are your thoughts on synchronicity or coincidence?**

Everything has a connection, and I have experienced it all my life. I find that I take advantage of unusual opportunities. I don't question it, I just go with it. Take notice of what I call "theme days." There are certain days that something is constantly making itself known to you, no matter where you go. Try to find out what message is trying to make its way to the surface. Just literally stop what you are doing, and take a few minutes to analyze this. This is great to do with the family too. I find that it usually affects everyone with whom you are connected.

**What is your definition of a mystic?**

Well, how about the Hollywood gypsy image... just kidding. When I think of the word, I think about places rather than people. Sedona, Arizona, is one of those places. In my opinion, Sedona has gone so wacky with people who do channeling, Akashic records, the Atlantian thing — it freaks me out. To me, mysticism is centered on things I can't understand or tap into. I don't strongly categorize what I do as mysticism.

**What advice do you have for those with children who have abilities?**

Let them be open to it. My daughter took me to high school one year for show and tell. They were doing a psychology unit and happened to be covering extrasensory perception. I took a chance and went to class. I was thinking, OK this will be fun. I didn't realize I would be lecturing for an hour. When I got home that night, I was actually terrified that parents would be using me for target practice. I expected to see pitchforks and torches coming down the street to run me out of town.

A few days later, the teacher called and asked me if I'd lecture for *all* of his psychology sections, so I did. This is now my third year at it. Kids even get passes out of other classes to attend the lecture and participate. My youngest daughter has abilities and she visits the class to lecture a little bit too. This is knowledge that doesn't need to hide in some dark corner.

**Do you think there is a dark side, especially when we talk about notorious people?**

There is a dark side to humankind. It's all in the choices we make. As far as notorious people throughout history — again, it's all in the choices they made. "Darkness" is a human condition or trait; it is not a spiritual attribute. When I have worked in the area of people who have passed over, I have never experienced anything like that. The communications from people, who were not exactly stellar in life, come through as messages of apology or understanding. I have never experienced a dark side in the spiritual realm.

**Do you have any messages concerning psychic ability?**

Everyone has a different talent and a different level of ability. Some people can learn psychic talents and tune up what they already have. We like playing with psychometry around my house. My daughter, my father, and I can touch things and get feelings off the objects. It's terrific fun to go to a garage sale. We can pick things up and compare notes to see if we are getting the same vibes. Your right hand is a receiver of information, so it's a good idea to use that hand to pick things up.

If you are trying to work on psychic ability, it's wise to write things down initially to look for *patterns* and *correlations*. Don't dismiss things. Try to categorize. Be open and aware. If you are ready to embrace it, those things will really start showing themselves to you all the time. In any event, I always recommend rocks!

# Dante

Dante began experiencing strong psychic ability and use of intuition as a young child.

He began doing psychic reading at that time, and began observing paranormal activity in his environment. One of the tools he frequently uses is the Tarot. Dante is a former special investigator. He was born and raised in Wisconsin. Dante currently lives in the Waukesha area and has a thriving client base throughout Wisconsin and beyond. He makes special appearances in person, on the radio, and throughout the Midwest.

**Contact Information**
Dante
2430 N. Grandview Blvd.
Waukesha, Wisconsin  53188
**Phone:** 262-549-4784
**E mail:** *dantemail@tds.net*
**Web site:** *www.houseofdante.com*
            *www.psychic-carnival.com*

**What mystical arts do you practice today?**

A little of this; a little of that. I psychically read as much as I can from a person. I sometimes use psychometry, which is divination through holding an object or being in the proximity of an object owned by the person in question. I pick up on whatever tends to be around a person in the form of entities or personalities. Generally, what survives is the obsessive part of a personality. Really, I do as much or as little as I can get away with. Tarot reading is one of my strong points. Lately, my work is more serious and involves memory and history. I seem to fall into things and it is tough, because I'm a little more "off the beaten track."

**How did you develop these talents?**

I tried to make them go away! I didn't like them. I can't figure that part out, really. When I was seven years old, I had "problems" with inanimate objects. Perhaps it was a response to other mediumistic or spiritual tribulations going on with me. For example, in the basement, my parents stored antiques they had collected. Portraits of the family would speak to me prophetically and correctly. I interacted with imaginary friends. When I predicted my grandfather's heart attack, people started to notice. My father likes to think of himself as an existentialist, not coinciding with anything. I couldn't live like that even if I wanted.

My grandfather was a lively musical and lyrical person who taught me to play piano. He was a person larger than life who learned piano by "deprivation" while quarantined during a polio epidemic. Strange the way some gifts arrive. When Uncle Art passed, I saw him standing next to the casket, and he made his usual gesture to me. Mother was upset with me when I told her this. When it was time for burial in the cemetery, he just walked away. My grandparents did the same thing. Astonishingly visual as this all was, it meant a lot to me because I knew there was not an end. Essentially, I had the opportunity to witness unexplainable things. It was very comforting to me and I could in a way, sort things out and write history. I think we can all do that.

### How did you fine-tune the abilities?

I don't think I have. I run from this! When I was working as a private investigator, it was interfering. I became good at knowing who was going to steal the money in an armored car. These abilities rather screwed up my childhood, my marriage, and so on. I don't know why I'm so far to one side. I'd like to be where everybody should be, which is somewhere between here and there. On the other hand, I think everybody should have the opportunity to open him or herself up. Survival of our species depends on this. I think we are at a point in our evolution where the next step is inward.

Our psyche needs to look at things from a distance and surround things as if they are larger than we are, but actually we are larger then they are. A good example would be the calculating savant twins who can be thrown multiple digit prime numbers and literally converse in a language of numbers. They somehow seem to look at a number from a distance and get their minds around it instead of trying to figure out if it is a prime number or not. *We* need that. We have that when we drive down the road at 75 mph and there's a good song on the radio, but unknowingly we slow down to 35 mph. A huge buck jumps in front of the car just as we are about to press down the gas pedal for more speed. Fortunately, we avoided an accident. What was happening here? The answer is survival intuition taking over, and that's not likely an accident. However, we live in a left-brain socially acceptable life, so punch that speed up to 75 because that makes more sense. But does it?

How many times have you heard, never trust your first impression? Well, why not? If you don't, you should at least make note of it, because more often than not, it will be right. We are so close to being right that it's eerie. But one way or another, we go out of our way *not* to do these things. I think that somehow and in some manner, that's what I'm supposed to be doing here. Sadly, it would be a waste not to have a purpose with what I do.

I will not just say I can read cards and tell you things no one else will know — so what? I can bend spoons — so what? How useful is that? The fact is anybody can do these things. Why are we not doing them? The answer is because we have found scientific methods in the left-brain that refuse to extrapolate at will unless trained to do so. If you could remember everything that you ever read, saw, smelled — what a library of information! We need to get deeper into that. There are things that you can know about me that you would have no physical way of knowing. Where does that come from? It comes from the gray area just above your head that exists as an aura, as some people call it. I think it's our "hook up" and communication with the rest of the planet.

**Let's talk about spontaneity of intuition you referred to previously.**

We are living our history at this moment and our spirituality is important. But now, and *especially* now, there is a part of you that detects danger and signals survival. A police officer, detective, or any agent that has to work an involved case or where something terrible is going on, usually ends up with some kind of "dumb luck" as it is referred to, or some "coincidence" happens, and the case is adjudicated.

I remember talking to an officer in Chicago about a particular incident. He was telling me that he had to shoot back and forth and he had never even shot his gun before this, let alone do this kind of thing. Suddenly he was shooting at one man, and unbeknownst to him, another guy was making an "end around" like in football. He said, "*Immediately I thought of football.* It was because of that *specific* impression that I turned around to shoot the guy in the stomach because he was coming at me. He wasn't making any noise so there was nothing to hear. The man's last words were, 'I didn't think you saw me.' Then he was gone." The officer turned to address the other guy, but he had disappeared. If the officer had not used the instinctive "Faculty X" moment, he would have taken a shot in the back of the head.

The officer swung around to this man's fatal surprise. Football was the archetype that made him think, "end around." Many people will not understand this. You have to know how to read your own head. For this cop, it saved his life. That's just one example. There are numerous pathways to choose from and accomplish this. However, it can work with you or against you.

It is dangerous, yet important in our times. We will see things get darker, and we need to practice that instinct.

### Are there other areas of mysticism that you study?

I study the Kabbalah much of the time. The concept of using meditation to learn Kabbalah is beautiful. I have an interest in the Kahuna of Hawaii and in Tao. The Bible and Martin Luther were interests of mine as a child. I have avoided the Celtic concept because it doesn't feel right to me. Judaism and Hebrew mysticism leaves us open to a wealth of interpretation, and that's excellent. Christianity is "this" and if it's not "this," you're going straight to hell. Islam seems to be difficult for me to understand, although I have studied the religion. It is poetic and striking, but difficult for me. I think about the "Gypsy" history of my family, and that is quite intriguing because it takes from everything else. Allistar Crowley is a favorite of mine and I continue to study his work. Development of my own methodology is aided by reading about recent mediums and mystics. There is so much to absorb. With the exception of Judaism and then Christianity, almost everything is alike when it comes to spiritual concept. Everything is basically oriented around nature.

### Is there a common thread among those who practice mystical arts?

Lying? Just kidding. A dear friend taught me a lot. It's kind of strange that she was there to teach what I couldn't learn from my grandmother. Intuition is certainly foremost as a common thread. Madame Blavatsky was a wonderful psychic aside from the fact that she smoked a half ounce of marijuana a week and would generally cheat when she had the chance. She just simply didn't want to do the work. Most psychics that really do their stuff are usually people who are suffering and/ or have health problems. They are typically burdened by their abilities. Sometimes they have a hard time holding jobs. Sometimes they are diagnosed as mentally ill. They are often medicated and frequently kill themselves or die at an early age.

Mystics, on the other hand, take better care of themselves and can do just as good a job as a psychic. They may not be pin-pricking accurate or perfect as you want them to be, but they are an easier group of people to deal with. They are more light-oriented, more Christianized, serve a great purpose, and do a good job. Most psychics and especially mediums have suffered some type of damage that causes the door to fly open unintentionally, and the better ones are those who can manage it. The ones who aren't up to par let it manage them.

### What's your opinion about the 1-900-call-a-psychic-now hot lines?

"When I grow up I'm going to be a psychic." Be careful what you ask for, because you'll get lost in a city with two roads. You will forget phone numbers, faces; it's a silly way to live. 1-900 has ruined the business. In 1967, nobody did this except for little old ladies in homes and at carnivals. Now you can't shake a dead cat without hitting a psychic. University studies say that eight to ten percent of the people on the planet can actually tune into psychic stuff, three percent can handle it, and one percent can perform it.

Everybody is looking to the right and to the left to attach themselves to something. It's a dangerous point in time for us because people at this moment in history are easily misled. You've got to look inside. *You have to know that.* If you're getting a hot line reading, and obviously are not across from the reader, you can't tell what they're doing and you can't tell if they are real. How do you know they are not reading off a script, especially if they are good at the script? Secondly, where is the transfer, where is the intimacy, and where is the exchange of information? There is none.

True psychics can work these lines, but it's hard and it hurts. Essentially, the psychic ends up dealing with people who are horribly depressed. They called because they needed mental health services, wanted someone to talk with, and didn't mind spending $250-plus an hour to do it. I saw how my friend worked on one of these lines. Sometimes you can help people more as an entertainer or as a minister than a therapist. What you end up with is a mix of entertainment, social commentary, mental health, personality issues, mediumship work, and gossip. Conversely, if you are having a reading as you sit across the table from someone, that reader is trying very hard to read for you and give you quality information. Why would you want to talk to someone in New York on a psychic hotline?

### Any words about the skeptic?

Skeptics are an interesting lot. They have lost the ability to actually seek out the unexplainable and then attempt to explain it. Science doesn't necessarily have evidence of life after death. We have evidence of survival of personality. The skeptic must at least acquiesce to that. In addition, psychokinesis has been proven in the lab. Transfer from mind to mind, or mind reading, has been proven in the lab. We just deflated the skeptic. Near-death experiences (NDE) have been studied for years and they all fit a pattern. Methodology? Program? Model? Isn't that what the scientific mind is trained to do? Define by pattern? How did Galileo do it? Yet we refuse the people who have the scientific mind of Galileo to work in this field... "Oh stay away from that parapsychology stuff." Yet, the fact is, these people are on the only cutting edge that we have. If we at least do not get a grasp on it, history will run out. I love skeptics. I eat them. I have a hard time with a lot of these people. I blister at those who say this or that will happen to me. You are your own God. With that information alone, we should be doing wonderful things.

### What criticisms do you hear?

"You're wrong; that's bullshit, I don't like those earrings." The earrings are a family thing. Hematite earrings make me more susceptible to psychic energy. Maybe it's the grounding part of it. I don't know. I feel better when I have this stuff on. A psychologist would say that's just because you are taking a character. Okay, I'll go with that. I use what works — stones, rocks, pebbles. Everything has a different vibration. Hematite keeps my brain working and is good for my spine.

Satan and "the work of the devil" is another criticism that chokes the air. I have nothing to do with a devil. The devil is a purely Christian creation. "Devil" is taken from a Sanskrit word meaning "diva" which is female goddess. We see yet another attempt to detract or minimize the female by turning her into evil.  Greek mathematicians created the plus sign as giver of life (female) and the minus sign (male) as taker of life.  The devil — he owes me money; he won't be around.

### What about a dark side?

The dark side, on the other hand, is a very different thing. When a person dies, there are two parts to distinguish.  One of the components is, as some people would say, the soul, but I call it the personality.  This personality part of you was loved, positive, cared for things, and so on.  This element went off to Heaven, New Jersey or wherever that part was created.  Other people have different jumping off points.  It is a point of familiarity and you go there.  Sometimes there are relatives, pets, or Woodrow Wilson.  Things depend on how your personality (Soul) handles its own memory.

Part two is the obsessed part.  The element drank too much, drove too fast, put too much make up on, molested children, smoked pot.  That's what is here as the dark side.  Very often in working as a medium, I can feel the dark part and I use it as a springboard to bring out the better.  This fraction is what worries me the most and it interests me.  The dark, negative, dank side of survival is an important and interesting part of psychology and psychiatry, and much more than any of us understands.

It's nothing for an obsession to travel after death from one person to the next especially when the person is geographically and bloodline related.  This is almost impossible to throw into the lab, but evidence for that kind of survival is strong.  The case of miniature possession by disgruntled entities is quite important and misunderstood by the psychic community.  We see novice healers and novice people, including magicians, working with energies they don't understand.  This can be very dangerous for the innocent person.  The case for possession is very strong.  There again, is that obsessive personality that gives us a lot of what we perceive as the dark side.  I could go off on this topic for days, but I'll spare you.

### Is there anything unique about practicing in Wisconsin?

Wisconsin is mixed with a curious level of liberalism and conservatism that works well — Wicca, German, Polish, and

Swedish, just to name a few of the prominent ones. The Polish and Germans have a tremendous tendency to be mystics and very religious. This is an interesting place for me to do my work. There's also a lot of haunted material out here too.

### Do world events affect your abilities?

World events make me more paranoid. Right about the middle of July, I was buying survival gear. I have a friend at Hebrew University in Israel, and I am very worried about him. Future events make it important that you do this book, and that I do whatever I have to do, and that we all are involved in trying to educate the public. In a very strange way, I think this will mean a lot. We need to pay attention right off the bat, first impressions, and dreams especially.

Many people that I've talked to said they prophesized September 11, 2001. If you cut those people in half, take half of that, and then cut that part in half and determine half of these are screwy, there's still a number of people who had intuition present to some degree. Whether they knew it or not, many people felt something was coming and didn't go into work that day—these were the people that were *trying* to pay attention. *Something* bothered them. That same feeling could have saved *all* of those people. That is the kind of intuition I'm talking about, and we need to develop this. If we don't do this, we are going to war ourselves into oblivion, not to mention all the aerosol spray cans eating up the environment.

### Do you have a belief in a structured religion?

Structure is a wonderful thing if you need it in your life. People desire freedom, however. The greatest trick any religion, except for possibly Judaism, played on the Universe, is to prove to humankind that you "need" religion to be a religious person. That you *need* religion to be spiritual…this is the man you *have* to see…you *must* go through this man. He will tell you to do jumping jacks and six pushups; your prayers will be answered, and you will be saved. Well, NO. That's exactly why Jesus said, in so many words, no that's not what this is all about. He said you are your own savior, and if you're not, don't count on us, because we made you like this. If you expect some entity to come down and save you, you're screwed. If you accept Jesus in your heart, great; now go out and prove this. People need to know that religion is right here inside of you. So use it! That's the biggest fit I have. Repeatedly, I have people who come to me who are responsible for their own destruction. It's all you. Get to work!

### Is there power in prayer?

The *will* is a wonderful thing. I think the will does better with ceremony and the ceremony should be purposeful (whoops, I'm talking about spells). The greatest place to see witchcraft is in the Bible. That's where the concept of witchcraft comes from actually. The will is really the same thing as prayer. A prayer is a spell or a charm. The power of positive prayer is a fantastic thing. You can pray to the microwave and you'll get good results because you believe in it. So pray. I don't think it makes a difference that you pray to something, but that you believe in your heart that it can be done. Call it whatever you want. Just don't force everybody to do it the way you do it, unless of course, they want to come along.

### What has been your involvement in police or investigative cases?

Yes, I have been involved in so *many*. Recently, a guy called me because he was looking for his stepdaughter. He was worried she was dead. I told him that she was going to be pulled over by the police, and that she would show up tomorrow. It was also my strong sense that she ran away because somebody was interfering with her. For me to do this kind of thing for people is very easy. On the other hand, when a person has passed, you really need to be objective. Working with the dead in criminology, and getting information from the dead, has to do with first impressions, but it also has to do with your soul.

I was an investigator on one particular homicide case involving a vehicle. The person I was representing had been accused of killing his girlfriend and best friend in a motorcycle accident. I went to the scene of the accident after many months, and the spirit of the dead woman rushed me. She said it was wrong. Her biggest concern was that the man not be prosecuted in a manner that he would be unable to see his children. The woman's family was alienated to the situation and despised this person. Her spirit gave me the tools I needed to do this. She told me what to look for, how to look for it, how the accident took place, how the fork in the motorcycle was bent together, and where I would find the evidence. I finally found an expert to testify. He confirmed everything she described, one thing after another, and we were able to get the case dismissed.

Unfortunately, the man did not pay attention to his *intuition*, refusing to listen to what messages were coming to him about caring for the children. I had to walk away from it because it was too much for me. This case bothered me the most because it involved a bizarre form of third party innocence that I had never encountered before. A woman was plucked from the Earth with babies on the Earth, and no recourse. It was truly a tragedy, and a ripple in the delicately woven mesh where time and space meets.

The location where the event happened is cosmically damaged now. I know this very strongly. People are going to have bad experiences at that location, no matter what. I liken it to the area near Lake Michigan where people throw themselves off the bluff. It's the same kind of thing. When you feel creepy and you look over and see a cross, there is a reason for that creepy feeling. This person lost her life right there. She is tied to that spot. I don't know what to do about it, because it feels incredibly heavy and sorrowful. I look for missing kids, I'll give you family stuff, I'll give you clues, but this other matter hurts. It makes me relive the entire experience and this is indescribably painful.

### Do you have a belief in reincarnation?

Do we need to check out the obvious? Just throw a photo album in front of a two- or three-year-old child. They know names. The more intelligent the kid is, the better.

### How do messages or intuitions come through to you — voices, feelings, images, symbols?

All of the above plus! Yelling, screaming, loud angry voices, quiet whispers, weird smells, flashes of memories that don't belong to me, there is a "shouting" obviousness, there's delicate intricacies with hidden little parcels that explode. Need I say more? There's an instant flow of psychometry from one object to the next which is very annoying. *All* of our senses can obtain extrasensory information. We have to get out of our own way to avoid some of this. I wish I just had a switch...

**What is your view on the idea of coincidence or synchronicity?**

Everything is connected. That being true, what is coincidence? Déjà vu is the same thing. You have a *feeling* of living this experience in the past, and dismiss it as simply that. Well, you may *actually* have lived this experience at a different time. I frequently find coincidence occurring when I am in some sort of amnesia or blackout. I end up having the weird synchronicities later on, and I essentially think they might have been things that were happening when I had the amnesic experiences. When I do channeling or mediumship work, I disappear and I don't know what I end up with. The synchronicity might be something that I have taken from somebody else. I don't know at that point.

**Do you have any advice for people going to a reader?**

Do you like the reader? Do you feel they are giving you a line of crap? If so, then walk away. Always pay them because they are trying to make a living. But don't go back. I've seen some people totally hate the experience when they could have merely left the situation. Don't go back to a psychic any more often than ninety days. You're not going to find out anything new. It would be a waste of your money. A psychic is only as good as the fresh experience, and they are only as good as their own experience. Another caveat is the moment anyone tells you he or she wants to bless or cleanse your money, run fast.

**Is there any thing you would like to say about hardcore scientifically minded people?**

I love empirical people! They remind me of old police scanners — engineer types. Communication for them is only on two channels, and the rest of their crowd tries to figure out the problems on the two channels while at the same time being oblivious to all else. That's great, but it is precisely this kind of thinking that hastens the demise of the right brain into oblivion. I guess that's OK too, but if you want to marry an egg or be an egg, you will never come out of your shell. I suppose some people are satisfied with this. These people subsist on a strict philosophy with no edges or openings for anything. It is generally not a very healthy life or happy life, and death comes early. Unfortunately, and I really mean it is truly unfortunate; these people have a tendency to hurt themselves or get hurt. As we go through this spiritual revolution, or evolution, science will strangely mix. I genuinely look forward with openness to that day.

### Do you have any messages to leave with us?

Anyone can do this work. I don't care to amaze people anymore. I would rather teach people. Pay attention to your intuition, is my main message. It will save your life. When you have a feeling that something is out of the norm, *please give it attention.* Plan your life, live your life, and don't let it control you. Use it in a balanced form.

### I know there are some additional comments you would like us to hear.

Nobody should be fighting. For God's sake, why don't we go to war and…PAINT? Who can make the most hideous, the best, the angriest or happiest looking painting? Why don't we go to war and…COOK? We went wrong when men began to dominate the thinking process. Believe me, they developed late. In the next decade, it will be women who get us out of the mess. Strong females such as Golda Meir come to mind. As far as things related to September 11, 2001, I am still afraid of Christmas time, and I'm also up tight about July 4. What is going on will not be as organized, but they are not finished. It will happen here on American soil. Foreign policy has distanced us, and that is sad, but I don't disagree with it. This is a different place, and I am not responsible for what happens in other places like India or Africa. Generations before me killed my family. I have to accept that.

It is a very nasty thing to say, and a bizarre thing to say, but in a very strange way, killing can be positive. I have worked in large cities on the streets, and I have seen what happens when murders and killings occur. Communities suddenly lose their drug houses. People rapidly change because of it. Look at killing in Afghanistan. If not for the bloodshed, the women would still be sexually abused and murdered.

Government as we know it will change. Look at history. An old example, but nonetheless a prime example, is Adolf Hitler and his "Thousand Year Reich" that lasted twelve years. There was nothing positive about that. When things don't fit right, things change. People change and consciousness transforms. We have to be open to it and not be our own worst enemies. Intuition, awareness, courage to *listen*, and change; it's all within us individually — that's my final message.

# Patty Martin

Patty Martin, a Reiki Master Teacher has practiced Reiki in her home since 1995. She conducts workshops and teaches healing techniques involving subtle energies, Reiki, and essential oils. Patty also teaches guided meditation, the use of pendulum dowsing, and Native American hoop drum making. Her focus is advanced bodywork technique promoting high-level wellness. She also works outside of her home as a professional recruiter and account executive placing engineers nationwide. Patty lives in Waukesha, Wisconsin, with her big gold cat, Buddy.

### Contact information
Patty Martin
2507 Pebble Valley Road
Waukesha, WI 53188-1531
**Phone:** 262-542-2991
**E-mail:** *martinpr@att.worldnet.net*
**Web site:** *www.3dconnections.com/angels*

**What mystical arts do you practice today?**

I am a Reiki Master Teacher. I love the opportunity to introduce people to Reiki. I have a certification in Neurolinguistic Programming (NLP), Light Bodywork, and Harmonic healing modalities. I also support wellness using herbs and essential oils.

**How did you develop your talents?**

In 1994 I was reaching the end of my rope physically. I had my first heart catherization and was on eleven medications. Physically, emotionally, and spiritually I was a huge mess. I had to leave my marriage that I did not want to leave. I loved my husband, but it was a dysfunctional one-way effort. It was not a healthy situation. All of the doctors we were seeing and the couples counseling were just a bust because it wasn't going anywhere, and I was losing…me. I stumbled across an article on Reiki and bought a book about it. I liked what I was learning and called people on the list of Reiki healers listed in the *New Avenues* magazine. Now I was looking for someone to introduce me to Reiki. I wanted this.

My efforts in calling that list produced answering machines and businesses. The last thing I wanted was contact with another sterile office with a receptionist-type arrangement. On one of the calls, a lady answered the phone and she sounded like one of my sisters. This wonderful lady became my Reiki Master through all the levels of training. I believe everyone on the planet is here today because they are highly developed Masters who are in various stages of remembering and reclaiming their mastery. People are stepping forward one by one at different times, and now it's my turn! It has been a great adventure for me. My health has improved dramatically beyond belief. Of course, leaving a bad marriage has helped as well. It was very difficult departing from a marriage of twenty-one years. My life has changed so much.

Reiki pulled me through the physical challenges, which I now believe were stress-related — you know — heart, stomach, allergies, skeletal things. I presently take only one medication, and remain in the best of health. I like who I am and where I'm going. Things have really shifted. I was hanging on to a dream that wasn't going to happen.

### How did you fine-tune it all?

I continually read, attend lectures and classes, plus I host a weekly healing circle at my house. Every Tuesday night the group gathers to share Reiki and learn from each other. My appetite for learning keeps on ticking. I am rather eclectic and use other tools, other modalities as the person's soul calls it forward. I don't decide that. I wait to "hear," to get the nudge as to which direction to go with the person. This is not my agenda.

### Do you think there is a common thread among people who practice mysticism?

YES. Among my circle of friends in general, I believe there is a basic love for people, soul recognition. It is the desire to reach out and to help.

### How do you receive messages — voices, symbols, scents, images?

I don't bill myself as a psychic, but when I am tuned in and doing work for people, messages come through and I pass them on directly. I suppose it is a power of intuition and the openness to channel allowing the information to flow. If I don't pass the information on, the messages keep coming until I do. Not only that, but if I don't relate things correctly, I am corrected. My prayer, before I start any work is to be a clear and perfect channel, and a pure and simple servant. Even when I use a pendulum, this is my prayer. The purpose is to get my stuff out of the way — my ego, will, and biases.

### What is your answer to the skeptic?

They can be skeptical; that's OK. I invite them to let me introduce them to their energies, to their ability to receive and channel the energy. If they don't accept the invitation, that's OK. They're not there yet. Most of my family is skeptical. I think that's another common thread that we carry — skeptical family members.

### What are the criticisms that you hear?

I try not to listen. Criticism from my family has stung. It surprised me to be criticized as a know-it-all. It's taught me to be more gentle in how and what I offer. When I am quiet and focused, the answers are right there. I am more discreet in offering information. I am also more discreet when channeling. I don't work on a public forum. When answers come through, I may talk to the person later, and maybe not, depending...but I think that's where the know-it-all came from. I've never seen myself in that context. I don't see myself strutting through life blasting my opinions and knowledge, but maybe I have.

### What do you find unique about practicing in Wisconsin?

I have lived here twenty-six years, but I was born and raised in Chicago. When I started practicing Reiki a number of years ago, we offered it free at a bookstore in downtown Waukesha. At the time, it was novel, a curiosity. People received it well, and yes there were skeptics. Now it is much more widely accepted. On the other hand, some metaphysical bookstores in our area have been closing. That's sad, because we are losing our resources for a variety of metaphysical books, incense, sage, crystals, and places for like-minded people to meet. We must be letting the stores down. The big bookstores don't sell the smaller things like pendulums and other tools.

### Do world events affect your abilities?

Yes, they do affect abilities. September 11, 2001 was a huge shift. Celebrating the New Year the last three years has opened big shifts and links to the next step forward. Things are falling into place. When we have a tremendous windstorm or thunderstorm, the immediate geographic area is cleared and there is a huge lifting and cleansing of energy. September 11 was a similar shift for people who don't normally use their abilities to feel and understand. We were conditioned to forget them; to essentially "leave the invisible playmates at home." September 11 was very tragic, but on the other hand, many could feel the release and the wave of exultation of those who left. We who were left standing are hurt. The pain and the loss are real. Social and political shifts influence the world.

**What are your thoughts on belief in a structured religion?**

I'm very universal today. I am cradle Catholic with seventeen years of Catholic education. I finished college in my late 30's. I am grateful for my Catholic heritage. It is an important part of who I am. Catholicism is the foundation that shaped me. My family is very Catholic. Religion has an important place in society, the way kings and their caste systems had a place. It provided a formation and order to society. Churches formed an order of society, but I think we have stepped way past that. We don't need the hierarchy.

"I am better than you are. I am more important than you are. I am going to control and intimidate you. You are nothing. You need me to give you blessings. You need me to talk to God." Well, BALONEY! God is not *only* in a church or in a tabernacle. These places are wonderful and I'm not dismissing them. I have great respect and reverence for our places of worship. I believe we are all one and I believe God is within everyone and everything. The Divine I AM resides within each of us (Din view). It was a struggle for me to search and come to my decisions on where my views of church and religion have settled. Like the interdenominational church that I attend and support, I don't promote a "brand name"; it's not Coke versus Pepsi.

I find the phrase "I am a recovering Catholic" to be *very* offensive. I think that is a crock. What are you looking for? Sympathy? Deal with it and move on. It might sound harsh, but that is how I feel. I am a Catholic, and I have expanded my view to much more of a global focus. Catholicism was a great microcosm for me to learn in and get my training wheels assembled. Then it was my choice to learn and broaden my view. I needed that information to get me where I am. I went through a phase of passionately studying world religions. They all have great elements, and I am aware of them, but I am not a scholar. I am open and accepting that you don't have to be from my background or think as I think.

**When you are out and about, are your abilities on hold or are they in action?**

I shut down. There are times I choose to make myself "invisible." There are other times when I am just wide open. What really gets to me is if I see mothers being nasty to their children. That is painful. I will bless them, send them love, and send them peace as they wish to accept it. I ask my angels to talk to their angels. When people are in conflict is when I kick in, and I don't want to know why. My interest is to support. When people are stuck on the road, I use my Reiki symbols and send a ray or even just a cross. As far as reading people without permission, knowing their history, knowing their insides, I don't want to know that. I'm not interested.

**Do dreams have a significance?**

Yes, certainly. My dreams are great teachers. They have been deeply encouraging. It used to be just in dreams, but it has moved beyond that now. My mom and my grandmother are present in my life even though they have been gone for seventeen and twenty-five years now. They are in my dreams and are great sources of encouragement. I've also received very clear instructions in my dreams and I recognize their voices. I pay attention to this. There are times I have been with them, and I don't really write it off as a dream. It's more of a "dream state" and I love it. I have come to a point where I can just settle down, meditate, not be in control at that level, and just be with them. When that door opens, I will be high for weeks, if not longer.

I endorse Carl Jung's interpretations of dreams. When I'm working with someone, that's where we go. Every element of the dream is an element of me...so I am the chair; I am the car. To look at it from that perspective is extremely interesting. It has taught me much and I believe it has turned the light bulbs on for many people. When I have an exceptionally powerful dream, I write it down. I want to talk to someone about it, because verbalizing it is another way to discover the intricacies of it. The way to remember dreams is to ask. At bedtime, I tell myself that I am going to remember my dreams and I ask the angels to assist me. My job is to get to bed early enough so I'm not flat out exhausted. That's sometimes one of my mistakes.

### Are their any specific experiences in your work that you'd like to discuss?

It is a privilege to share Reiki with people. I don't use the term "healer." I view myself as a coach and a guide. The universal life force energy, which is a description of Reiki, is drawn to you as you need it. I can help people open to receive and open to release. One woman I worked with for years was very bristly, opinionated, and difficult. Whoever comes here is an important lesson for me too. What I find is that we have a lot of similar issues. As I worked with this woman, I saw her transition to soft and gentle. Even her short, abrupt, spiky hairstyle has changed. It was difficult for me to stay open, nonjudgmental, and be available to her when I found some of her actions to be quite rude. Now I just speak up, which is a lesson for me to practice and live. We have talked together about this many times. I find that we have commonalities in family issues and other things too.

### What are your views on charging?

That took some getting used to, and I think that was a self worth issue. Now I am completely comfortable with it. I believe there needs to be an exchange because the perceived value does not exist if there is not an exchange between us. Something for nothing is nothing. If you are given this beautiful treasure, are you going to treat it with respect and value it, or if you worked hard to earn something, will you place more respect and value on it? I'm not saying an exchange in money is necessary. Sometimes barter is involved such as services or other methods of exchange.

### What do you think about the 1-900 psychic hot lines on television?

*Everything* can be distorted or exploited by the drive to make money. Some people have a need for their names to be out there — in lights, in publication, whatever. I took my name out of my fliers for several years because I was disgusted with the "look at me" name recognition stuff that was going on in Milwaukee.

It's not about me, and it's not about you; it's about what we offer, what we share, what we support, and what we can build together. The drive to make money can taint the goodness of the work that is offered. Sometimes I have been criticized about not doing this work full time. If I did this full time, I'd have to ask myself if my clients were becoming a means to cover my mortgage and my living expenses. I think for me personally, I like my day job and getting a regular paycheck. My efforts come back to me.

I think psychic hot lines can be a tool to introduce people and help them to make a first tentative effort to check out the psychic world. They serve a purpose. Psychics in general can really tune in when you are open to let them in, and they can offer tremendous insight; however, there is a caveat. I believe psychics are looking through their veils, through their life experiences, and through their biases. My advice is that when you go to a psychic fair, select the person you will have a reading with by using your heart and follow your gut feeling. Ignore glitz and glamour, or the size of the sign. Shop around. If you are in a reading, and it does not feel right, it's not. Don't stay there. Don't ask permission to leave; it's already yours. Trust yourself.

### Does your outside work have any influence on things?
Last month I was putting in eleven- and twelve-hour days. I help make people make decisions and connections, and change their lives in my outside full time job. It is really an extension of what I do in my home. There is a balance and I love my outside work. Twice a year, however, I put a real push on my Calling All Angels Program. I have my speakers lined up twelve to eighteen months in advance. My mailing list has 444 people on it at the moment. I was thrilled with that; 444 is a cool number. The work is consuming, and I think one job supports the other. I don't evangelize and I'm not out to "convert" anybody.

### How about your family and friends? What do they say?
My friends accept and respect my abilities and support my work. A part of my family is threatened by what I do, and therefore shut the door. It took me a while to figure this out. I

am from a typical American dysfunctional family. I had to learn that I am much healthier just to step out of that system. I let their dramas, traumas, scapegoats, and crises go. Instead, I concentrate on the joy in my life. I really need to be careful, however, about stepping back into that system. It's always a test for me. There are certain people in my family with whom I feel safe. Sometimes I debate about visiting on holidays because I don't know if I want to fall into the same pit as the rest of them. Basically, I withdrew from the family dynamics. I am the second oldest and I abandoned the role of little mother, fix it, and over-achiever. I am grateful to Al-Anon for helping me over the rocky times. The organization taught me key lessons, such as, "whose problem is it? I didn't cause it; I can't fix it."

### Do you believe in the power of prayer?

Power of prayer — absolutely! I'm not just talking about the prayer that I was taught as a child praying to a God. God is within. I believe wishful thinking can be positive prayer. One type of prayer can be in the form of affirmations. Simply state your affirmations in the present tense and believe that they are. We are the script writers of our own lives. Distant healing work in Reiki is another form of prayer. It's gathering your thoughts and your energy and offering it to someone to accept or reject as it supports that person. It's real — absolutely real.

Prayer books are good things, wonderful treasures. I have a wide variety with beautiful prayers, thoughts and poetry. They can be very stimulating. I will use them often to get a group focused. My prayers are the joy of my heart. I sing my prayers and dance my prayers. They are centered on gratitude. I use my prayers when I am scattered or looking for help or don't feel the right direction is coming. What we focus on we draw to us. If you say, "I really like that house on Elm Street, but I'll never have it," then that is correct. You will never have it. Focus your energy *and* word choices. If you say, "Oh that guy makes me sick," be careful, because you are calling that in! Thought is the most powerful creative force in the Universe, and whether we put it into prayer or "pain in the butt," we have given it energy. When we take the thought, the prayer and put it into song, we have given it that much more energy. Take the thought and add joy-filled dancing energy to it, and the power is amplified even more. Indeed, it is real and exciting. Prayer has the incredible ability to change things.

### What are your thoughts on reincarnation?

As a good Catholic girl, I believe in it. Deepak Chopra emphasizes the concept of the time line that we use to organize and define time, as simply a human constraint. We look at past, present, future; but in the quantum soup of life, it is all happening now. It's a great privilege to be alive and kicking on this planet right now. People are more and more aware of their inner wisdom. The children coming forward are incredible.

### How do messages come through to you?

They come through as a "knowing." That knowing is always here in my heart. My struggle at first was to get out of my ego and allow my mouth to open, and let the information flow, not necessarily knowing just how the sentence would end.

### What is your definition of a mystic?

Good question. I believe mystics are those who know — they've cut all the crap — and they just *know.* They have the courage to stand fully in their development and in the Divine essence. They dare to be different and have the courage to keep going. There are marvelous women and men who have had the courage to be *blatantly* different in their lives and have the perseverance to continue to live their truths. I'm not there, but that's my goal.

### What is your advice for those with children who are showing abilities?

Respect your children. They are magnificent beings. Be careful of the social conditioning that we have been taught to lay on them. *Let them be children.* Don't force them to fit into the "square peg" that a particular teacher may want all the children to fit into. *Please* do not dull them out by stomping on their individual spark. Encourage the individual sparks to bloom and flourish. These children are coming in resilient. Switch gears from social conditioning to nurturing their inner wisdom.

## What is your view on coincidence or synchronicity?

In my interpretation, coincidence and synchronicity are one and the same. An old saying taught me that coincidences were simply the hand of God evident in my life. Yes, I believe everything has a connection, and it's great fun watching and recognizing the connections. I don't always get it immediately, and perhaps there are some things I may never get!

## What's your view on the hardcore scientist?

Science belongs to them. That's their skill and that's how their minds work. I work with engineers in my outside job. They are very linear, and they are very talented and gifted people. That's how they naturally view the world. It's just on a different plane, you might say, than most of us. Socially, some of them can be rather difficult because of their perspective on the world and way they analyze it all. But, nonetheless, these are their gifts. I have a lot of admiration for them.

## Do you think there is a dark side?

Oh, yes. I'm not all sunshine. I have shadows too, but I'd rather show you my sunshine. My aspect that I am not proud of is that nasty little witch who surfaces. It's a part of me, and that's OK. I need to know it, understand it, and determine what drives it. I very much subscribe to the Pagan tenet of "harm to none." It is a good foundation, but shadow can go against that. I have to stay honest and in tune with me to recognize and embrace my shadow. That's life.

The "Devil," or good and evil, is another human construct. Good and evil, right and wrong, ...I don't live there, but I give the construct recognition. It serves a purpose, and it has both a lesson and a gift. I've met people who have lived in the dark. It has been painful in my experience, but it has taught me a lot. I developed a rigid, zero tolerance for abuse such as lies, disrespect, discourtesy — I'll give you three tries and we're done, and then I shut the door.

What about criminals? They too serve a purpose. One concept that really spun me around was the whole idea of author Neale Donald Walsch that "Hitler is in heaven." Such a horrible man and the wretched pain that resulted from his actions, but…he served a purpose. His purpose brought forward lessons and gifts.

### Do you have any final comments for us?

Mysticism is the mystery of becoming. It is the esoteric. The great mystics and the great knowledge of centuries ago were driven underground as the Catholic Church became so powerful. The Church attempted to abolish this knowledge and these ways, but the sacred teachings were hidden in the Tarot cards with symbols and Hebrew letters to keep them alive. They have survived the ages. Now is the time to take the knowledge and be clear and open. The world is in need of peace with a strong foundation of understanding and acceptance.

We are not simply human beings. We are humans *becoming.* This concept is attributed to Og Mandino who wrote *The Greatest Salesman.* I am not a great mystic, but I am *becoming.* I fall into judgment, I recognize it, and I move on. I don't live in that world 24-7, but I live there more often than I did last week or the year before, so I am *becoming.* I like who I am and where I am going. It's a great adventure. Mysticism is the becoming.…

# Maureen St. Germain

Maureen St. Germain has a spiritually based practice that enables her to pursue and consult in several arenas. She has been a certified facilitator of Flower of Life workshops for over seven years and has lead study groups for over twenty years. Maureen has studied the teachings of the Essenes, Edgar Cayce, the Ascended Masters, and the Esoteric Mysteries. She has conducted many dolphin swims in Hawaii in connection with Merkaba Meditation in the Flower of Life transformational workshops. Drunvalo Melchizedek, a graduate of the University of California at Berkley, who pursued Physics and Fine Art, trained Maureen. Merkaba Meditation is based on Sacred Geometry.

Maureen is also a consultant in Feng Shui, the ancient Chinese art of space alignment used in homes and in many businesses and large corporations. Her very active, creative, spiritual life takes Maureen from coast to coast and internationally in her work.

**Contact Information**
Maureen St. Germain
307 Crossing Ridge Ct.
Sun Prairie, WI 53590
**Phone:** 608-837-9648

**E-mail:** *maureen@ maureenstgermain.com*
**Web site:** *www. maureenstgermain.com*

**Tell us about your talents and the development of them.**

I grew up in a family of psychic women. My brothers and sisters are psychic as well as my mother. My brothers don't use it much, but once in awhile things surface. While working in the corporate world, I was a CEO, but I began doing readings little by little with the express idea that it was about building a focused practice. Eventually, my time turned into a waiting list of people. The readings were accurate and people could find out information such as, oh you're going to get married next month, you have three children and your job is about to fail. But my readings are positioned to give succinct information about your spiritual path. That is really my specialty. I suppose I could continue to focus on the reality of things, but reality changes very quickly around us and all bets are off.

My psychic abilities developed over time. When I was very young, I was fired from a job because a secretary complained about me. The boss returned from Europe and the message struck me immediately and directly that I was going to be fired. A friend of mine disagreed with me, but I insisted I was correct, so "just give me a game plan," was a request I made of him. He was kind enough to tell me all the things a young person would need to know to maintain composure and things. Whenever I am out on the edge, another plan steps right in for me.

I don't believe in karma anymore and with the skills I teach in the workshop, people can literally have a clean slate everyday. Angels have given me the answer to my question of why can't a person ask for any gift once, and have it happen? They said every day is a new day and every day humankind gets a clean slate. Because humans experience this phenomenon, they also must start over in asking for things they want.

There is a blueprint, but it is not a blueprint. It is actually a diverse matrix coming out of the creation field, a lattice holding a climbing vine. I have been shown this image, and I was given the metaphor of the lattice.

**How did you fine-tune the talent?**

My husband was intuitive in a different way, which rather blocked my own intuitiveness. It was similar to a shadow. In my family, my older sister was very funny, but nobody knew that my younger sister was also funny until Chris (older sister) went off to college, and then the younger sister took over. My husband was able to pull things from the ether spontaneously and he really did not even know it. For example, one of our sons had gone to Europe with a couple of friends with no particular return time. A mother of one of the boys called and asked me when they were coming back. I wasn't sure, so I turned to my husband and he immediately said August 2, a date he pulled out of the air. We had a call from Minneapolis on August 2 and the boys had just landed in the United States. Once I stepped out of the shadow of my husband, I was able to express more of my abilities, and really developed by staying one step ahead.

### What is your definition of mystic?

A mystic is not just a psychic. The mystic is connected to the spiritual realm. They bring forth a new understanding of religious thought and of mystical thought about what is going on in life, how to interpret what's happening, how to get a portrait of the big picture of reality. It can mean a deep connection to God. One who does channeling quite possibly has a connection to God but comes across as a bit more secular. The words "mystic" and "psychic" have different connotations. Mystic has a feeling of reverence, whereas psychic sides with worldly. In terms of religious tradition, particularly the Catholic religion, there was a huge dividing line between the mystics. Some were having visions and others were having interactions coming straight through as messages from God.

Another element of "psychic" is that this person might be bringing forth information from somebody's ancestors, from deceased friends or relatives, or from entities that are not necessarily connected to God. Ultimately, everything is connected to God, but some forces may not have a strong or direct connection. Compare that to buying your phone service from the main company or a subsidiary. In other words, how many tiers are in your information system? Various people scrutinize the psychic as a charlatan — the used car salesman image. But take a look at the great Christian mystics of the church. They were getting information all along too, and in the same way.

Study groups exist today where people go into a meditative state and get information from a very focused and spiritual basis. The information comes through effortlessly. This is the mystic tradition. The mystic often challenged himself or herself in the experience. Was it real, was the question. I think we all do that. It is a healthy stage fright. A good mystic or psychic has to question seriously his or her work.

### What is a common thread among those who practice these arts?

I think everyone has the capability of being a psychic or a mystic. We are in an incredible age of growth, challenge, and evolution. People's ability to obtain information for themselves and those around them is growing exponentially. The common thread is that we all have the skill. I have used other means such as numerology, graphology, and common sense, and with these, sometimes messages coming through are clearer than anything. We just have to learn to work with it and follow through. In the last ten years, there has been a greater awareness of possibilities.

### What is your answer to the skeptic?

Oh yes, the skeptic…I preserve their right to believe whatever they want to believe and for as long as they want to believe. I was with someone who said he could not explain his connection to me and that he felt he did not know me well enough to justify the feeling. I said I had an opinion about that. It was possible that we were acquainted in another lifetime. When we met in this lifetime, we picked up where we left off long ago. His immediate response is that we die and go to heaven or hell, and that's it. I immediately said, "And I champion your right to believe that." As soon as I made this statement, his resistance dropped. My friend then said, "Well, does that mean your grandparents and my grandparents were married?" He was trying to bridge the gap here. From his perspective, that was a big leap.

A rational explanation is not always imminent. Another thing this person said was that I could not describe a personality just on such little information as a birth date and a name.

Then I made an offer — come up with someone that you know, and whom I don't know, and give me the accurate name and birth date. I told him the results would be so upsetting that he would be unable to deny my accuracy. He didn't take me up on the offer.

Often times, the skeptic does not want to know the truth. The skeptic wants to be *right*. There is a difference. If the skeptic finds a different truth than what he or she was taught to believe, then this person must accept that error is involved and originated from an individual or an institution — very tough thing to do. If this is true, the question now becomes, "Should I trust someone else?" Ultimately, it comes down to owning the fact that *I* am the person responsible for my reality and my understanding of the truth. In the world of the skeptic, trusting another person or institution or theory is safe because the blame for error can be laid upon something externally. Frankly, it's where our whole western society has carved a niche for the past 200 years. The bottom line for me is that skeptics don't interest me, and I have no need to prove or disprove anything.

**Do you run into criticism?**

Generally, I have not experienced criticism. My mother was clairvoyant so I grew up in a very accepting household. In a lot of ways, I do care about what people think because I like them to know my values.

**Is there anything unique about practicing in Wisconsin?**

People in Wisconsin that I do readings for have a very sweet nature. I attend a fair in a rural area of northern Wisconsin where people pay a minimal price for readings and some readings are just free of charge. I like this unique fair because people show up with relatives, particularly teen-agers. Teen-agers need a great deal of support these days and they will not find it anywhere else. A woman I read for had a boyfriend who committed suicide at the age of 16. She was carrying the common guilt feeling that perhaps she could have prevented it in some way. During the reading, I was able to get the information that she asked about and give her new information that instructed her in a very specific way to do certain things and have a conversation with the boyfriend. Two months later, I was at the show and she thanked me and confirmed that she was ready for the next level. It was empowering to me to make a difference in the life of the woman.

Wisconsin has some things going on that are serving as a block. There are people who are well meaning, but their "unhealed" ways are expressing themselves out in the business community where enemies are being made and people are experiencing hurt. I jokingly said to a friend of mine that anything I do people would love — kind of like the new salesperson who follows the bad salesperson. Anything the new salesperson does will make the company happy. It makes me a hero very easily. I think we have been held back in the Midwest. The east coast and west coast are more open in numerous ways.

### Do world events affect your abilities?

If I ask specifically for information about a world event, I will get it. Relating back to September 11, 2001, I was in New York City the weekend before the event happened. When I bought the airline ticket, I was told not to hang around and go shopping, which is something I like to do on my trips to New York. I departed on a September 10 flight and went straight home. I was home by 4 p.m. on September 10th. On September 11th I was getting calls from people who had just attended the workshop that I held in New York. Some of them wanted to know if I had arrived home and the others wanted to know information about what was going on.

When I went into a meditation, I got one word. It was the word *sekmet*. I did not know *sekmet* was even a word. As it turns out, the word is *Sekhmet*,[1] an Egyptian word. Sekhmet

---

[1] Several mythological versions of the Egyptian Goddess Sekhmet (Sakhmet, Sekhat) exist. She is a woman with the head of a lioness. The translation literally means "powerful one." Daughter of the Sun God Ra, she is often portrayed as extremely destructive. Sekhmet accompanies Pharaoh into battle as the "Eye of Ra" and is able to send not only weapons, but also plague and disease. In stark contrast, healers, physicians, and surgeons fall under the governance of Sekhmet because she was also involved in the avoidance of plague and in curing disease.

was the Hathor cat sent out by the God Ra to straighten out humankind. Sekhmet was so carried away in her destruction that she had to be stopped before destroying everything. I had no information on this, so to me it was a profound message with a huge meaning. From my perspective, there was a direct attempt at some level of spirituality to bring everyone's attention to what is going on in the world. This was accomplished by a horrific act of terrorism to raise awareness world wide to change how we look at life. I believe it was a collective choice we made. It was a collective consciousness choosing to do something to get our attention. My wish for the world would be that we respect others' rights to be and think, to the extent that it does not cause harm to others.

**How do messages come through to you—symbols, voices, images?**

Messages come through in several ways. They are primarily thoughts and visuals. Sometimes the visuals are metaphors and at times, the image is very clear. Words pop out of my mouth.

I am also an empathic. That is someone who feels what the other person is feeling. If I am giving a reading, I can sometimes go into that person's emotional body and feel what the person is feeling. Sometimes that person can't cry, but I can. I can feel the feeling and express it. I am not caught the way that person is caught. The experience frees them. Think of it as you're carrying something and your knees lock. You can't carry it any further. I step in and say this is really a heavy load, and we don't have to carry it. The person who sets it down is then free. I think beyond where the person is at, and I present permission to choose differently. The person may not even know the load needs releasing.

**Do you have a belief in a structured religion?**

I love structured religion. I don't care for the *practice* of structured religion, however. I grew up Catholic. I went to a Mass everyday. Structure has promoted the knowledge of God immensely. We have also committed a huge disservice in promoting misinformation. Do I think one outweighs the other? Yes, the good outweighs the bad, but there is still plenty of bad in there. Structured religion I am opposed to is any construction that prevents a person from pursuing that person's spirituality. So, if your religion says to you that you can't get a reading from a spiritual person, or a psychic, or a clairvoyant because that's "the devil's work," I would be strongly opposed to that doctrine and way of thinking. As you can see, I am opposed to a system that says my way is the only way. My beliefs say my way is *one* way. It is a sure way and it is a good way, but it is not the only way. I refer to the Bible where we learn that in my father's house there are many mansions, in other words, there is more than one path to God.

Actually, I think truly structured religion came out of the Roman invasion of the Church. The Romans were very adept at order and rules and when applied to the Church, a controlling rigidity resulted. However, I have contact with diverse people, and if I know that person is a Catholic or a Jew for example, I tune into that template so the person can receive the full benefit of what he or she is already respecting and honoring. It does not affect me personally. I do not want to go into a battle where the person is choosing between the reading and the structure.

### Reincarnation?

Yes, of course. We have a lot in life that we don't know about. There are layers and layers and more layers. What we observe about ourselves is the outside layer. When I speak of incarnations with people, I often refer to layers because somehow that's easier to live with for a number of people. There are multiple selves (not referring to multiple or dissociated personalities).

### When you are out and about are your abilities on or off, like a light switch?

I use my abilities all the time. If I am told something, I don't even question it anymore. I just go with it. I was told to depart New York on September 10 even though it would have been fun to hang around another day or two. I am at a place where I am *connected* to the information.

### Is there a meaning in dreams?

A lot of information comes out of dreams. I have interpreted dreams for many years. Some dreams are precognitive and are without metaphors. On the other hand, dreams can speak in a veiled language. As Joseph Campbell talked about the commonality in myth, I talk about the commonality in dreams. The Jungian theory suggests that the principal personalities in the dream are the dreamer — it's all you. Very often, if you allow yourself to see the dream from that vantage point, then you can ask what else is going on. We discover what those metaphors are. Sometimes they are a play on words and sometimes they are a play on concept. Step back and see what it is you are trying to discover.

There are three kinds of dreams. One dream functions to collect data around you and mixes up the reality enough to give you hints at what is happening. The dream speaks to you, but not always in an instant way. This is the most common type of dream. The second kind of dream is something going on in your immediate reality that you are not aware of, but may be aware of subconsciously. Maybe someone is being nice to you, but behind your back, the person is shooting you. Your psychology is telling you that things are not as they appear. This is more of a hidden type of dream. The third type of dream is a precognitive dream where information just blatantly comes through and it is very clear. My dreams are generally of the latter two types.

### What is your view on charging for services?

I charge a fee and make sure the client has a reading that meets expectations and is meaningful. Some readers are better than others are. Just to do readings at a party does not interest me. However, if somebody came to me and really needed information, I would just give it to them.

### What are your thoughts on the psychic hot lines advertised on TV?

Some of the people hired are true psychics; however, the business practices of these lines are harmful and dishonorable. They want to know your name and your birth date. I believe they can plug that information into a computer and get astrological information immediately. Much research has gone into astrology and the information is readily available, but they are using it as a short cut. You could have gotten the information without their help, so it is not truly a free reading. If they spend five to ten minutes collecting data and then the credit card kicks in, there is nothing free about it.

As a result, psychic work acquires a bad reputation.

On the other hand, all of the advertising has raised people's awareness and to many degrees, their acceptance of it. Thirty-five years ago if a woman dyed her hair, she was considered jaded, but today nobody thinks twice about it. So, in some ways "1-900-Take-A-Chance" has actually helped people get over their distrust and consider the possibility that this work may be helpful in their lives.

### Any cautions for people consulting a reader?

We all have free will. A psychic or clairvoyant is only able to give you information on possibilities and probabilities. I encourage people to glean what can be learned from a reading. Don't let the reading rule you.

### How does your family view your work?

We have a tight knit perspective. My four sons rely on each other for friendship a lot and we have traveled together. There is a sort of closed system there, and they have not been able to experience other systems as well. They learned about this work at an early age. Once in awhile they probably think I'm off the deep end because I'll say I've lost something in the fourth dimension, which is weird. Then when the object, keys or whatever, shows up in an obvious place, they begin to think, well maybe she's right about that fourth dimension.

### What is your advice to those who have children showing abilities?

Accept it! We train them *not* to see and we train them *not* to look. If a child is psychic, it will come out in other ways. There are other signs. Everyone should be told strongly to develop his or her own abilities. The goal is not to go to a reader, but to seek information within your own abilities and this is where children also need to start.

### Do you have any messages for us?

My advice is to do what is put in front of you, be sincere, and put your love in it. Don't resist. Allow it to serve you in a way that you may yet discover. At times, I feel fear, but I am guided as to what to do. A long time ago, I was whining, "what do I do, what do I do, what do I do?" A booming voice said to me JUST SHOW UP! So that's what I did. I established my business and my office and it took off from there. I had an outside job for a long time, and then I began intentionally living in the moment. I moved in baby steps, but whatever presented, I went with it. I had kids going through school and things like that, but I had been instructed — just show up. I landed a high paying job and paid off my debts within a year, then left the job to set up my own business. Amazingly, it was all literally from the answer I received — just show up.

An array of people in day jobs are doing mystical work on the side because to try to support themselves in another way, would put a strain on the spirituality and cause a failure. The outside job gives them the freedom to be what they really are in their spiritual practice. And that is very powerful. This is an enormous gift. Eventually this will lead to the right thing. Sometimes a floodgate opens. Taking care of your physical reality is extremely important. If you find joy in whatever it is, your spiritual path will follow; it has to.

# Jerry Christianson

Jerry Christianson graduated from Marquette University, Milwaukee, Wisconsin, and entered into the world of business for many years as a mortgage banker. His journey into the mystical actually began when he took up the hobby of public speaking. Jerry then proceeded to professional motivational speaking. He incorporated magic into his performances, but kept his banking separate from his other life, knowing people probably did not want wizardry mixing with bank loans, depending on perspective. Jerry is an avid humorist, at the same time takes his work seriously, and views his psychic work with clients as life changing. He has been practicing palmistry and Tarot reading for more than twenty years. Jerry reads privately for individuals and couples in his office, and reads at commercial events, and private parties. He has participated professionally in over 500 corporate and organizational gatherings. His psychic gifts continue to grow and he has received much attention from the media.

**Contact information**

Jerry Christianson
14100 W. Park Avenue
New Berlin, WI 53151
**Phone:** 262-641-9033

### What mystical arts do you practice today?

I practice palmistry and read Tarot cards, involving channeling. What got me interested in all of this is palmistry. Palm reading done in the classical way is dull. A lot of my work comes from studying the English author Sasha Fenton. Readings are complex and if done correctly, they are comprehensive. They vary widely in specific areas. We look at aspects of intellect, imagination, career, love, sexuality, vitality, potentials, and more. I also read the minor lines and use a magnifying light to do this.

Many of the minor lines are not present in every hand. There are several examples. The Line of Apollo, which is the line of the sun, shows us the potential for exceptional achievement. The Samaritan line shows a natural healing ability for both emotional and physical ailments. The Via Laciva is a line on the hand of those who have a potential weakness for addictions to drugs, alcohol, and gambling. This line, in addition, indicates someone who is easily bored. I sometimes find lines of intuition, adventure, travel, and worry lines. The Ring of Solomon line indicates the ability to understand and influence people, and this person has an interest in psychic phenomenon.

I like to pride myself in practicing ancient arts in modern ways. I belong to the Psychic Entertainers Association. The title of that is a misnomer. It is an exclusive organization with around three hundred people, some of whom study and interpret palmistry among other things. Over the years, we have changed some interpretations.

### Describe your Tarot practice.

Five years ago, I had dreams for a week that were very vivid. I don't even know if they were dreams or not. I was told it was time for me to help people more. In the dreams, I was shown how to handle the cards in a different way and switch back to the Rider-Waite deck. This deck is considered by modern standards to be the classical deck. The usual way to read is to place cards face up in the layout. Then read and discuss them. The dream instructed me to place them face *down* and turn them over individually as I read them. I think that with this approach, I get messages or thoughts that need to be passed on to the client before we even look at the card. Ever since I've done this, there seems to have been a change that I can't explain, but it has been a good change. The readings are right on target. Some think it's a trick, but it's definitely not.

Some readings are very difficult. People have cancer, domestic abuse problems, and affairs. Specifically in these cases, the Tarot cards are very helpful to the client. The private readings are especially interesting and amazing. I want to emphasize that short readings people receive at an event should *not* be minimized. People think the readings are just for fun and not real, but this is untrue. Minimizing is a big problem, and I don't know how to fix that. The readings are accurate, so keep that in mind.

### How did you fine-tune your abilities?

Well, it's been a long path. I was a banker for years and worked in business development after graduating with honors from Marquette University in 1964. I was offered fellowships to New York University, Northwestern University, and the University of Pittsburgh and I threw them all aside. I went to work for Sears because I just had to get out there and work. Mortgage banking and real estate were stressful, but I was very successful in those careers. I earned $102,000 the first year, and I didn't know much about mortgages. It went that way for about 17 years. Somehow, I came through life without killing myself. I was an only child and I still am! Mom would say, "Oh Jerry, what's wrong with you!" Her intentions are good, although she accents on the negative.

Eventually I came out of the Dark Ages, and around 1980 I decided it was time to start doing what I do now. I always liked public speaking, and I began doing breakfast talks and added magic tricks — you know, like make a pair of silk underwear fly out of someone's jacket sleeve. Over time and with studying, I went into palmistry and Tarot. It made sense to me and it was motivational. Now I do banquet talks but don't use my "slapstick" magic tricks, although they were popular. I still love the humor.

**What are some of the things people should be aware of when seeking a reading?**

There are two kinds of people who seek readings: the average person and the chronic readaholic. The later type goes from psychic fair to psychic fair. I'd say probably twenty percent of the clients are that way. I find that people going from one reader to another compare notes and these are people who wish to perpetrate negativity somehow. They don't wish to resolve problems, and therefore, really use the problems as a crutch. This is something to beware. Don't get caught in that trap or that nightmare. When I read at psychic fairs, I would usually read for twenty to twenty-five people. The negativity from some of the patrons was intense. I finally stopped doing the fairs. Readers earn some money, but go home with their brains exhausted and relocated.

I try to do well for people by working in a conventional classic way for the most part. Discussion during readings is channeled, I believe. Truthfully, I am extremely skeptical about readings and I question strongly. So if I tell you something — it is.

**Why do people go for readings of any kind?**

People enter into readings hoping to capture an uplifting and recharging energy. During a reading I use Tarot, palms, pendulum, psychometry, or simple "shut eye" reading while holding the seeker's hand. Sometimes they want an affirmation of their own thoughts in a particular situation — yup, I'm right sort of thing. A reading can involve personality exploration and trying to find a hidden talent. They come for entangled love problems, but all of these factors enter into their particular niches. If you are a Tarot reader, I advise not reading for yourself. There is too much subjectivity in this, and what you get is awful inaccuracy when you look back on the reading.

**Do you find anything unique about practicing in Wisconsin?**

Psychic readings at business and corporate events are accepted now as an interesting and mysterious entertainment, but Wisconsin is conservative. I average around two events per week including home parties lately. Even those brief readings, however, are meaningful to people, and often times they make appointments for longer readings. Lately, people are seeking to become more spiritual. This seems to have started around January 2001. It does not mean they are more religious. In spirituality, the person is seeking to find something bigger than they are, but this is not necessarily a religious experience. In a January 2001 article, I stated that businesses and people were in a rut of half-truths and we still are. This is especially true of large business and corporate America and applies to Wisconsin as well.

### Elaborate on the skepticism you talked of earlier.

Such a plethora of readers has erupted in the Milwaukee area. I am *always* skeptical. I don't mean to disparage the good work done by several area readers, but there are some that have a do-gooder attitude, but not a lot of good comes out of it. They are sincere and honest, and they think they are psychic, but it's doubtful. Reporting on anything that pops into your head is not necessarily psychic. Refinement and intuition are lacking. A corporate event lasts about three hours, and fortunately, these readers don't tangle with that kind of intensity. But I too, do not have all the answers.

### Would you like to share a sample Tarot reading?

Let's look at a short card reading for C.G. (C.G. is a friend who accompanied me on the interview.) We'll ask her to come up with a question, shuffle the cards or mix them up, and then cut the cards. Your question is about an outcome with a certain man in your life, and looking at the situation currently. Sometimes the cut card will answer the whole question the seeker has given me. In the next step, I lay the cards face down in the Celtic Cross spread and explain the position of each card and anything else I want to say before we turn a card over. I consider card readings strong and accurate for approximately six months to a year, but the second year holds some accuracy too.

In the card cut, it shows C.G. is carrying a huge burden, but there's an end in sight. Ultimately, the sticks you are carrying will find their destinies. I see in the brief layout that in the recent past, which sometimes goes very far back, there entered the presence of a strong-willed, argumentative man — kind of a jerk really. He wants or wanted to run the show. The state of affairs regarding your question is in the next two cards (representing the present). It is puzzling to me, but true around eighty percent of the time, that what is going on in the situation shows up in two extremes in the two cards. In the relationship you inquired about, there is difficulty and sadness. The Spirit is telling you there are new beginnings, energy, creativity and business...but it does involve the man. The challenge to overcome is this (another card is turned)...hmm...looks like he makes a lot of money or else he will be making a lot of money...but nonetheless, the challenge as far as *you* are concerned is to catch up with him and be with him in an ongoing relationship, potentially a marriage.

Right now things are stuck, or in a pattern of slow progress for six months to a year and a half. The lack of activity brings up the topic of money and sex. The near future has movement in this situation, and the Chariot, a very strong card in this position, indicates travel or move. There is strong activity in a positive way. The stress and bumping around goes on for quite awhile. In the seventh card, we see that you have fears he's treated you dishonestly, but those are only *your fears*. I pound my fist on this card (which Jerry actually does) when something like this pops up because these fears are without content.

The next card shows that some people question this relationship. This is how people who know you see it. There is indecision and there may be a choice by either one of you to hop out of the relationship. It is interesting that people think what is in the Tarot cards will come to pass. This is not necessarily true, and I talk to people extensively about what to do to make it happen or avoid it. We have free will and choices to make.

The next card is very significant. Something will happen with this relationship to get it out of the rut. The card has tone to it that life is too short to be toe dancing around like this. What do you want to do to face this situation? The outcome is especially strong. Either the man in this relationship will come through to you in the next six months to one year, or you'll be meeting someone else who will just blow him right out of the water, and then this guy will mean nothing to you. The final card is the psychological indicator card, which tells me you are secretive and keep most things to yourself. That is your nature regarding this situation and this question. (C.G. perceived a strong connection and interaction with her reading. She has things to work on.)

### How would you begin a palm reading?

When I look at C.G.'s hand, without using the magnifying light, I see that she has a strong Line of Life—she must be taking care of herself, or is praying to an angel, or something. There is strong energy and a "pop" to life with much vitality even though C.G. is a quiet person. She has many inner lifelines (some say angel lifelines). These represent people who have passed on, but are available to her. The lines can also represent some childhood person she admired — like Buffalo Bill or Elvis — but that does not mean she knew the individual personally. They can be saints or guardian angels.

Palmistry is non-psychic, fascinating, and fun. I have a small guidebook that I wrote and give to people so they can recall what was discussed during the reading. The readings can get complex and there are many lines to consider. Just one line has a wealth of information. For example, the Head Line can be mental, creative, or mixed, and each type dictates particular characteristics in a person that leads to compatible careers, romantic relationships, and so on. I try to be a practical resource for people.

### Do you have any comments concerning events on September 11, 2001, or world events?

Since September 11, 2001, people have a desire to be a bit more honest and take a slightly more sincere approach to life. Initially after the event, people were beginning to think we have changed our philosophy to life. Perhaps we have, but it is minimal if at all. What I saw in my practice was that there was less cheating on husbands and wives. There was a tendency to break off relationships that were on the side. I get so much of that in my private readings — triangles and double triangles — such a mess and just bad. We try to work through them fairly, but fairy tale endings are not always an option. After September 11, people were trying to reorder their lives and live for the "now."

### Do you have a final message for us?

There are truckloads of serious things to deal with in life, but we have to keep humor on board also. Balance is a good word. I find that humor, time and again, whether it is within a reading or in real life, can bring important messages and even make them more digestible and memorable. Bear in mind that humor has the power to lighten and enlighten — and that's my magic wand. I am very grateful to be able to help many people, even if it is just for a brief moment in time.

# Beverly Kay

Beverly Kay is a notable and popular Milwaukee area Numerologist. In addition, her practice includes the use of Rune stones, *I Ching,* and various cards including angel, dolphin, and Mayan. She has combined her psychic ability with numerology for more than thirty years. Beverly has made numerous appearances on television and as been a frequent guest on various radio shows. Other pursuits include lecturing, writing, business consulting, teaching, and studying world religions. She has aided police and other agencies with her psychic abilities. Beverly is available for individual readings and social and business events. She lives in Mequon, Wisconsin.

### Contact information
Beverly Kay
11431 North Port Washington Road
Suite 205
Mequon, WI 53092
**Phone:** 262-242-0422
262-512-1178

**What mystical arts do you practice today?**

My focus is in numerology. I use other tools such as Rune stones, *I Ching*, and the cards. Combining all this with psychic ability, I can come up with some amazingly accurate answers for people. Numerology is a reliable friend, because numbers tell the truth. A lot of my work is in spiritual counseling. Sometimes instead of turning to things like alcohol or cocaine, people will seek spiritual answers and discussion.

**How did you develop your abilities?**

I've been using my abilities for more than thirty years. Initially, I was looking into astrology and taking some classes in it, but eventually I drifted into numerology where I really just took right off, launched you might say. Once I seriously started using numerology, it held such a fascination for me that I naturally fell into putting it to work. My true goal is to help people, and this is how I do it the best. I have always had a deep interest in spirituality and the mysteries that it brings to us, not that we can necessarily solve all those mysteries.

**How did you fine-tune your abilities?**

I spent hours and hours and hours of practicing with people — day after day after day — sometimes seven days per week. You have to have people to practice with and get feedback. You cannot do the practicing on your own. After a *great* length of time, you can do strong interpretations with many kinds of tools as I mentioned before. Time, serious effort, and study are all critical. Get your feet wet because you cannot just take things off the top of your head. Until you have keen and dedicated understanding, you absolutely cannot establish a business or a practice. Only after you have this firm understanding are you a professional. Learning something, such as card reading, does not give you license to just run with it. Much practice and much experience is what comes next, and I'm not talking about pulling out the cards now and then on a weekend. I now work with all types of people — business people, law enforcement, ordinary people seeking spiritual growth — you name it. Feedback from them tells me that what I say is accurate.

**Explain more about Numerology.**

Each number has certain characteristics. My birth path for example is a number 7. That's the number associated with radio, television, books, art, and ministry. Take a look at what I do in this career, and you'll see the characteristics of the number 7 pop up all over the place. If you want to know how to calculate, let's take the birthday of 1-9-1950. This boils down to the number $1 + 9 = 10$ and $1 + 9 + 5 + 0 = 15$. This can further be reduced to $1 + 0 + 1 + 5 = 7$.

The letters of the alphabet are also associated with a number. To find daily, monthly, and yearly paths of a person's life, we add up the numbers associated with the letters of the original birth certificate name. Adding the numbers assigned to the vowels in a person's name correlates with your motivation in life. I believe the numbers actually tell you what you are capable of doing. When people literally associate the numbers with themselves, they can find direction in their careers. For example, people with the number 5 make good sales representatives — always trying to sell you something.

In numerology, not everything is a bed of roses. Realize, for example, if someone hits a number 5 or a number 9, these numbers can edge toward negativity and these people can become highly accident-prone. When you get a 9 for the year, a red flag should go up. That 9 signifies a conclusion to something also. We are usually looking at the numbers 1 through 9. When we hit a number 1, a new beginning or a new direction is at hand. The numbers actually become guidelines, and from my years of experience, this has been a great help to people. I want to say that we need to use numbers in a directional way also. For example, when someone goes from a personal number year of 4 to a personal number year of 5, we know that in year number 4 a foundation should be laid for the changes that will inevitably be coming in the year number 5. The year number 5 is a time to follow your intuition and take some risks. The unexpected is likely to happen in May and September, and things that are confusing will make sense later.

**Is there a common thread among practitioners of mystical arts?**

Yes. They have to be spiritual, have a belief in God or Spirit, and have a liking for people. The story of like attracts like is true. I meet people who do the same thing or nearly the same thing as I do, and there is a commonality. The common thread for us is mysticism and spirituality.

**What's the Beverly Kay definition of mystic?**

Mystery with a capital "M." It does not have to be more complicated than that.

**Do you have any comments about the skeptic?**

I give the skeptic knowledge. It's one thing for me to say something and then it's another thing for me to prove it. That's when the skeptic starts to believe, although cautiously. I have had business executives, police officers, detectives, and others say to me, "How can you possibly know that about me?" I tell them it's because I know their numbers and this gives me troves of factual information that applies to them.

Its OK to be skeptical, but there needs to be a balance at some point. Math, logic, and intuition are all important. If you are heavily into left-brain, then what I see is a robot. On the other hand, if you are weighing in on the right brain too much, you're just nuts — really you are out of balance.

**Is there anything unique about practicing in Wisconsin?**

Wisconsin is very reserved. I don't mind that. I am a logical person who likes mathematics and therefore I employ numbers. That too could be considered conservative, but nonetheless, they give me solid information and help me to decipher what's ahead. For years and years, people of Wisconsin have rather isolated their minds when it comes to this type of work. After September 11 however, people are paying much more attention to numbers than they ever did in the past.

**In regards to September 11, 2001, do you have any numerological comments?**

That is a complex matter, but the short version for me is to look primarily at the number 9. Middle Eastern terrorists had to wait until 9/11/2001 because the numbers had to match the event. The number 9 can go negative, and it did. Mars, God of War, rules it. Nine is associated with bombing, the color red, blood, and fire.

When the 9/11/2001 destruction stopped, we went into the positive attributes of 9, which is associated with humanitarian acts. The world goes full circle, balancing out the negative and the positive. The circle can't be closed until it is balanced — just like balancing the books. When one circle is closed, we enter another circle, and life goes on.

We are in the Aquarian age right now. It is the age of unity of man and woman, but the opposite sign is Leo, and that is Christ Consciousness. So, we are all going up in consciousness, one by one by one. Nobody can do this for us. We have to do this for ourselves. The Unites States had a birthday on July 4, 2001. If you take $7 + 4 + 2 + 0 + 0 + 1$, the total is 14. Take $1 + 4$ and we have the number 5. The five represents a major turning point in this country, but not the rest of the world. You see then it peaked again in September with a number 5. This is calculated by adding $9 + 1 + 1 + 2 + 0 + 0 + 1 = 14$. We get the number 5 by adding $1 + 4$ again. The year 2001 for the world is a number 3, indicating the world would spring back. The year 2002 is a 4, indicating preparation for change. The year 2003 is a 5, bringing the change into being.

### Do you have a belief in a structured religion?

I study many religions and like to associate with a variety of ideas from the different religions. It is important to remember that what is right for one person is wrong for another. I decide for myself. Nevertheless, the bottom line for me is worshiping God and practicing the worship of God. I do practice what I preach, you might say.

### When you are out and about are your abilities on or off?

They are mostly on and I stay open, but I don't really do any numbers unless I am asked, and then I'll say something. It would be difficult for me to push information on to someone who is not open or inquiring about it.

### Do dreams have significance?

Yes, absolutely there is significance. Some people, who are really advancing in consciousness or changing their thinking, will get things in dream form so these messages will not scare them when they are in a more conscious state and walking down the street. In some form, the dream materializes. When that person is busy in daily activities, and something that originally came out in a dream hits that person right between the eyes, he or she is more prepared for it then. I believe this to be a right-brain phenomenon related to psychic ability and intuition. Incidentally, looking at the year 2000, or the number 2, we can say there began a merging of logic and intuition. Some would say a merging of information from the right and left brain. We can do things differently that did not come to light in the past. We can balance the logic and intuition and have things running in sync. If not, we end up fighting some part of ourselves, either mentally or physically.

### Is there power in prayer?

There is a lot of power in prayer. Really, prayer is a form of electrical energy and this kind of force doesn't stagnate in one place. One of the greatest assets of prayer is its ability to heal. Maybe healing does not always happen directly, but through prayer, we can help people to help themselves in a healing process. Prayer needs to be taken seriously and not frivolously.

### What do you think about reincarnation?

Reincarnation is a Universal Law. It was written in the Bible. When you think about it, the idea does make sense. For someone to be born blind or handicapped makes God look like a villain. There has to be an explanation for that. It is part of a greater plan that is incomprehensible to us. We try to nip away at understanding bits and pieces, and I think reincarnation is one of those snippets. It's a law that works. We are recycled.

### Are there any caveats for people seeking a reading?

I advise seeing a professional psychic reader who is also spiritual and who lives by a belief in God or Spirit or whatever name you choose to give that energy. Check out the experience and the credentials of that person. Beware the power of suggestion. Don't forget that you are walking into the unknown, so you must be very careful.

### What do you think about the television psychic hot lines?

The same message goes out to people — be careful! Also, be cautious of psychic hot lines advertised in the yellow pages, and what comes in the mail. Some of these mailings are setting the hook. Once they have your name and address, and perhaps phone number, they keep on sending you "bargain offers" that are increasingly more expensive. Personally, I advise staying away from all of this.

### Is there a dark side to things?

I believe so. I see a dark side as negativity primarily. How does one avoid the dark side? Use common sense, use spirituality, and be strongly aware that you need to analyze and examine your thinking. Does that kind of thinking make sense to a sane society? Is that thinking destructive?

### Have you worked on any police or investigative cases?

In criminal cases, scenes come to my mind. I have helped in police cases and assisted families trying to locate missing friends or relatives. I've also helped people to find lost objects. Mequon, where I live, does not have a high crime rate. So, when something out of the ordinary occurs to me, I take notice. An unusual case came up and I reached into my abilities for some information. In my mind, I could see a young woman riding a bike. She was on her way home and had been swimming in the Cedarburg area. She stopped at an intersection with traffic lights, and the name of the street she was traveling on popped into my head. I did not know it was a street name however. A man ahead of her in a van got out and went around to the back of the vehicle, hit her on the head with something, and abducted her. She was later found murdered around Davis Road. I knew the name I was coming up with was important, and that it was not the name of the van driver.

I didn't want to work on this. I was getting calls, and I felt an obligation to help the family. I called the detective on the case, and he said, "Bev, you would have to be there to know things." I gave him the information and then I let it go. I didn't hear anything more from the detective for a long time. A few years later, I ran into him in a restaurant, and he said to me, "I should have called you to apologize." I asked him why. He said that the name I gave him was later determined to be the street where the young woman was first abducted.

**Do you have any advice to those with children who are showing abilities?**

Encourage them! It is a talent and a gift that can serve them well. Why stifle that and "dumb" things down? They are developing and what they are saying and seeing has a truth to it, although you may not recognize it immediately.

**Is there such a thing as coincidence or synchronicity?**

I believe there are connections. Things happen in a certain manner and sequence and there is a reason for it. Meaning may not be evident, however. It's important not to read things into events also.

**Do you have any final messages?**

We are all here on a mission. We all have unique paths. When I first started working with numbers, I viewed the numbers as "favors" or "clues" from God. If you have a number 7, that number has specific things in store for you. It's very important to find out what the numbers are about. If you are carrying a number that lends itself to science, then pick and choose within that category. Do you want to be a water analyst, a nuclear physicist, an engineer, or a biologist? There will be no stopping you. Without the knowledge of this number, you might be saying to yourself, "Oh, I'll sell paint and hardware because it's a safe job, even though my passion is nuclear engineering." Don't do that! If you know your numbers, you can push yourself to your full potential and find happiness for yourself and others. There won't be that longing and nagging voice saying, "I should have gone into nuclear engineering." If you don't know the blueprint of your soul, you will find yourself in conflict.

# Sheila Graves

The Reverend Sheila Graves is the presiding minister at the Living Spirit Community Church in West Allis, Wisconsin. She has a B.A. in English, a M.S. in Linguistics, and an A.B.D in Linguistics. Reverend Graves is an Ordained Minister and a counselor. Prior to this, she taught at Ohio State University and the University of Wisconsin-Milwaukee. Eventually she left teaching and went into sales, then "walked out of the Main Street of Life" only to walk into Pathways of Light, a spiritual college in Kiel, Wisconsin. At Kiel, Reverend Graves taught spiritual classes and was ordained at this college. (This interview was conducted in the Living Spirits Community Church, which is housed in an old church at 66th and Beloit in West Allis, Wisconsin, that reportedly has resident spirits of its own.)

**Contact Information**
Rev. Sheila Graves
Living Spirit Community Church
P.O. Box 341444
Milwaukee, WI   53234
**Phone:** 414-604-0444
**E-mail:** *livingspirit@ameritech.net*

**What mystical arts are you practicing today?**

I would not call it "practicing." I would call it awareness, though some people may turn it into a regular practice. To me it is more of a river that flows through everyone and everything. Awareness that I receive is often translated into the messages that I offer as a minister of nontraditional approaches to living a spiritual life. The understandings come through images and knowing that often hits me unexpectedly. Frequently, I don't entirely know what the messages are about at first. I sit with them awhile, and then I begin to find a meaning. I also work with dreams and meditation, and decipher on a symbolic level — almost like living in a land of metaphors.

I get feelings in my own body that "belong" to someone else. For example, I was recently talking to a person who was having some eye problems, though I didn't know that at first. Yet, I had been talking to her for fifteen minutes and was getting an odd sensation in my eyes that I knew was not originating in my own eyes.

This also happened to me after September 11, where I had several days of knowing that I was carrying energy that was not my own. I had lost much of my own energy and felt like I was dragging around a huge weight. I came to understand later that it was the weight of human grief and confusion — shocked lodged in us.

**How did you develop your abilities?**

I have been fairly left-brain all my life. My abilities did not come naturally. In fact, I probably denied them for a long time. About ten years ago, I started working with energies and just started asking to feel my own. I see energy grids. For example, if you ask me what fear is like, or if you ask me what is going on with a particular person, I am able to see a geometric figure with a color and an energy to it. I'm not sure that I ever went about developing it. I think I just *allowed* it. However, I have to be very respectful with this ability. I don't go around "invading" people, just because I can. Sometimes I am reluctant to see that the ability is there, and downplay it. If it feels anything like a gimmick, I quickly back away. Understanding is the sweetness of who we are, not a tool for gaining powers over others.

**Do you study any other areas of mysticism?**

I would not say I study other areas; however, I am aware of people around me. Sometimes my father is here. At any time, if I close my eyes, ask a question, and quiet myself, the answer is evident. In that way, I actively work to use that ability and develop it more. I also focus on creating intentions that turn into results. The intentions must always be helpful and loving — always. Wiccans believe that whatever you send out comes back to you threefold. So sending out little nasties is not a terribly good idea.

When I gaze at a picture or a painting, I let myself feel these images. As a left-brain person that is a difficult thing, but in fact, it turns out this is my strong point. I am a carrier of emotion and a speaker of emotion. I end up balancing this with equally strong mental activity.

I am very analytical and it is a comfortable place for me. My thinking focuses on writing, talking, logic, and rationality. I can *avoid* anything by getting into my left brain to analyze it, but it doesn't get me where I often have to go. I'm not a believer in discarding thinking, but there has to be a marriage or a dancing of interaction between thinking and feeling. I would suggest reading Candace Pert's *Molecules of Emotion.*

**Books?**

In talking about books, my suggestion for you is to go where your interest carries you. If it leads you there for five minutes, or five pages, or five years — fine. Stop tying yourself into "I have to finish this — I have to read the whole book." Envision it as a strange land, as an exciting land. When it no longer holds your interest, let go, and conclude your visit. You are reading for a reason, and trust that you don't have to know what that reason is.

**What do you think is a common thread for those practicing mystical arts?**

Start a little lower than that. I think there is a common thread that we all share. I think we must soften our contact with the world at times. The common thread at the very least is one of opening up and practicing integrity. If we are psychic and can touch understanding of what happened in the past or understanding of what will happen in the future, that suggests all time exists now. It suggests that the divisions we draw between us or amongst us, or between human life and Divine life, are not really there.

**How did you develop your abilities and from what age?**
Mysticism is a way of life. It is living your life as if it is all about spirituality in a transpersonal and transcendent level of reality. It is very freeing. There is a possibility that if a person starts out with right-brain orientation, the left-brain characteristics develop later. Maybe I'm prejudiced, but I think it is easier to start out leaning on the left brain. I was raised a Born-Again Christian, left the church at age 18, and then became an agnostic and then an atheist. In the mid 1980s, I walked out on almost everything.

Around that time, I read Shirley MacLaine's book *Out on a Limb*. In the middle of reading it, I had the experience of beings hovering over me with so much love and softness, though they weren't angels. I was beginning to come back to an understanding that I don't think really left me in the first place. Then I began reading Deepak Chopra and Marilyn Ferguson, who wrote *The Aquarian Conspiracy*. It was a comfort to me that both of these people had strong scientific backgrounds. I waffled around with this spirituality for a while and found myself at Pathways of Light, a spiritual college in Kiel, Wisconsin.

I had a background in linguistics and English, and taught at the Ohio State University and then the University of Wisconsin-Milwaukee. It was not my intention to become an ordained minister, and I missed teaching, but it was clear there was another plan in store for me. I started teaching some spiritual classes, doing some readings, and performing marriage ceremonies. It has grown from there.

I think that by giving up the mainstream life, as I did for a time, the message was no, you are not supposed to go back to teaching. I was not making much money and had left a relationship. At three points in my life, I pretty much lost or left everything. After all that happened, the Universe finally said,

"OK, now I'll help you. We were waiting for you to make up your mind because we were not going to help you until that time." Once *I* made up my mind to do something else, then a job came forward and it led to my current full time position.

### What is your answer to the skeptic?

Skeptics believe what they *need* to believe. Part of the skeptic might be tired in an emotional sense. The skeptic also does not like the idea that outside of him or her, there is something that can tell the person what to do. The mystique really should be blended with the idea that you are a powerful being. You are not a worm that someone had to die to save. I think skeptics are looking for an affirmation in their lives that they make a difference. They are willing to believe there might be more information other than what is right here on Earth. But essentially, I have to say my answer to the skeptic is, "Do what you need to do, and believe what you need to believe." Those of us who trust in transcendent understanding will believe what we believe. I don't think we have an obligation to address those who do not. Our obligations are to stay true to what is right for us and not judge those who don't agree with us.

### What are the criticisms that you hear about mystical arts?

The most obvious is the line "oh, that applies to everybody," in reference to intuition, astrology, Tarot reading, and so on. The other criticism would be with astrology in the question, "How does anything millions of miles away have anything to do with me?" Again, the critics are pulling understanding from only *this physical world*. Energy is continuous. Quantum physics now theorizes that when something happens on one end of the Universe it is felt immediately — *immediately* — across the Universe.

"It's the Devil's work" is another popular criticism. I don't believe there is a devil. When I hear this, I don't fight it and I don't argue. I try to find a common ground. My understanding of "the Devil," whether we see the entity in form or not, is that it is the manifestation of human fear. Hitler used the same creative spirit as any of us. But he drew energy from it, and created more fear. We are Divine creators. If you truly believe in something, you can create it. He did. Yes, if you get enough gullible people and people in fear, they are going to follow you. This was the picture in Germany and other parts of Europe in the 1930s. To me, the devil is merely a model constructed for the mythology of personifying fear.

With any negative comments about alternative healing and spiritual beliefs, one can also find just as many of the nicest explanations in the world. However, if the criticism is coming from those with a traditional Christian religious background, they will not accept your premise of opening this up to discussion.

### Do you find anything unique about practicing in Wisconsin?

Wisconsin is a fairly conservative place in some ways, but here in Milwaukee we have a very interesting spiritual community. I would classify the Living Spirit Church as an interesting metaphysical community. I think there are pockets of understanding opening up everywhere.

### Do world events affect your abilities?

Certainly, September 11 affected me. In ordinary terms, it affected my talking about what we do with all this. I probably realized ten or more messages that related to these events. It took me a long time to depart from the topic. The energy in this church was different from what it had been. People were droopy and sluggish in here. I know that was a statement of what was going on in our country and other parts of the world. There is a shift coming or occurring now, but we don't entirely know what that is yet.

### Do you have a belief in traditional structured religion?

This church is independent of any other church and religion. So it would be considered unstructured in the traditional sense, although we certainly have strong beliefs. We consider God to be within us and that we are Divine beings. I basically believe that just about anything is possible, even on a human level. I am only in this form, because we have agreed that I will be in this form. If I could set myself free of that belief, I could shift. Most people in standard America don't buy that idea. Bringing the potential into form, and gathering molecules or particles is simply (not so simply) condensing energy into a template created by our mind.

**When you are out and about, do you put your abilities on hold?**

I can go on or off at will. I don't try to feel people's energy. It is intrusive. I use this resource only when I need specific information that I have a right to know, or that I need to know for a reason. My personal abilities are not so strong that I must make a special effort to control them. Some people, on the other hand, consciously need to turn their capabilities off.

**Do dreams have significance?**

Yes, absolutely, dreams have significance. Some dreams have a literal meaning. Others have symbolic meanings. Generally, this is the kind that I have. I consider sudden images as symbolic too, and if you are doing a meditation, the images that come are symbolic. I can't stress highly enough the importance and usefulness of meditation. There is so *much* information for us to just strive for and grasp. If we do that, we don't have to feel so alone.

**How do you feel about charging for services?**

It's an option. People have a right to make a living, though it is also important to disseminate this knowledge to as many people as possible. For a while, I thought that if a person is spiritual, that individual should not expect a payment for services. I no longer believe that. In this church, we don't have tithing. We don't require anybody to be here, and there are times when it can be a little tight.

We do need to give back to what feeds us spiritually. There must be an exchange of energy. That suggests what some call "payment." It doesn't matter if it's food or money or whatever. If someone gets a reading or a service free, that person is not as likely to benefit as much. Another issue we might address is the tremendous discrepancy between what we're willing to pay for entertainment, and what we're willing to exchange for spiritual connection and understanding. What does that say about our values?

### How do your family and friends view this work?

My friends are almost entirely the people in the church, and I guess they are quite happy with me. I'm not so sure my biological family takes my views as seriously as I do or as respectfully as I do. I don't discuss this with them at length because I have no wish to impose upon them my understanding of the world. Even in talking with my son, I did not approach him with this until he was 14, and even then, I did not ask him to sign on to my beliefs. He has his own, and they are somewhat different from mine.

### Do you believe there is power in prayer or wishful thinking?

Wishful thinking is rather anemic and does not get you very far; however we can *intend* into being. We can change our lives in the world with active intentions. Affirmations are OK, but they are not nearly as powerful as the affirmation, *plus* the feeling, *plus* the vision in our mind. We have the ability to walk in a certain image. Yes, absolutely, I believe in prayer, especially as a group of people. Remember that we are quite powerful beings. On a regular basis, I pray for friends or relatives of people. Whenever there is a worldwide vigil or prayer happening, I announce it in the church so that the congregation can be part of it if they choose.

### Is there such a thing as coincidence or synchronicity?

Things have their own timing. To change that is like trying to push a river. On the other hand, every choice we make sets us up for another choice. This suggests synchronicity. We could drive ourselves crazy—I have done this—trying to find the meaning of something too soon. The meaning will become evident at its own pace, and this may coincide with events that all tie in at the proper time.

### Do you have a belief in reincarnation?

Yes, I believe we have incarnated many times. I believe that when we pass over from the physical life, what happens to us immediately depends on how we have left this life. Have we left in anger or have we left in acceptance? We are given choices and opportunities to move forward in continuation of growth. I don't see reincarnation as a vehicle to learn lessons. I see it as an opportunity to grow in wisdom, compassion, and spiritual strength. It is my understanding, right or wrong, there are similar threads or themes, or functions that run through many of our lives. For example, I know that I have been a teacher, writer, or leader in many lives.

**How do messages come through to you — voices, feelings, visual symbols?**

All of that applies. We are limited by our assumptions, however. I generally don't get words unless I ask for them. I am good at words, and have been all of my life. If I were to get words, I'd spend my time analyzing them, probably unnecessarily at times. So instead, things come to me in intuitions. I am most likely to receive images, or sentient information. When I look at messages that I talk about in church, I start out with a goal that further helps the messages evolve. Some of the messages I deliver in church come from experience. I sit down to write about a topic and things just end up on paper, especially if I light a candle and ask for help. That ritual creates in me a certain receptivity.

**What is your definition of mystic or mysticism?**

Mystic means living in mystery. That's what you heard in my message to the church today. And that particular talk came about because of your phone call to me. It was not at all what I had intended to talk about two weeks ago. So there's an example of opening to the mystery and allowing the different things that can happen. It is an example of living in the mystery of the Divine. Our partner is the Divine Spirit, but we are in that partnership with a desire to both "be" in the mystery and to "know" more about it.

### Do you have any cautions or advice to give those wishing to consult a reader?

Trust in yourself. Don't give your power away to anyone else. I have no problem with seeking help from someone else, but don't believe for even a minute that they have an understanding that you don't have. Don't let them direct you to do something that you otherwise might not do. In this society, we are indoctrinated to think that the experts are outside of us, but really, the expert is inside of us.

### Is there a dark side?

Energies exist that are still in fear. Some of them have been in bodies and some have not. It is my understanding that some attach themselves to bodies to prevent them from moving and growing. I would not call this a devil or a demon. It is an unbalanced energy. I believe there are people who are able to transmute that energy and they shift and interact with the energy. We do the same thing. If a friend comes to you and is in a bad mood, you may decide to sit down with that person and say, "I think there is something going on with you." With that visit, you talk to them with softness and an understanding and you transmute that energy. It's the *same* thing. Only we *accept* more easily the conversation with the friend because it is in human form and human words. We don't accept as easily if this same phenomenon occurs in another way, but I believe that it happens nonetheless. We are just the tip of the iceberg. So much energy and understanding in life is not always humanly possible to explain.

Humans, collectively, in their fear and in their negativity, and in their cruelty, have set certain energies into motion. The pooled energy has to be released, and sometimes that comes through something like Twin Towers and September 11, 2001. Usually it is less catastrophic. I believe that at a soul level many people sign on to do something difficult. They don't necessarily say, "OK, I'll sign on to starve to death." or "OK, I'll be killed when a plane hits the building." But at some level, we know we are in this together. When a young child dies, we ask how God can allow this or do this. We are created in this world to have free will. I don't believe God has retribution. We are experienc-

ing the consequences of the choices *we* have made. These people
"volunteer" for lack of a better word, to show us the consequences of our choices on a collective level.

### Do you have any advice for those who have children who are showing abilities?

Encourage. Encourage. Encourage. Don't shut them down.
Don't downplay something into wishful or imaginary thinking.
If they like stones, bring the stones into it. If they say they see
friends, engage them in dialogue. If suddenly they seem to know
another life, believe them. Engage in their wonder.

### What answers or comments do you have for the hardcore scientific minded?

I would say two things to the hardcore scientists. Number
one is that they are only touching one part of the elephant.
They are doing a magnificent job organizing the information
they have about the part they are touching, which is the humanly empirical. But in another dimension, what we consider
empirical would be irrelevant.

Secondly, how can scientists who have seen their models of
some aspect of "reality" overturned time and time again, especially in the last century, believe that they have an absolute version of how the Universe works? Life is change and growth.
Perhaps there are those who are not viewed as scientists that will
lead the way into a newer understanding.

Another point I want to make is that if we are to be studying psychic ability, we have to throw in the factor of *belief.* The
power of belief can be absolutely *astounding.* Half-hearted belief isn't going to do it, however. Humans have done so much
by default. Yet how can we pretend to do something with ten
percent of our brain or fifty percent of our awareness? We must
bring our intention and our entire presence into this moment.
Don't give energy to the fear and worry that some disagree with
you. Step into "I am what I am and I know what I know!"
Then create within that context.

In summary, the scientists are doing a wonderful job, but
they are only one piece. When I was sixteen years old, I thought
that magic, science, and religion were all the same. Guess what?

They are!  In the 1960s scientists did not believe that, but now more of them are signing on to this concept.  Look at quantum physics, the healing power of prayer, and the ability of emotion to affect our bodies, just to give a few examples.

### Do you have a personal goal in your work?

My fervent goal is to become more and more open.  I am excited about it!  I passionately accept whatever way openness arrives, and whatever roads I need to change.  The purpose of my being open is not to be seen as a psychic or to practice in that manner.  I just want to *know*.  I am an Aquarian, and we just want to know everything.  I want to dance with the Divine. I desire that experience.

### Do you have any final messages for us?

My wish for the world would be that it comes alive with life. It's not all about holding on from one experience to the next. It's about being vibrant with awareness.  I don't buy into the view that it is *all* about peace.  *Some* of it is about peace.  *Some* of it is about understanding.  *Some* of it is about freedom.  We are creative and we need to use the creativity.  This is an incredible time to be alive.  Specifically I am talking about love, understanding, wonder, and excitement.  I think of the line from *The Walrus and the Carpenter,* "The world is so full of a number of things, I'm sure we should all be as happy as kings."  If a *single word* for excitement and enjoyment, eagerness and passion exists, that would be what our world is about — that "word" is in our grasp.

It's time for us to move from experiencing spirituality and Divine Mystery as that which reins us in and judges us, to that which exalts us and our human expression of Unconditional Divine Love.

# Chief Blue Hawks Shadow Walker

Chief BlueHawks Shadow Walker has been a spiritual reader, teacher, and healer for over twenty-five years. He feels that life-threatening and near-death experiences have enhanced his abilities as a spiritual counselor. His work currently involves developing an expanded interpretation of the Medicine Wheel into an Intertribal Universal Medicine Wheel. The chief is an ordained minister who performs weddings, officiates at funerals, and participates in speaking engagements. He was appointed Chief of the Bird Clan for the United Cherokee of Ohio for the State of Illinois in 2001. The Chief lives in central Illinois. His land has a Medicine Wheel and an inipi (sweat lodge) where he conducts intertribal ceremonies. He works in Wisconsin frequently as well as Illinois and other states with his tribal arts.

### Contact Information
Dr. L.M. BlueHawks Sander
P.O. Box 122
Mossville, IL   61552
**Phone:**  309-579-8202
**E-mail:** *bluehawks48@hotmail.com*

**What mystical arts do you practice today?**

I practice the Earth medicine of my ancestors, and Earth medicine of the Earth, so to speak. I know that sounds simplistic, but I follow a philosophy. Everyone has rituals, even just as simple as brushing teeth in the morning. The things that I teach can be mystical and magical. We need to be what is called *hollow-boned.* The Cherokee also have a word, *eggahmatu,* which means "it starts within." We are responsible to the Earth and for everything on the planet. Many people are looking to the indigenous past because they become disheartened on other journeys. I'm not saying that people are unsuccessful on a chosen path. When they select a path and believe in that path, Creator guides them on the voyage to true happiness. These passageways are within each individual from the time of birth to the time a person passes to the Creator.

I do channeling and look into past lives. I conduct sweat lodges. I practice in the use of sacred herbs. If a person comes to me and is a healer and wants to have a leather Medicine Wheel, I pray about it. If they present me with two hides and a gift of tobacco (tobacco in the traditional sacred sense) which is the proper way, then it will be prepared for them. The Medicine Wheel is a healing instrument. It absolutely is not a decorative piece to hang on a wall. Basically, the traditional Medicine Wheel was used to help males, the Earth, and animals. The woman is totally respected as Walking Medicine Woman — many steps ahead of us all!

**You mention a Medicine Wheel. What part does this play in your work?**

Yes, a very strong focus of mine is the Medicine Wheel. This tool of ritual dates back to 7000 years B.C.E. The oldest formation found so far is in Big Bear Mountain in Wyoming. Others are in Saskatchewan. There are approximately 28,000 Medicine Wheels of varying sizes, or I would call them sacred circles, throughout the world. This permanent wheel is assembled and integrated into the ground. I have been happy to build these for many people. The center stone is known as the creator stone. I do not use Sun Bear's wheel. The one I use is an intertribal wheel. A Medicine Wheel starts with a main stone and has pinnacle points of north, south, east, and west. Numerous Medicine Wheels have three stones at each pinnacle point. This intertribal wheel has five stones between each pinnacle stone.

When all the stones are laid out this can be viewed as a pyramid if we imagine looking down upon it. At the same time, the concept of roundness is with us from birth to death—heads are round, blood vessels are round, the earth is essentially circular, trees are circular, even molecules are considered rounded. This creates a vortex of energy that can enhance or de-enhance a situation. If you come to my wheel feeling you are depressed, much of the time you will leave feeling happy, but only if you want to get rid of the depression or sadness. But a caution is that if you come into the wheel desiring to retain the depression, it can get worse.

Medicine Wheels sprouted over the centuries in different cultures from the Americas to Asia. One thing about the sacred circles is that they are always evolving.

Even back in the 1970s, people were thinking the appearance of crop circles was a sign from Creator to get us back into the loop again. We come into this life, follow our path starting in the wheel and go from birth to adolescence, to adulthood, to elder. I hope that we are collecting wisdom on this journey.

**How do you use your leather Medicine Wheel in your readings?**

As far as I know, I am the only person in the country who makes a Medicine Wheel out of a hide. One of its uses is as a divination tool. When people sit down in front of my wheel, I do not know what will be said. Sometimes I use cards and sometimes I don't, but when the person leaves, he or she knows what has to be done next. In my Tradition, we are all individuals, and we all have the opportunity to make voices for ourselves. Some people who do divination say this or that will happen — bing, bang, boom — but that is not adamantly so, because things *change* for a person. The mystic and the magic in the Medicine Wheel are awesome.

I have observed situations before wearing this leather Medicine Wheel, after wearing the wheel, and during a time of healing. If an aura photo is taken, the person jumps from a picture with yellows and reds to one with light violet and light pastels, which is what people look for in a good aura picture. After two days of doing readings with my Medicine Wheel, I had an aura photo taken and had pure pastels and white in the middle of the photo and believe the Medicine Wheel had a direct effect on this.

In the technique I use, the north represents the earthliness of a person. The south is the passion of spirit. If I lay the wheel out properly, the person will be in the north, and grounded, even though the person may not feel that way. I ask the person what brings him or her to this place. From that point on the person usually says nothing. Sometimes the person is shocked, and totally blown away by what comes out in the session. This is also a tool to channel the spirit world as well. Scores of people go to readers. I happen to be a very blunt chief and I say it like it is. If it's red outside, I will say it's red. I won't beat around the bush and say it's pink and purple and polka dotted. A good reading just does not work that way.

Life sometimes has hard things to offer. I have done readings with people and cried all the way through. When I do a reading, I tell the client that I am here to honor and respect him or her. I believe the Medicine Wheel has the gift of Mother Earth; especially this gift is given to the men to help their female side. It helps men to connect with mother and women in our lives. There is far too much testosterone on Earth these days.

**From what age and how did you develop these abilities?**
I had this ability since I was very young. I went through two comas in my life. I was allergic to a medication as a child and that put me into a coma. I think I learned many things from the experience. We all have the ability to channel and we all have eyes in the back of our heads. Go back to the basics and that tells us we are all connected. That is the way Native Americans have always felt. We are all sacred. At the age of 12, I was shot with a bullet in the leg. The friends I was with were frightened and ran off. I stayed beneath a cypress tree all night. The next morning I was found. When I was 17, lightening struck

me. I believe that all of these experiences heightened my ability to listen and develop an imagination of reality. Imagination of reality is in every word you speak—watch what you say and watch what prayers you send out there. A person examines facets in his or her personal life when a life-threatening event happens. Two things can occur. Either the person will be wacky the rest of his or her life or the person will learn from the experiences and use the knowledge to help others. But really, life can be a celebration; it doesn't have to be a bummer.

I was fortunate to have been raised in an educated family. My father was a professor at Wesleyan, then Ohio State and NYU, and my mom was a biologist for the University of Texas. Reading was very important in my family, so undoubtedly that helped in my development too.

### What is your answer to the skeptic?

I love this. Actually, my wife started me going back to the fairs. I was always too busy with the Earth. Now is the time for that. When I was in my 20s and out of college, I did an eight-day vision quest in the Painted Desert. It taught me a lot of things. As an adolescent, I used my abilities to figure people out in a heartbeat, no problem. I was youthful and stupid and having lots of fun. Now when a skeptic comes to me, and there have been quite a few, I start stuttering. That is Creator's message to me to *seek*. When I seek, everything is as if Spirit puts the person through the ringer and shows the dirty underwear. The skeptic steps back, eyes as big as silver dollars, and then I hear, "You know, nobody has ever done that to me." Then we can get down to business. The person knows there is just something they cannot explain going on with the Medicine Wheel.

I'll tell you right now that I am the biggest skeptic there is. You have to show me…and I'm not from Missouri. I have spent time in many Medicine Wheels or sacred circles and there is a difference. It is amazing. You can take a dull razor, come back four days later, and it's sharp again. You've heard about "pyramid power," well, Medicine Wheel is the same. Skeptics walk away in a different light and they don't treat what I do as hocus-pocus or witchcraft. It becomes real for them.

**Can the Medicine Wheel be used by anyone interested, even if the person is not a healer?**

Yes, that is possible. However, remember that the Medicine Wheel can *enhance* or *de-enhance*. A situation can actually become worse. You must want the change. The worst thing that happens is when a person can't express this and says, "Well, you tell me!" I am currently putting my information into a book to train people in the art of the Medicine Wheel. My clan mother works in essential oils and Medicine Wheel oils — no, not "bears in a bottle" or "essence of skunk." These essential oils represent certain animals that are traditional figures in the Medicine Wheel. She petitioned me to make her a Medicine Wheel. She laid the hide on her dachshunds that have some crippling in the hind legs, and the dogs can now stand very well on those legs for longer periods of time.

After I construct a Medicine Wheel on leather, I take it into lodge and pray on it, and bless it. It goes to people who petition me in the traditional form — always tobacco and a gift. What kind of gift, you ask. The question I would ask is, "What does this mean to you?" How much are you willing to give to have this in your life? It could be tobacco, it could be a stone, it could be a set of tires, it could be a bag of groceries, or it could be a sacred item of yours. In other words, Spirit is asking you to pass it on. It is not necessarily monetary. A 10-year-old child came to me, gave me tobacco and a feather — that is all she had. Our purpose in life is to honor other people, and until that time, we cannot honor ourselves.

**Do you find anything unique about practicing in Wisconsin?**

The energies are very different in Wisconsin. I occasionally work in Madison, and find the people to be pleasant, outgoing, and respectful. There is something about Madison that emits a positive energy.

**Do dreams have significance?**

Yes, dreams are visions of the past, present, and future. If a dream comes to you three times in a row, it will come true in some form. You can't stop the reality of that dream. The dream may come in symbols, but at some point you will interpret these. Sometimes it may seem like something is affecting to you, but it could also be intended for someone close to you. I have studied dreams quite a bit. Pay attention to warning dreams. If you dream the place is on fire, get up and get out of there. There have been actual cases of this happening. Yes, dreams are significant. They can be messages.

**When you are out and about do you put your abilities on hold or are they in action?**

I use my abilities all the time, and I don't want to turn them off. It's my radar. On the other hand, I don't read for people unless they ask. My wife and I were at an event and we ran into an acquaintance, a skeptical person actually. He was astounded when I told him he was into some illegal activity. The law caught up with him.

**Have you worked on any police or investigative cases?**

I have done this, and I offer my services to police or investigators, or anybody in situations along that line. I don't charge anything and I keep it as quiet as possible. I have worked on quite a few cases in Virginia, North Carolina, and here in Illinois. I don't advertise this, however.

**What do you think about charging for services?**

What I tell people is that this pays the bills. I have to eat. I don't charge for doing sweat lodges or sitting in the Medicine Wheel. I charge for knowledge.

**What is your view about the 1-900 psychic hot lines advertised on TV?**

Now you've opened Pandora's box! I worked on a line for four years; however, I was never dishonest. I did not read out of a book, as some did. In the beginning, the business was trying to do the best things for people, and then they branched into different things, always adding more and more. Talk about greed — that was greed. They wanted a Native American to do a TV ad. I did a take and they were not satisfied but could not make up their minds whether to use me or not. Before I left, and this will sound crazy to you, I said to them that they needed to let me know, because if I were not treated with the same respect I gave them, the business would be no more. Then they went out of business. I recall the first part of the Torah when Jacob talked to Joseph and said, "Whoever blesses you I will bless; whoever curses you, I will curse." I am glad they are off the market. They hired too many people that were incompetent, unreliable, and BS artists.

The business was unkind. Many callers would be put on hold. I reported this. Part of the problem was that those hired were not checked out for quality of work and that's why the businessman who started the line got in a lot of hot water. I would rather be talking to someone face to face, and many people ask me if I do phone readings. The answer to that is yes, but only after I have met the person once. I receive calls every day to do readings, participate in a show, or teach. The bottom line is that there is no reason for a person to use one of the psychic hot lines.

### Is there power in prayer?

It works! Just watch what you say. We can create our own destiny by what we put out. If a lot of negativity goes out, then you'll get a lot of pucky. If you are able to balance physical, emotional, spiritual by following your heart, speaking the prayers that you need to pray or the words you need to say, then you can have what you *need*, which is not necessarily what you want.

### Do you have any comments about structured religion?

My eight sisters followed the Jewish path. I happened to follow the Native American path of my grandmother. My mother allowed me to do this after my bar mitzvah. We don't need a building to worship in, and we don't need a person to lead the way. We live in a negative society with too many people that spread the negativity around — well, do something about it — smile and find spirituality. That can happen in many ways, and there is no requirement of involvement with a structured or traditional religion.

Part of the purpose of life is to give. The term that is used is "turkey feather." The Cherokee tribe holds the turkey in high esteem just as they do the eagle. Turkey feather represents "give away." I teach many people how to connect with the spirit and how to do rituals for themselves in their own way. You are part of the Earth no matter what your blood type, ethnicity, or religion.

**How do messages come through to you?**

They come to me in several ways. I get a picture of a person's face, and sometimes a voice. When a person does what I do, you literally have to channel, and you have to remain quiet in your mind. If I am holding a picture or some object, I will actually experience the pain that the person experienced. Many times, I have cried. I go through the same symptoms, and it's something I can't control. The more a person fights intuitive abilities, the stronger the abilities will struggle to come through. As society grows, there will be people who come forward to help. Christians talk about the return of Christ. It is common for Jews to talk about a Messianic Age, however, more so than a single Messiah. I believe the Messiah is in the people who are following their hearts. I try to be a *hollow bone*, or conduit, and not a judge.

If you are getting messages, you don't have to stop and think. One thing about the spirit realm is that they do not command. When or if you hear people saying my guides told me to do this and my guides demanded that, there is something wrong with that picture. In the beginning of creation, God gave us choices. Go with the intuition. When you listen to your heart, ninety percent of the time you are going to win. Every person I have interviewed that said they went on "commands from a guide" and did not use their own choices and intuitions, ended up with disastrous results.

**Do you think there is a dark side?**

A positive does not exist without a negative. Your car battery has two wires. Take the negative wire off and you have nothing but positive. Where are you going to go? Looks like you'll be walking. See how many TV shows you'll watch with a one-prong plug on the TV. When there is happiness in one area, there will be chaos in another. This is meant to teach us to stand strongly and learn to serve people.

I have talked with so many people who speak about demons, and they are afraid of the darkness and the spirits. This darkness is real, and I have seen ceremonies in the western U.S. and in South America where this plays out. The "evil" is known as manipulation. When I say this, I think of voodoo, satanic worshiping, or Wicca that is not true Wicca. Manipulation also occurs in drug use. The Creator did not mean for us to be as high as a kite. Scare tactics are out there. I tell kids that the spirit realm is not what you see in Hollywood.

I have done many "house cleanings." Usually people get into trouble when they don't know what in the hell they are getting into. What I wipe out is the negativity in the house, because these energies do exist. Sage, any type of vanilla or vanilla candle, or tobacco (not smoking) helps to alleviate negative energy in the house. Have you ever had anyone come over to your house and that person left a "cold feeling" in the house? You don't know what to do. You've tried odor-eaters and everything else, and nothing works to get that damn energy out. Try the sage, vanilla, or tobacco. A positive person will love the smell of sage. A negative person will walk away from sage as if it were stinkweed. I don't believe in a devil. The "devil" is in us all, because each of us has positives, negatives, and choices.

**What's your answer to hardcore science?**

Hardcore science is like hardcore Christianity or hardcore anything. Look at all the dogma happening in Palestine. In parapsychology, we try to explain things as best we can, but we are human and ask too many questions. If a person wants to analyze things, whether it is the Kabbalah or Science, that person should wear a tee shirt that says, "I can't please everyone." Some soul is bound to criticize or make fun of what you are doing or saying. The scientific community has to do what it wants to do. We have learned multitudes from them and we need them. Native Americans believe we are all connected. When science came around and said look at all the molecules and we are all connected, we really could have said we've known that all along. We'll use science as confirmation in this case.

### What are your beliefs concerning reincarnation?

For a long time I did not believe in reincarnation. My sister Joanna in Maryland was preaching to me all the time on this. We had debates, I was hardheaded, and I was not going to accept it — thought it was a bunch of bull. Nevertheless, I continued to read about it, and then ran into an account of a man who was shot between the eyes and died in India. A baby was born around that time and there was a birthmark between his eyes. When he was about five years old, he began to have weird dreams of someone shooting him. When he was older, and as the dreams continued, an investigation led the authorities to the murderer of the man who had been shot shortly before the boy was born. The deceased victim is thought to be the young man's former incarnation. This interesting account began to change my thinking on the topic of reincarnation.

As a hypnotherapist, I do past life regressions. I have interviewed women who have aborted children. They may have guilt and have had dreams about that child, but what's really interesting is that the child that they have ten to fifteen years later, reportedly has the soul of the aborted child. Man's ways are not Creator's ways. In Native American tradition, until a child is two years of age, he or she has the choice to leave or stay. At least ninety percent of the women I have worked with who have had abortions, *felt in their hearts* that it was the right thing to do. How do you think the child notifies a parent that it has chosen to leave? It is through the *heart*. We put far too much emphasis on "you're going to hell; you aborted that child." The woman is not to be condemned. Too many people out there playing God — let go; he's doing a good job.

### What advice do you have for those with children who are showing abilities?

Kids are very intuitive. When a child is born, he is a fresh spirit and he is in tune with the Creator. Eventually the Creator steps aside a little as the person comes in touch with reality and reconnects with the Earth. Children I have talked to have so many dreams and visualizations. It is so sad that in this country we have video games and the like. These marvels of technology rob us all of imagination. Building tree houses and flying kites has gone the way of the dinosaur. Those who are able to "escape" you might say, and manage to cultivate imagination in a positive way, can cultivate abilities to exceed and succeed in life very strongly. Imagination creates leaders and healers.

### Do you have any final messages for us?

You would ask that. Mysticism is real. It is in the perception of the individual. It is something given to us in a sacred way. To the skeptic it may be something else. Books are good to learn from, but don't view them as a Bible. Remember that a book is one man or woman's idea of what he or she sees. Learn for yourself. The path is a simple thing. It is developing your own medicine. When I say medicine, I refer to knowledge or things that can help you develop to help other people. The indigenous path is to keep it simple. Don't confuse it.

My advice about going to a reader is that you need to keep in mind there's not one side to a story, not even two sides to a story. There are many. In other words, if you come to me for a reading and then move on down the line to another reader, you'll hear another side and then another and so on. It is up to *you* to bring all the pieces together. You are gathering information from a metaphysical family.

# Ley Guimaraes

Ley Guimaraes is from Brazil and is the founder of the Akarma Institute. She was initiated, ordained, and trained in Brazil as an esoteric teacher and healer practitioner. Since 1976, she has been teaching, leading workshops, and giving private consultations in Brazil and the United States. Akarma Institute was founded in 1985 as an educational institute dedicated to esoteric studies and practices leading to raising spiritual consciousness, personal growth, and self-healing. The institute is not affiliated with any church or religion. Ley is a certified massage therapist. She lives in Baraboo, Wisconsin, where she offers massages and Tibetan bioenergetics treatment based on the study of Tibetan tantric healing. The holistic healing treatments are designed to help balance psychosomatic symptoms caused by emotional and mental distress.

### Contact information
Ley Guimaraes
Akarma Institute
504 8<sup>th</sup> Avenue
Baraboo, WI 53913
**Phone:** 608-356-5126
**E-mail:** *akarma@sauk.com*

### What mystical arts do you practice today?

I practice spiritual reading and guidance and teach people the esoteric principles for healing and spiritual education. My students are part of my karmic family. The key to it all is discipline in the field itself and control in personal manners. The teaching, as in any religion, must be taught with respect. Overall, this involves a discipline of the person, but to reach this point you must discipline your emotions first. Sometimes we take the opposite way because we want to free ourselves and express ourselves, but with this, we lose the discipline. Mystical arts are not about freedom, but about discipline. This involves higher thought. The beauty is that everyone has his or her own rhythm and a temple for the soul.

### How did you develop these talents?

To do this kind of work, you must study. So, of course I went to school. I was initiated in Brazil through The Order of Crown by one of the most remarkable charismatic teachers and clairvoyants, Xazyr I. How old was I? That's an interesting question, because I believe that everything is tied to my experiences from a previous lifetime in Greece where I was also devoted to spirituality. So really, I don't have an exact time. My training in Brazil took seven years of practice and learning. Esoteric teaching demands a very intense discipline — it's the icing and the cake. To look at ancient teachings, we must look at their origins.

### What is your view on karma?

A person must pass through a cycle. We create karma, and it is based on the law of action and reaction. Every time we make a decision we must ask ourselves, am I creating karma or not? It is not much about who you are, here and today. It is more about your ancestry and what you accomplished and how you existed in a previous life. What is running inside you from that former life? Biologically, we look at things the same way by studying the dynamics of the cell and analyzing DNA. The mechanics of spiritual dynamism operate in the same manner. Every individual is unique and has the ability to transmute karma.

### What is your view about soul mate?

Many people ask about this and there are many views. People look for a soul mate within a relationship. But a so-called soul mate is not necessarily another person. It could be your solar angel or, in other words, your higher self. My soul mates are my Masters. They are my friends and they are the ones I trust. It is amazing how many people ask about soul mate. It is an indication of the limitations in our thinking to believe that a soul mate is physically another person — well, maybe yes and maybe no.

If your thinking is improved, a soul or soul mate can help you and guide you. People mistakenly interpret some unknown want as being resolved by finding a soul mate. In effect, they are saying we need a companion. Look for the soul within you.

### Do you think there is a common thread that practitioners of mystical arts share?

That is a hard question. We cannot separate from ourselves and everyone has his or her own frequency. In that sense, I do not believe there is a common thread. On the other hand, if everyone who is related to spirituality has the desire to help humanity, there is a common thread. The way each person expresses it is different.

### Do you have any comments about the skeptic?

I run into some skeptical people. My students and people who come to me for consultation are not skeptical. They know in advance what kind of work I do and what they can expect to experience or obtain from a session. At times, people do not accept what they are hearing, and in that case, they are not ready for this kind of work. They return to say, "Now I am ready."

### Is there anything unique about practicing in Wisconsin?

It is America! Wisconsin is part of the American culture. In Brazil, spiritual healing is part of our life and culture. I think all the mediums were sent to Brazil! It is much more open there. Mediums are part of every family. We also have many centers that focus on the concepts of spiritual healing. Brazilians are openly accepting of shamanism and the esoteric. Healing in a mystical way is a part of our life in Brazil. Medical professionals in Brazil many times will recommend their patients consult with spiritual healers or mediums. In that culture, the medical healer, the spiritual healer, and the medium are integrated.

In the United States, people value these abilities as a "gift." In Brazil, these same things are considered commonplace. Brazil is part of the tropics located near the equator, and it has been said that people are more sensitive and touched by the energy. I have heard this about other tropical regions of the world also. In Brazil, as in other cultures, there are practitioners, sometimes these are shamans who are working or channeling lower spirits, and sometimes they are known as "lower psychics." We need to be cautious when dealing on these levels.

My discipline is to educate people, and this requires a lot of time. There are levels that you never thought existed before. We go like a wheel that keeps on going and we never stop. How do you get to those other levels? Meditation is absolutely and unquestionably the key. I am talking about *a lot* of meditation and *a lot* of discipline and *a lot* of knowledge again. People in the United States are very open and they have respect for this work. I am not aware of any school in the United States, as we have in Brazil, which prepares and teaches mediums how to channel and improve their qualities. When I talk about schools, I am referring to true esoteric teachings where there is comparison within levels and a measure to determine levels.

### Are there any cautions or things people should be aware of in consulting a reader?

Yes, recognize where you are. What is your ideal? From what perspective are you looking at things? People need to understand this so they are not attracted to the lower psyches. In Brazil, some people can "mystify," referring to a trance-like state, and we know who these people are. It is very easy to reach a certain state in your mind where you may be vulnerable to lower thought forms. To raise your thoughts to higher ideals, you have to channel higher thought forms.

Some days I can give wonderful readings and on other days, my readings are not as strong. Frequency, vibrations, environment, diet, emotions, or stress play a role for me. It is the same for the person who comes to me. There is no separation. I have to accommodate my frequency to the person's frequency. Whatever the frequency is on that day will be determined in a consultation. Sometimes I have clients with a high frequency and things go well.

People ask various practical questions. Should I change jobs? Where is my soul mate? Information from previous lives comes through, but not always on that particular day. These are psychic questions. My expectations are more and I try to work for a Divine purpose. People need to know what their purpose in life is! They need guidance.

### Do world events affect your work?

World events cannot affect a spiritual work. They give us more spiritual maturity. World events are the consciousness of humanity. How much responsibility do we have? We should be asking this question over and over. We have to change ourselves to change the world. Crises are a call for taking responsibility of our creations. A crisis is also a call for our courage to *examine* what we have created. We have to strive for this even though it may be painful. Certainly, we must stop the hate.

### Do you believe that a dark side exists?

I wish I could send the book *The Battle of the Dark Forces* to all the world leaders! Dark forces enter by way of those that don't have knowledge. Darkness comes in the forms of obsession, possession, and infiltration. This is why channeling has to be respected and used carefully and wisely. Who and *what* am I channeling? Channeling is not to be taken casually.

People may use big names and say, I channel so and so. But I ask the channeled entity, for whom do you work? There is definitely a hierarchy. When a spirit presents itself, the spirit must have an identity and state what entity or group is represented. This is recognized through studying the esoteric. For a person who channels to say, "I work for the light," is far too vague. What light? To channel does not mean the person who is channeling is well developed in this experience. Anyone can channel — through development, through imitation, or through mystification (referring to trance)! We divide channels into three categories: well developed, not developed, and in the process of development. If a spirit takes you for a channeling ride, this does not always mean the spirit is well developed. We have to see if a spirit is a helper or knows things from a higher level. People tend to believe without adequate knowledge.

Questions are important. If someone claims he or she is the reincarnation of a certain being, for example, Apostle Paul, then we must question. Who has to come first — the Christ or the apostle? We need to recognize by the actions and the teachings. A healer who is a channel needs to know how to teach. Divine channeling is a result of higher ideals, virtues, and a lot of discipline. A person who is a psychic or medium is not automatically spiritual. We must be alert and discerning. Channeling is not necessarily a part of spiritual teaching.

### Do dreams have significance?

Most of my clairvoyance and predictions come through dreams. It is important to pay attention to how you were feeling before you go to sleep and how you are taking care of yourself. Rituals and meditations prepare you for astral travel. I record my dreams in writing so they are not forgotten. If I need guidance, I ask my Masters and they tell me in dreams. Emotion can play a part in dreams, and we have to be careful not to channel lower entities. We must make a strong attempt to connect with higher rather than lower spirits.

### Do you believe in the power of prayer and wishful thinking?

Of course, I believe in prayer. Prayer works. That is as plainly as it can be stated. Prayer of some form is found in all civilizations and all religions. Prayer is a like a "free phone call" and does not have a requirement that it be part of a religion. Meditation is different from prayer. In prayer, we are asking for ourselves or for someone else. On the other hand, in meditation we are seeking and finding. I try to be in a meditative state every day with the purpose of advancing my thoughts. Like much of

my work, meditation is too a discipline. Wishful thinking, I
believe, is not as intense or as eminent as prayer. We have to
develop our abilities and effectiveness through prayers as individuals and as a nation to help humanity. To do this we have to
drop some of the baggage on the way up the mountain or we
won't make it to the top.

### Define mysticism.

Mysticism is to know God and to trust the power of God.
Power comes through in rituals. The Spirit loves rituals. Rituals discipline our mind. When we expose our spirit to rituals,
doors open, and we learn. These are all parts of mysticism.

### Do you have advice for those with children who have abilities in these areas?

Do *not* look through your own perspective. Look through
the child's perspective. We cannot impose our beliefs on a child.
We must respect. When a child has a question, answer it respectfully. It is unwise to teach meditation to a child until the
child is 14 or 15 years old. Compare it to not driving until the
age of 16 or drinking until the age of 21. Meditation can take
a child into the unknown. Parents should be the best examples
they can possibly be for their children when they are dealing
with these areas.

### Do you have any advice for the hardcore scientist?

Scientists are *guided* in what they do, although they may not
accept that idea. All science, art, music, and creativity come
through the Divine Masters. Some magnificent things come
out of dreams. The Universe is an orchestra of sounds, colors,
symbols, and wisdom. Answers to scientific questions have arisen
out of dreams. Songs and works of art have been created from
messages coming through dreams. People are surprised when
this happens, but if faith is considered a factor, perhaps this
phenomenon is not so surprising.

### Do you have any final messages for us?

Do not make decisions based on emotions. Raise your
thoughts to a spiritual level. God sends us back again and again

until we reach perfection. My goal is to educate and teach. I'm not just here to be a psychic, but to have a discipline in place. People can help find the meaning of life through the Teachings that were before us. The religions are to be respected too. So much hopelessness is in the world and we must teach that there is hope. There is a Divine plan, and it is protected and orchestrated through the Divine Masters.

# Sue Joy-Sobota

Sue Joy-Sobota is a hypnotherapist working in the area of past-life regression. She is certified by the National Guild of Hypnotists as an advanced hypnotherapist and as an advanced instructor of hypnosis. She graduated from the University of Wisconsin, and studied intuitive communication skills with the Institute of Analogical Psychology in Milan, Italy. Sue studied past-life regression with Fr. Marty Patton of Ohio and with Henry Leo Bolduc, a noted regression researcher and author from Virginia. She lives in Madison, Wisconsin.

**Contact Information**
Sue Joy-Sobota
Labyrinth Center, LLC
1105 Gilbert Road
Madison, WI   53711
**Phone:** 608-274-3454
**E-mail:**  *sue@madisonhypnosis.com*
**Web site:** *www.madisonhypnosis.com*

### What arts do you practice today?

Much of my work is in past life regression, which is a journey where one may see and experience another lifetime. These experiences can be visual for some people. They report scenes similar to watching a movie. For others, it can be as if they are in the situation while seeing, smelling, hearing, and feeling just as they do in this lifetime. An experience can be kinesthetic, meaning an individual gains an understanding of the experience without actually seeing or reliving it. When I am working with people, I use psychic ability to facilitate the journey. It is really a "self-guided tour" however. I don't ask leading questions, but the questions that I do ask pop up and out of my mouth rather unexpectedly at times. Meanwhile, I'm asking my brain, "Where did you come up with that?" Questions are important to the work because sometimes clients see the surface of what's going on, but they don't understand the depth.

### How does one investigate a past life?

I use progressive relaxation hypnosis technique, which is what I think most hypnotists use, although not exclusively. This involves using a trance to set the conscious mind aside to experience the regression. Compare the trance to driving a car and missing an exit because your mind was busy thinking about something else. Understand that regression is not a tourist event. It is really a healing journey. The lives that one chooses to regress to are lives that parallel what is going on today in this life. Issues that were present in another lifetime are still with us. By going "back" we can see how the issues were dealt with in that lifetime — beginning, middle, end. We'll know whether or not it felt right, whether or not it worked for the person, or whether or not it was a good thing. Does the person want to address the situation in the same pattern as in a past life or is there a desire to change it? Is there something that can be learned?

### How does astrology fit into this?

Astrology is supplemental for me. I studied astrology to do some past life charting on an astrological chart. Information is available on past life matters that appear in this life. It's more of a "sketched" blueprint, and is not cast in stone. Obviously, I have a belief in reincarnation. You choose the family you will be with; souls that you likely have been with in the past. They are to teach you, and you are to teach them. It is actually a complex mix. People who are born into traumatic family systems where abuse is present, learn from that system. It is not a choice to be born into an abusive situation, but it is a choice to *learn*. Although it is not an easy and comfortable situation, the ability for a child to leave that environment and grow from it is immense.

As I said, astrology in my work is like a skeleton that is not hardened bone. However, issues you come in with are things you will be addressing in this lifetime. Look at a natal chart and see what this individual is choosing to do. Some people really pick a lot of stuff and others opt for an easier, less challenging life. A decision can be made within that lifetime to revise, and not to tackle it all. You know how it is if you bump an ankle, and then you bump it again and again. Soon you're saying, "Darn!" It's called "2 x 4 therapy." Wake up, this is occurring repeatedly for a reason. Don't turn your back on an experience, because you'll smack that ankle again. Allow yourself to get through it. Astrology is not my primary work, but it helps to enrich what I do.

### How did you develop your talents and where are you headed with them?

I was very young. Things started happening when I was about 7 years old, but it was not a surprise. My grandmother was very psychic. The women in my family have strong intuitive natures. There is a universal energy field that wraps the Earth, and we humans are able to access that. The field has all the knowledge and information that you need to know.

My studying and interests are ongoing. It's like going out to eat. When you have finished eating, you leave the table. The next day, you're hungry again and so you try a different place to eat. Right now, I'm "dining" on Celtic and pre-Celtic study. I have visited several sacred sights in the United Kingdom. I want to know more about Native American culture, and I have "sampled" here, but have not "dined" on this yet. Aboriginal culture and Egypt at the time of the Pharaohs is intriguing. These are cultures related to Earth-based religions. I want to understand their belief systems and apply them to the underlying belief systems of humankind.

### Do you think there is a common thread among those who practice mystical arts?

I think it is an accessing of the universal energy field. Some people are more aware of it than others are. I don't know why; interest perhaps. I studied art history in school, and when my husband and I were first married, he had an interest in this too. I had the art books. Some people play cribbage, but what we would do is experiment. We'd go into separate rooms and one of us would have an art book and the other, a piece of paper and pencil. The one with the book would try to send the picture telepathically to the other one to sketch. Did it work? Surprisingly enough, it worked more than one would predict.

My son is city planner. When he was in Maricaibo, Venezuela, he had to do some research on how to lay out a mass transit system. When he came back to the United States to work on the project, he was insistent on naming train lines in consideration of the people living there. The project people here wanted to name them the red, blue, green line, but he said no. The people in the city are very proud of their mountains, the water, and the sunsets and that's where the names had to originate. When the presentation was made in Venezuela, the people were grateful for the consideration and sensitivity taken in naming these transit lines. This is an example of a "people intuitive" sort of phenomenon. It wasn't as if the people were saying anything, but he knew it underneath. It is an example of accessing what it there for us to know in an intuitive way. I believe that entering this flow is a common thread.

### Is there danger in past life regression?

I think there can be danger, and it is unwise to embark on this if an untrained individual facilitates it. It can be unnecessarily traumatic. I have never had a client experience what is known as an "ab" reaction, which means the person just freaks out. I myself have had an ab reaction while in training. Clients of mine have experienced some horrendous things, but I know how to re-guide them by letting them put it on a "movie screen" and not experience it at present. I always ask, "Do you need to experience this?"

The choice is theirs. Training for past life regression (P.L.R.) is a specialized field in hypnosis. It should be considered carefully.

### Is there anything unique about practicing in Wisconsin?

This area of Wisconsin and the La Farge area are great, but this wasn't always the case. I think things changed in the early 1990s. The white buffalo, Miracle, was born in Janesville around that time. There is a reason the buffalo was born in Wisconsin. It is a very mystical place. The Lakota story is that the buffalo's coat would go through changes to the four colors of skin—white, red, yellow, and black. This occurred. The story also said the sire would die shortly after the birth of the white buffalo, and this too has happened. The buffalo has a purpose and that is to usher in an era of community and reunion of all the races.

### Do you think world events have an effect on your practice?

Sometimes this happens. Events can trigger a need for an individual to come in for a session. The event might trigger a memory they were unaware of, and then the accompanying question is, "Why am I suddenly obsessed with something that didn't bother me before?" We'll use that as a direction in which to take their journey into a past life.

### Do you subscribe to a structured religion?

There is a great gap between religion and spirituality. A religion can be one way of expressing your spirituality. Religion is the structure of a "group" called "we will express our spirituality." As a child, I resisted this. My parents were Episcopal. When I was supposed to be in confirmation classes, I would simply hide, because I didn't want to learn all that stuff. I ended up confirmed anyhow, but the important distinction is that I was not *indoctrinated*. Consequently, I was free to develop what

I thought was real and distinguish what wasn't. In a child's mind, there is not much difference in what a Native American, or an Aborigine or a Celt would see because the child will be looking at nature and fitting into a belief system of an Earth-based religion. I have a strong sense of spirituality and a very loosely structured religious practice around it.

I wish those who are fanatics with their religion would embrace their spirituality as well. Maybe there would be less hate in religion. It has been going on for thousands of years. It needs to stop. This is the time.

**When you are out and about do you turn your abilities on and off like a light switch?**

I can't exactly say I'm a light switch with my abilities. I play a lot of amateur golf, and I was at a golfing competition in Florida when I met a woman whom I felt I would like to get to know. It was as if I knew her, but I wasn't thinking I know her, the way we sometimes do. When a person is drawn to another person for a rather vague or even unknown reason, my belief is that the two are connected from a past life. In any event, the woman ended up talking to me about places she would like to travel. She talked about Alaska and at that point, I instantly knew she had been from that region in another time. I think my light switch is on alert status. Then she revealed that it felt strangely like she had already been there. Our paths crossed two years later, she mentioned this, and I had the same reaction all over again.

I have what I call the "Parking Diva." I know that if I am supposed to be somewhere, there will be a parking space. It is not always spiritually based; instead, it is whimsical and pedestrian. Fortunately, my younger daughter also has the Parking Diva. She needed a prom dress once and we went over to the West Towne area near the place she wanted to shop. There was no parking space, so I said, "Well let's just look around." We found a place next to a different store, and so we parked the car and walked into the store. Right in front of us was the dress she wanted. We looked at it, put it on hold, and went to the original store that we set out to visit. She didn't find anything she especially liked, and we went back to the store that we had parked next to, and then purchased the first dress. So, the diva is whimsical.

### Do you believe dreams have significance?

Sometimes they do, but not always. There are times when a dream is just "download." Sections of our brains just need to fire some things out. If a person is having a boring day, that individual sleeps to download. If the person is having a stimulating day, I don't think as much sleep is required.

### Do you want to discuss any specific case of yours?

I am very excited for my clients and I love my work. They return to me and say, "I finally realized this, and it's something I needed to look at." I get to share in the "ah ha's." The child in me is just always there. One time I worked with an autistic child who was a kleptomaniac and had poor self-esteem. This was not a regression case. She came to me because she had stolen an heirloom diamond ring from her mother and the family could not find it. It was a very prized possession. She wanted help from me in locating the ring. I had read about autism, and I was delighted that the child could drop into a trance immediately. She was able to relocate the ring in a matter of a few minutes. I felt there was something else going on with her, but I didn't know what.

I told the mother that we had finished, but the little girl wanted to come back. We scheduled a session for the following week, and I had no idea what it was we would be doing. Interestingly enough however, in the previous session, I brought her in trance to a point immediately before she was going to take the ring. Here, at this junction, she heard a voice that told her to take the ring. Through hypnosis, I gave her a way to *turn the voice off.* While she was in trance, I told her there was a dial and she could simple turn the voice off by using the dial. Autistic children can have a sense of hearing that is unbelievable, so the child is turning and turning and turning this "dial." Finally, I said, "There's a switch next to the dial, so you can just flip that switch to the off position." She flipped the switch. Then I told her she could use that same switch anytime she needed to turn the voice off.

The child wanted to stop stealing. I checked back with the mom a week later, and she said the child had a horrendous week, but she had not stolen anything. Apparently, this was the first time in her life since she was very young that she had not stolen something daily. It's the same thing as when a person quits smoking. The person is a little on edge for a while. So we dealt with that in another session and I reacquainted her with her soul energy. This is light within her solar plexus that allows her to grasp love from within herself. She did this and it enabled her to release the knotting tension that was agitating her. It was such a revelation to this child. I told her that she had this within her and to open it up anytime she needed it.

### What are your views on charging?

This is my profession and I charge for the services. I charge by the session and not by the hour. The client always knows that when he or she comes in, we work until we are finished.

### What is your view on the psychic hot lines advertised on television?

They charge a lot of money, so I truly hope they are helping people. Unfortunately, people whom least can afford it are washed into the business. It is in no way a panacea, and people desperately want it to be just that. I wish people would not spend their money on these networks. I know psychics who work over the phone, but they are privately in business and do not, nor would they, work through a network.

### What advice do you have for people consulting a psychic or a reader?

I believe it is better to experience things using your own filters rather than someone else's. A psychic is valuable, but a psychic is entering the universal energy field using *their own* filters and then informing you. When a person is seeking past life regression, personal filters are on cue. A caution would be to know that what you are in receipt of has been filtered through someone else and possibly through that person's belief system.

### What do you think about the problem of some people putting up walls?

What about walls — depends what your goal is. If your goal is to be a friend with that person, you cannot reach them if the wall is in place. For me, that means the energy fields can't intermingle. The thinking part of me says, "Isn't that too bad?" The heart part of me is feeling sadly sorry that it can't intermingle. I will talk with the person and search for a spot where the wall is not such a strong structure. People who have walls feel safe with their walls, and that's always the issue. They can talk, and you can respond, but it's always head stuff with them.

### How do messages come through to you?

I am a visual person. I am also accepting of auditory, but if I can see it, seeing is believing. If I can hear it, hearing is believing. I am clairsentient, which is a "just knowing." I did some energy work and training in Chicago, and had the opportunity to experience clairvoyance. We were working on releasing energy from the individual through hypnosis. The energy is observed in various colors that are near or on the individual. This was my first experience with the work. One woman had so much light around her that I had to tell her to move the light because I couldn't see. This was while I was in trance, and later I found out that she is a Reiki practitioner. So I have seen, but I don't see when I am awake or not in trance.

The messages I get are not messages for me. On the other hand, I believe everyone has guardian angels or entities that are agreed upon before you are born. This Soul energy, the guardian angel, will "nudge" you from time to time. It can be subtle. It happens when you are asking yourself, "Why did I look over there?" For whatever reason, it was important that you did so. Recently, I was sitting in an airport lounge engrossed in a book. I suddenly stopped reading, looked up, and saw a friend of mine that I had not seen in ten years. That was a nudge. My energy field was familiar with her field even though my brain was not noticing what was going on here. Sometimes the nudge smacks you upside the head and says *take a look!*

The book, *The Story of Edgar Cayce: There is a River,* by

Thomas Sugrue, is fascinating. Cayce didn't choose his eventual occupation, and he was not raised in a religion. The man had to be in a trance to accomplish his channeling, and he was never able to experience what he did other than reading the steno notes about it. He had extraordinary and powerful abilities. The point is we have to be open to whatever may appear on the horizon. Messages may come through in the least expected way.

### What is your answer to hardcore science?

The hardcore might want to do some homework. It is not my campaign to make people believe. If they come to me and ask, then it *is* my campaign. In Bethesda, Maryland, the energy worker Mietek Wirkus, was tested and hooked up to instruments to see if he was actually changing the energy field when praying. The conclusion was that he was working in a "different place" where we don't know what's going on. The power of prayer is amazing and mysterious. Science looked at this. The answers, if there are answers, baffle them.

### What do you have to say about a dark side?

I believe there is a dark side that we must be careful and aware of. I think the saying, "love conquers all" is true. Love is frightening to the dark energies, but we can move them toward this as opposed to the dark side. People such as Adolf Hitler and other members of mass destruction have profoundly dark energies that consume them.

I believe in "balancing" sorts of karma. I don't believe someone like Jeffery Dahmer is going to come back and have a horrendous life. He will come back and his *soul* will have a horrendous experience. It does not mean his life is necessarily going to be dreadful. In order to understand the pain he inflicted, there needs to be a balancing to understand that. It doesn't mean an eye for an eye; a tooth for a tooth.

I think I have a guardian angel that takes care of me. Clients I can't deal with have not appeared for me. I have had a couple of clients who were on the edge in terms of their level of functioning, and this can be scary. They had very dark experiences in their current lifetimes. I never had a client who was frightening to me, however. I trust they don't come to me and I trust there is a wonderful "filter" taking care of that.

### What advice do you have for those with children who show abilities?

Talk to a two or three-year-old and ask the child, "Do you remember when you were big?" It's a great question. They might say to you, "I remember when I was my mommy's brother." By the time they reach the "age of reason" at about six or seven, the "veil," as it is referred to sometimes, comes down. Historically, children were not even named until they reached that age because of the high mortality rate in children and secondly, the age of six or seven was *officially* considered the "age of reason."

### Do you have a personal past life regression to relay?

When I was in training, I had to let go of a fear that I knew I was going to experience in regression. It was very difficult to do this. My past life took me to Ireland. I had a sister who was seventeen years old and another who was three. I was somewhere in the middle. While in this trance, I was recognizing people and their roles in that lifetime. My sisters and I ventured into a stone circle. This was forbidden by a keeper of the stones. This act was pagan and sacrilegious. My older sister and I were imprisoned. I remember the windows where we were confined, being long and narrow. My older sister and I were hanged. The platform was built so that we had to step off the edge.

When the group I was training with came out of the trance, I recounted that I had been in a prison. The woman next to me stared surprisingly and immediately said, "and we were hanged." Coincidentally (or not so coincidentally, since all things are connected), we must have been close in a previous lifetime.

Thinking back on the regression, before I came to that disastrous end, I recall climbing some rocks and looking over a fence. I was perplexed when I looked over the fence because I hadn't climbed that high, but it was a long way down. There were men loading boats and they were busy, which meant we could go off into the sacred stone circle because they wouldn't be watching.

My brain was having difficulty with this picture. After coming out of trance, I tried to locate this place in the here and now. I thought that perhaps the water I was seeing was a river. I was thinking inland. I took my pendulum and dowsed on a map. I ended up at a point near the southern coast of Ireland. I visited my "previous sister" in Iowa and we stopped at an Irish pub restaurant. A map was on the wall, we went over to the map, and I said, "OK, Pam, where was it?" She pointed exactly to my same river near the southern coast.

Amazing to me too is that when I traveled to Ireland, I searched for the stone forts. I had to find the right one. I remember it as forested, but it no longer is that way. I found the fort in County Cork. The whole layout is there. It exists. I needed the personal experience of finding that in order to let go. It is the skeptic within me. My conclusion is there is no endpoint. Life is a circle, although it is a complex circle.

It gives new meaning to the phrase, "going around in circles."

# Pat Ross

Pat Ross is widely recognized as a gifted trance medium, palmist, Tarot reader, counselor, spiritual teacher, and healer. She has traveled extensively throughout the United States and has appeared on radio and television shows. Pat has been involved in the Noetic sciences for thirty years. Pat lives near Milwaukee, Wisconsin.

**Contact information**
Pat Ross
7550 Grange Avenue
Apt. 113
Greendale, WI  53129
**Phone:**  414-423-9468

### What mystical arts do you practice today?

I am mostly a psychic reader and Tarot reader. I practiced palmistry at one point. When I was seven or eight years old, I just knew how to do it. The information was there. At that age, I conducted little "fairs" and would receive a safety pin or a bobby pin as payment. Never did I realize where this path would take me. I am clairsentient and clairvoyant and I see Masters in my dream state. That's actually how I learned the Tarot. I use the Rider-Waite deck.

At the age of twelve, a being came into my room, held my hands, and said the 23rd Psalm, "Yea though I walk through the valley of the shadow of death...." I had a bad case of pneumonia at the time with a high temperature and apparently, I was hallucinating too. In a near-death-experience (NDE), I was told I had to go back because there was something I had chosen to do that was not completed. I didn't know what this entity was talking about, but the entity had a set of words for it. I think I figured it out when I was in my 30s or 40s however. It has been with me all these years, maybe because everybody thought I was dead. It was a very strange experience. After that little brush with who knows what, I started gaining psychic powers. It wasn't an acceptable thing, and I sometimes received a slap across the face for saying things I wasn't supposed to say.

### How did you develop or fine-tune your abilities?

It was through a number of dreams that I actually chose the Tarot. I *still* can't get over how strange this all was. When I was twelve years old, I saw the "Hermit" card as a man in a hooded gown in my dreams. Years later, I started seeing the Magician card, but I think I was the Magician because I was dressed in the same garb he was. My daughter purchased a Tarot deck and book at that time. Those dreams just kept right on stepping in for me. I had a dream where there were cans arranged on my hexagonal table. The cosmic lemniscate, which is the figure-eight shaped curve ," also known as the sign for infinity, floated down. I reached out for it, but was unable to catch it. Well, the thing started to open up every can, but the cans were empty. That was the end of the dream.

I went to my daughter's house and asked to see "that book." I found out the gold lemniscate represents the super-conscious and the silver represents the conscious mind. I thought about what that dream might mean. I interpreted it to mean that my super-conscious mind would be opening up. From that point on, I seriously started to work the Tarot cards. I studied and studied the Kabbalah,[1] which is actually Jewish mysticism, to help with my studying the Tarot. The Kabbalah is quite complicated, but it essentially refers to the Tree of Life, of which there are several variations.

I didn't incorporate Tarot into a practice for a long time. I started out doing it for myself, but it never tells me anything! It still doesn't, and I've been doing this for decades! I don't know why. At least it works for the people I read. I was doing a lot of radio and television for a time in Madison and Milwaukee. Eventually I gave that up. It was a while back and so many people would put me down for this. I endured disapproval and accusations of witchcraft in a negative way. What people failed to realize then was that this is *human nature*; it was not whatever their perception of witchcraft is. It's different now. We live in different times, for better or worse. I tie the Bible in very much with what I do.

### What is a common thread carried by those who practice the mystical arts?

We are all part of the whole. This includes the animal kingdom and everything. When I do a reading, I say a prayer and put myself into your mind and into your heart. I become you at the moment. That really is the common thread. What is God? God is love and we are all part of that.

---

[1] No historical evidence exists to back up the claim that Tarot cards derive from the tradition of Jewish mysticism known as Kabbalah, meaning "received doctrine" and implying an oral or secret tradition. At the same time, the links appear compelling between Tarot and Kabbalah, and the connection between the two has become the main line of symbolic interpretation, as well as the basis for many of the meanings used by Tarot readers in divination. Many readers do not give much thought as to where the meanings in Tarot readings originated. Nevertheless, Kabbalah (or *Qabala*, the non-Jewish occult version) is where they came from. (Pollack, *The Complete Illustrated Guide to Tarot*)

### What comments do you have regarding the skeptic?

The skeptic, yes, of course, they do compose an interesting clan. Well, frankly, they just haven't had the *experience*. My husband was very skeptical and finally before he passed away, I think he was more psychic than I am. I don't believe it was through me, but I do believe it was through his guides and forces. In addition, there was fear on his part. He was born Catholic and believed the Devil was out to get him. I simply said, "I've never seen a devil in this part of the woods."

### Do you hear any criticisms?

It's mostly religions that put us down. Many years ago, we were doing a psychic fair at the University of Wisconsin and some of the greatest psychics in the world were there. I was lecturing on the Tarot and a group came up to me and informed me I was doing the "Devil's work." I said, "If the Devil does good work, then God bless him too." They didn't bother me after that, but they told me they would pray for me so I wouldn't go to Hell...wherever that is...if it is.

### Is there anything unique about practicing in Wisconsin?

I was pulled back here like a magnet. I think Wisconsin, especially, is a psychic center. There are certain places that I would consider centers of psychic strength, and those would be Arizona, New Mexico, and Wisconsin. These were centers of Native American culture, and the people of these ancient cultures were astonishingly psychic. When I was very young, we were taught to "hate the Indian" or at least not respect him.

Wicca ties in with the Earth forces, and that's exactly how the Native Americans are connected. People don't understand the belief systems and sometimes they don't understand how another belief system different from theirs can hold credibility. By the time I was in eighth grade (after the pneumonia), I did a lot of growing spiritually and looked at *everyone and everything* very differently.

A time is coming when man will be awakened to his own senses. He doesn't use all his senses, and that's fairly obvious if we take a look at senses used in the animal kingdom. I see a time when people won't be able to lie to each other. We will see through the lies. Even now, if people are lying to me, my throat gets very tight, but what I'm really picking up on is their throats. When this happens, I must walk away quickly, because it's almost like something is choking me.

### Do world events affect your abilities?

They have in the past. I used to have dreams, but I just don't want to see this anymore. I try very hard to block it out. There was a time when I would do some work on murder cases and on missing people, but I would become the victim too many times and then go through horrendous nightmares.

### Police or investigative cases?

I worked with officers on a case in Watertown in which two people were killed. I also worked on a case in Atlanta, Georgia when I lived there. In the Atlanta case, I told them the victims' bodies would be thrown from the bridge into the river. So the authorities waited there and actually heard the splash. I called them with a name and phone number that came to me. Even I was surprised. It's one of the strangest things that's ever happened to me. Some of this came out on the Ouija board. When I was a little girl, I had a neighbor who used the Ouija board to find missing things, but you must be *extremely* careful with the board. You must ask it to do things only in love, not because you want to be nosy or something. This was part of my grooming as a child.

One time the police from Fort Atkinson called. I was able to describe a van. The police took me to the parents of a missing girl, and I was able to describe what she was wearing the night she disappeared. The girl was reluctant to go to a dance with a particular guy, but she had changed her mind and went anyhow. It came out that I was seeing two men in camouflaged clothing. The bodies of the two young people were found. One was in a cornfield and one was in the woods. I can't take this anymore, because I take on the whole scene — the murder, the suffering, all of it. It is almost physically disabling to me.

### Do you have a belief in a structured religion or follow a universal approach?

I'm a universal fan. What's important is loving your neighbor and your friend. Christ never had an established church. It is not necessary to pray or believe within a defined structure.

### When you are out and about do you put your abilities on hold? On and off switch?

I used to have the switch on all the time. I learned to turn it off. It wasn't fair to people. I began to see the results of leaving the switch on too much.

### Is there significance in dreams?

Are you kidding? I live in dreams! They touch the superconscious. I have had what I would consider out-of-body experiences. Once I was caught in a closet between two walls—talk about stuck between a rock and a hard place! At the same time, I could see myself lying in bed. I remember ducking around clothes hangers and things.

### My question is do metal clothes hangers really multiply?

Like rabbits, dear.

### What are your views on charging?

I never really wanted to charge, but again in a dream, I was told there was nothing wrong with that. "A laborer is worthy of his toil," so to speak. That's actually the way it was given to me. I would not charge if I felt that what I do was not helping the client. For people who have no means to pay, I do a free reading. My readings are one to one and a half hours, and I read reverse cards too. Materialism can't drive this work. It's still difficult to put a charge on it. When I am paid for the work, I bless the payment and hope it will come back to that person tenfold.

### What do you think of the call 1-900 psychic hot lines?

I've heard that many calls are no less than sixty minutes and you end up with a bill for $500, which is an awful lot of money.

Clients I've worked with have called those lines, and I end up asking them, "Did you learn a lesson?" Apparently, some of the lines "refer" you to a psychic. A man in Florida called me once to ask me to work one of the lines, and I told him that I simply could not do it.

### How do your family and friends react to your abilities?

They approve one hundred percent. I am amazingly fortunate on that end. My family uses me to find lost articles. I meditate to find things. I have a tendency to find things that are lost in the lake. I've helped a lot of people find jewelry. One woman lost a stone from a ring or something and I was able to locate it in her suitcase. When I meditate, I focus on the person and I see where the article was placed or lost. Meditation helps *so* much. It takes you out of your own body and into the Universe. It has to be practiced very often for those who are just learning, however. A pin can drop when a person meditates and it can sound like a bomb. Clocks and phones become very loud too.

### Is there power in prayer?

Gosh, it's like planting a seed. The seed grows if you nurture it and water it. Negative thoughts are like digging it up and this can be destructive. Definitely, there is energy behind prayer. When I was a girl, I saw little creatures, fairies you might say. I saw what were possibly angels, but I wasn't sure, because angels in my church had wings, and these didn't. I asked my mother where angels went to sleep and she told me they sleep on clouds. I had to think about that awhile because I played with two of these beings everyday.

As it turned out, I had two sisters who died before I was born, and now I believe these entities were the two children. I think they were with me from about the ages of six through ten, but I was a lonely child. There were no kids my age in town, so I think they substituted. My mother used to remark about the swings I played on, however. I'd sit in the middle swing and the other two swings would swing right along. They were with me.

**Do you have a belief in reincarnation?**

Definitely. I've seen many of my own lives. My husband was my son in another lifetime. I knew his life history when I met him. He laughed. Death is not an end.

**How do messages come through to you — symbols, visual images, sounds, knowing?**

In meditation, I can pick up voices. It is joyous to be in another state of consciousness. Symbols are a part of my ability. When I started working with Tarot, my guides were telling me no way will I see things the way they happen. If three people see a car accident, there are three different descriptions. Therefore, my guides tell me in symbols — as in the Tarot. As far as interpretation, people know what I'm saying when I give them the symbol that I see.

**Your definition of mysticism?**

There is no concrete explanation or definition. Things happen and the spirit world works with us. Some will say, they can't see spirits, so therefore they don't exist. I see them often times, but I don't see the ones I often want to see, if that makes any sense. My husband came to me twice since his death. Once he was in a fishing shirt I bought him and on another occasion, he appeared to me in the hospital when I was ill.

**Do you have any cautions for people who may seek a reader?**

Always, the money factor is first. If they are a true psychic and want to help you, they will not put a high price on it. Some people don't listen to that advice and have to experience it for themselves. There are so-called psychics who want thousands of dollars. They should be reported, and they have been.

**What advice do you have for those with children who have abilities?**

Some children who are very young have quite an ability. So ask them questions. I had a three year old tell me once that she and I were from the same life stream, which is kind of an unusual reference for a three year old to make.

**What do you think about coincidence or synchronicity?**
I believe there are connections. I had a vision one day of a friend of mine stringing red heart-shaped beads. I took it to be a good omen and a spiritual gift. The next day, I got a call from my brother making me the beneficiary to a policy with investments. Was there a connection? Maybe.

**Do you have an example of how science is involved in this work?**
Marcel Vogel learned to work with flowers and their energies. In some way he had a connection between electricity and plants. He knew things we'll never know. I met him at a convention once and he told me I had to stop eating peanut butter sandwiches because they'd make me fat. Then he asked if I wanted that rose I was carrying freshened up. He put his hands over it and the limpness went out of the rose. Then he asked me if I wanted it turned into a flower instead of a bud. I said, "Go for it."

He put his hands over it again and I now had my flower. That's what he had been lecturing on was the energy in the plant kingdom.

Some branches of science are further advanced than others, and some people have to have equations for everything, but there are equations that we'll never pick up on. We have to go from one lesson to the next to get to a higher sphere. Vogel wrote a good book on crystals that is now out of print.

**Is there a dark side?**
Well, I don't know about you, but I've seen one. There's not a lot you can do except put the light around you. Some entities are Earth-bounds. They couldn't see the light when they lived, so they are still here. They can cause fear and unfortunate circumstances. Some souls have a long way to go.

**What's your mission?**
I'd like to be a great healer, hands on or distance, but I do not heal unless I am asked. Every now and then our time is just up and we need to take a chance and pray for that person. God

knows every prayer that you send out, no need to keep repeating. I had to learn to let go of the repetition. My mission is to teach others. There are beautiful lessons to be learned. There was a time when I said, "If you want me to do this work, then send me a teacher." A teacher who was a medium came into my life. I'd recommend reading Edgar Cayce or books related to his work.

### Do you have any final messages for us?

Some people are not meant to be card readers. Cards are chiefly an implement. If a person is not intended to be a card reader, and that person insists on it, karma is built, and the readings don't have a flow to them. People have a variety of talents. Excel in *your* talent. A few words about karma…some things are meant to be worked off in a karmic way. If a child enters the world crippled or blinded, take heed because the child may have chosen that, but on the other hand, don't get in the way of modern medicine. There could be a karmic situation here. Listen to your children in every way. They are always trying to say something to you.

# Debbie Smoker

Debbie Melichar Smoker specializes in several areas of metaphysics. She is a well-known Tarot card reader and works in the field of meditation and sixth sense development. Debbie worked as a freelance writer for *New Avenues Magazine* and published two books, *Turn on Your Magic Eyes,* and its sequel, *Joy of Jamaica.* She has appeared on several television shows and been a guest on many radio programs. Debbie has been a certified hypnotherapist since 1993. She has been an artist for twenty years in designing and constructing stained glass windows for businesses, public institutions, and private residences. Besides living in Wisconsin, Debbie has lived in Jamaica and Mexico. She frequently is a tour guide for groups traveling to Jamaica. Her most recent adventure and exciting project is in screen play writing.

## Contact information
Debbie Smoker
7857 East Oakbrook Circle
Madison, WI   53717
**Phone:**   608-833-0102
**Fax:**   608-833-5318
**E-mail:**   *dsmoker@execpc.com*
**Web site:**   *www.dsmoker.com*

### What mystical arts do you practice today?

I read Tarot cards known as Sacred Path cards based on Native American spirituality and wisdom. My other areas of work are in teaching guided meditation, dream interpretation, and developing sixth sense. I try to empower people, to help take them from role of victim to victor. People come to me looking for something, and in turn, things are going to be asked of them. This involves work by the individual. What the person gets out of a session depends what the person is willing to put into it. When a person leaves a session with me, that person will have information, direction, and help. The person can then make some mind-body-spirit changes, but the changes must include all three. My philosophy in life is *fun with a purpose*. Believe it or not, *learning* in that frame of mind is more easily accomplished.

### How did you develop the abilities?

As a child, I attended a strict Catholic school. From the very beginning, it was ingrained in me that we are all spiritual beings. Unfortunately, my upbringing was of the old school with all its fear, pain, guilt, and propensity for suffering. But the good thing about it was that it left me with a sense that I am so much more. My family was conscious of having a sixth sense. We talked about it often and naturally accepted it, despite the church warning that we would all go to hell. Still, we could not deny that we had this ability, because it was a natural part of our existence — just there, like an arm or a leg.

I feel my family gave me permission to continue developing this sense, and I'm grateful for that. It ultimately played a role in shaping the course of my life.

One of my missions is to teach people how to develop their own sixth sense. I'm doing this through a series of fiction books that I'm writing. Generally, around age 35 there is a shift for many people, and this is used in my character development in the books I write. Basically, we are divine beings in the physical. People often think of their bodies as being in conflict with spirit instead of in harmony, and that's a problem.

### What's your take on the skeptic?

I am, without doubt, a skeptic. I don't accept things just because a famous person wrote it down somewhere in a book. Always living outside the box, I have a tremendous curiosity, so I keep experimenting, exploring, and researching. I don't feel a need to prove anything to anybody, and everything I use in my work has gone through my picky scrutiny. When people come to me for readings, I tell them to take what they want out of this and leave the rest. I can usually tell how serious a person is when he or she comes into a reading. I do readings at parties, corporate and social events, and sometimes I run into skeptics more so at these events than in a private reading. Most people end up enjoying the readings and find them uplifting. For the skeptic who builds a wall, I say, "Let's not waste my time or yours. I wish you a good life. I wish you well." I don't hold resentment — takes up too much space.

### Okay, what about those lottery numbers?

Yes, people ask me that or joke about it all the time. Great that you want to win these bundles of money, but you are not looking at the issues. All that person wants is to think about what he can do with the pile of money. Take that one step deeper, and what that person is really looking for is happiness and fulfillment. That does not necessarily come along with winning lottery numbers. In fact, your life can suffer because of it. We see divorces, loss of friendships, and you name it. Problems they encounter never existed before their winning landslide. What happens ultimately, is that the person has to *back up* and find the path dedicated to *who am I and what do I want*. I'm not here to answer lottery number questions and other little "so what" things. I want to teach you how to develop your psychic power. That's what I'm here for.

### Do you think there is a common thread among people who practice mystical arts?

We know the power of our thoughts, for one thing. When we acknowledge this power, we must take responsibility for it. Our thoughts are as real as TV or radio waves. They have a similar energy and they have an effect on the world, just as when you flip on the TV, there's suddenly a picture on the screen. Have you ever given thought to exactly where it is that picture is coming from? It's being transmitted from somewhere. We need to transmit the same things we call to ourselves every day. A common thread is that people who do mystical work have comprehension of the power in thought. There is a warning that goes out with this, however. If a person loses sight of the abilities, and is carried away with power, and vulnerable Souls end up abused, this person has fallen to a level of psychic vampire.

### What are your thoughts on psychic hot lines advertised on TV?

Good reading is not fortune telling. It is done with the highest integrity to assist you in getting in touch with your own higher wisdom. Ask yourself what is your intent in obtaining a reading. People generally are looking for answers and are feeling stuck. Some of the psychics on the hot lines are legitimate and skilled, but on the other hand, I have seen people on TV who laugh and openly admit they are trained to give certain answers. They are doing the work strictly for the income. It is very expensive for the client. There is so much that you can learn about a *specific* psychic reader before you even go in for a reading, so why go the uncertain and chancy route? Be fair to yourself; do the homework.

### What are the criticisms you hear about this work?

I have nothing against Jesus Christ, and historically he was a teacher, just as Buddha, and just as many. He said, "Look, you can all do this if you want to," but most people are afraid to dive in and take the responsibility that comes along with it all. I have been accused several times of "doing the work of the devil," and I "had better get out of there," and so on and so on. In Jamaica, I had an interesting experience with this. I wanted to understand voodoo and obeah[1] and why people were so scared

---

[1] A system of belief chiefly in the British West Indies, the Guianas, and the southeastern United States that is characterized by the use of sorcery and magic ritual. The word is of African origin ca. 1760. (*Webster's Ninth Collegiate Dictionary. 1991.*)

of it.  Just as I suspected, people who work with this have a strong understanding of metaphysics and can use it *either* way. A number of obeah practitioners abuse it and play on people's fear.  It works because victims hand their power over, and they don't realize it.

### Is there anything unique about practicing in Wisconsin?

I have lived in Wisconsin, Michigan, Montana, Mexico, and Jamaica.  I was born in Janesville, Wisconsin, and I believe I chose to be born there.  Janesville is a very conservative place.  I knew my perception of things and my consciousness were different from many people.  It took me quite awhile to "come out of the closet" in Janesville, but I absolutely had to,  because I had such a passion for what I do and I wanted to share it with people.  My love overcame my fear.  Wisconsin is conservative, but accepting and opening up as time advances.

### What are your thoughts on charging for services?

At first, I absolutely could not take money for what I do. My upbringing taught me that people don't make money doing things they love to do…the rule is you have to hate your job. That was the mindset at the time.  The other notion was that money is not taken for spiritual endeavors.  I have done a lot of work on figuring out what my relationship to money is.  Get to the root of the beliefs you have about money—not the truths, but the beliefs.  I had to make a shift and realize that money is out there, and it is okay to have it.  It is an energy exchange, and I need it to live and do what I do.

I will work on a sliding scale with anybody.  I once interviewed a famous reader for an article I was writing about eight years ago.  At that time, she was charging $225, which I thought was outrageous.  I told her that I liked her books and her abilities, but I really had a problem with the fee she was charging people.  She said to me that she had "worked very hard, studied my entire life, and what I offer to the clients is extremely valuable to them.  If the clients are sincere about wanting to help themselves, and change their lives, they are willing to pay that fee.  It weeds out those who are coming for entertainment from those who are going to apply the information and use it." The concept made sense to me, but I still believe a sliding scale is most fair for me, personally.

### Do world events affect your abilities?

No, not really. I work more on a personal level than taking into account global activity. However, with September 11, 2001, I was very conscious of the major shifts that were coming to life. I focus on the positives in living, and I am so deeply aware that every person makes an impact on the universe. The only way world peace can ever happen is for things to happen on an *individual* level. After September 11, people were thinking, maybe we ought to love a little more and take care of things better than we have been. People are caught up in thinking they can't change the world because it is too big of a place. They look at taking the giant steps instead of the baby steps. We need to sort out what is thrown at us from governments, media, institutions, and other groups of people. Individuals become the collective eventually, but it can't start there.

### Is there a Dark Side? I'm not referring to the Queen of Voodoo or anything.

I'll answer that from personal experience. I find words interesting because I am a writer. People define Dark Side as darkness and evil, and a light side as good — opposites. I define Dark Side as a certain frequency or energy level that is dense. We talk about ourselves that way without even realizing it. When we are depressed or sick, our energy is heavy. "I don't have the energy to put my shoes on" is heavy. When you're in that frequency, it is hard to get out of it, and furthermore, it sucks you dry. I believe that when we are in that frequency, we are susceptible to other inhabitants of the same frequency. There could be energies of people who have died in a twisted state full of anger, hate, and killing. If we don't eat right, or we drink too much, and so on, I think we become susceptible to the dark place with it's own set of thoughts and influences. These thoughts can latch on to a person. Think about saying, "I don't feel like myself today." Well, you're probably not! Darkness is a place of fear. Are you making decisions out of fear or out of love?

Notorious people, such as Hitler, come into life with dark issues. Unfortunately, they play a harsh role in our lives. That happened to me in a violent marriage. I think the man to whom I was married, chose to come in and play that part. Maybe we agreed to this in between life times as some sort of itinerary. In the big scope of things, I think he was giving me the opportunity to love myself. So what appeared to be a tragedy to everyone around me, turned out to be a blessing. At one point, I was ready to say, "I've had it. I'm going to check out of this planet or get serious about the work I came to do, and honor myself as the divine being that I am." It still brings tears to my eyes. But the way I deal with it is that I thank my former husband, because he certainly did not choose an easy role to play.

### Do you subscribe to a structured religion?

Definitely, I do not subscribe to a structured religion at all. My beliefs are spiritual. Love is really everything. That may sound trite, but truly, it is everything. Think about it.

### What is your definition of mystic or mysticism?

Mysticism is that which appears to be unexplainable. It is involved with touching other realms and dimensions, laws of the Universe or cosmic laws. It is communicating on a higher level with all of nature. We have the ability to go beyond our five senses.

### Is there significance in dreams?

Of course, yes, there is significance. Our culture in the United States is one of the very few that is of the attitude which conveys the message of, oh, it was "just a dream."

That's plain crazy. My sleeping life has been such a major part of my waking life. The big joke in my family is that I have to get up so I can get some rest now! I have always paid attention to my dreams. I can't help it. I receive lots of information and help that I need. Trivial as it may sound, but for example, I was having car problems and the information came to me to pinpoint the problem. I had thought what was wrong with the car was totally different than what was coming out in the dream. It woke me up enough to pay attention to it, and the information probably saved me from a potentially serious accident. Sometimes I receive mathematical information on books that doesn't balance. I journal my dreams and then study them. It's like a free school, so why not take advantage of free schooling?

**When you are out and about are your abilities on hold or are they on all the time?**

My abilities are part of me all the time. When I was young, I tried to run away from this because I didn't want to deal with it and I wanted to play and party. Now I don't want to shut the abilities out. My antennas are up. I can go out socially and not talk about this work, but I am constantly tuning in to things. I am not invasive and I respect people's privacy. However, I see the spiritual aspect of people more than I see anything else about them. I have had experiences, especially in Jamaica, where people are of such frequencies, that they almost seem transparent to me. For some reason, the energy in Jamaica really accelerates my senses.

**Are there any specific readings you'd like to talk about?**

One time a client of mine asked me to look at a photo. He didn't want a card reading, just a photo reading. That's not generally what I do, but I went with my intuition. Sometimes I think I'm hearing little voices coming through the back of my head. In a reading, I just say whatever comes out in the direction that I am pushed. Most of the time, it is pertinent to the client. With this photo, one guy just kept jumping out of the picture so I said, "This person is around you and he wants you to know he is with you." The person in the photo was the client's uncle, with whom he was very close. The uncle had died a month ago. I've had similar experiences when people come to a reading with objects. Most of the time I use cards, and I find them to be beneficial because they are affirming to an individual.

I started doing readings when I was in an abusive marriage. Somebody recommended that I get the Native American Sacred Path cards, and it was as if I had been thrown a lifeline. They are a form of Tarot cards. I had gone for some traditional counseling, and I'm not knocking it, but there are some people who are good at it, and there are some who are not. The counseling I was getting was not helpful. I was frightened and I actually became very suicidal. My thinking was that no matter where I go, it can't be as bad as where I am now. Luckily, I had a brother living six blocks away who is psychically tuned to the family. He was watching TV, jumped out of the chair, and ran to my house in time to stop the dreadful act. It was awesome, really.

That was a turning point for me. I made the choice that I would do what it is I was meant to do. Shortly after all this happened, I took those cards and did a reading for myself. I thought, wait a minute, these cards are asking me to do too much, and I'm burned out and I don't have energy. So I put the cards away. A week later I hauled them out again and darned if most of the same cards didn't pop up again. This time I did some talking to myself and said, "Debbie, you have been asking for help, and it's right here in front of your face, so pay attention!" I took heed of the cards and went to work. It was no simple task, but my life has been blissful, creative, productive, and wonderful for many years now.

We are like candle flames. If the flame diminishes and the candle is about to go out, that means we are sinking and might die. When people come to me and say they feel like they are dying; and this, that, and the next thing is going on, I say, "You know what, buddy, sounds to me like you *are* dying. Thank God you decided to do something about it!" If we don't replenish ourselves, we burn out. This is the real basis of readings that I do. I look at where your thoughts have been, and where they have to go for you to remain healthy on an emotional and a physical level.

### Have you worked on any police or investigative cases?

I have no interest in pursuing these because of the negativity involved. I refuse to watch violence on television and I refuse to read about it. I'm not Pollyanna pretending it is not there, but I'm aware that when we put focus on negativity, we breed more of it.

Most people mindlessly watch or read the news but do nothing to change things. That breeds fear and depression. It serves a purpose for those people who mindfully take action to help.

We can all pray for peace without knowing every horrific detail in life.

### What do you think about the concept of coincidence?

There really is none. That's where the title of my book *Turn on Your Magic Eyes* comes from. What I'm saying is, look beyond the physical. We can use all of our senses superficially or on a deeper level. *Look and see* what is really going on instead of the illusion that is in front of you. We by-pass opportunities all the time because we have not learned to be open to them and conscious of them—these are supposedly coincidental things, but they really aren't estranged from each other. They are all connected. We put the thought out into the universe that we want something, it shows up right in front of our faces and in our lives—well, hello…wake up.

I love to tell people to sit in a room that they are very familiar with, and to look around and stay in the room until they notice something they have never seen. When you have the experience of finding this unknown, mystery item that you never noticed before, it will shift you into a place where you end up asking the question, "What else have I been missing?" Every morning I record my dreams, meditate, and ask for what is in my highest and best interest. I'm not only asking for the opportunities I talked of earlier, but I'm asking to be conscious of them. People and things show up in your life for a reason.

### Reincarnation — fact or fiction?

We can argue into the next millennium, and chances are we won't prove anything. But proof doesn't need to be an issue. Based on my own experience, I have no doubt that I lived in other times. I document things in my journal, and when I read over what has happened to me over the years, pieces start fitting together. Investigating a past life needs to have a purpose. Is this going to help you and what will you learn from it?

Hypnosis is a good tool for this. It makes sense as to why we bring stuff with us into the current life. Situations occur from which we learn. For me, it was being in an abusive marriage that I was finally able to let go of and move forward without beating myself up.

**How do messages come through to you — images, symbols, voices, thought...stained glass?**

Dreams are a good source for me, as I talked about earlier. Sometimes I see entities. Thoughts and voices come through. Occasionally, I sense a presence above me, and I feel like I'm being fed like a computer. In my journaling, I ask questions, pick up my pen, and allow myself to write whatever comes through. I receive some incredible information that way, and it benefits me personally. Journaling is one of the best tools we have. Don't hide anything in the journaling. Well, as for my work with stained glass, when my body leaves this realm, there will be things left here for people to enjoy — it's another avenue for touching the soul.

**Is there power in prayer?**

Thoughts are real entities, and they are out there. I tell people to think of them hovering in the air. Emotions are real forces and energies, too. People will pick up on love, compassion, and emotions that we send. Personally, I see a prayer as a hotline to the universe. Pick up that hot line phone and put your request in, but always ask for what is in your highest and best interest. I think of meditating as waiting to hear the answer. Too often, people put their request in and then slam down the receiver. They run off and don't wait for an answer, which again is why it is important to meditate daily. Answers are coming, but it is a matter of tuning in to them.

Everybody knows someone who has said, "Oh, that's a great idea. You should make that or patent it or whatever...." Okay, now the idea for this fabulous invention is out there floating around in the universe as a thought, thus making it a real entity. But you, the would-be inventor, are not going to act upon it, and furthermore you've told the universe that you're just going to skip it. You have said, "I don't know how to get it made, or patented, or whatever, but yes, that would be a cool tool." Well that great idea is still floating around, and what happens? Somebody else latches on to it; perhaps they prayed for an idea, and a year later, you see it on the shelf at Wal-Mart! Some inventor did not steal your idea. It was released by you, and given away to an ambitious soul who said, "I'll do it."

**Do you have any advice to those with children who are showing abilities?**

Encourage them and PAY ATTENTION. When we first come into this world, we are tickled pink because we know about our divinity and we are saying, "Hello World I'm Here!" As we go on, we bury or misplace that sense because of our programming. As children, however, it is natural for us to communicate in other realms. Denying this reality is called "progress," but it is actually regress.

**Any comments on hardcore science?**

Bless everybody and bless who we are. Some people are operating in the true scientific framework, and it is very important that they do this work in a powerful way. A bothersome tenet to me is that if one can't prove it, it does not exist. Our every day knowledge is limited to theories that we have, and not what might be around the corner. Therefore, what isn't proven has possibilities of existence…scientific thought of the day.

**Do you have any final comments or messages?**

I have a vision where I am looking overhead, and I see us all as merely visiting this planet. We landed here in our own little ships (our bodies) and our mission is to open the doors and leave our treasures and gifts before we depart. Our dreams, our passions, our skills are not happenstance. It's no meaningless coincidence that we are good at what we are good at, and that we are drawn to what we are drawn to. These clearly are messages. Don't put this on the back burner of denial, but look forward to it and own it. Some people make the mistake of not leaving their gifts here because of criticism or fear. They succumb to the "who do you think you are?" bullies. Their lives are not fulfilled and they feel like something is "missing." What's missing is the locked up passion. People exit with these gifts still locked inside the ship. I look back here on Earth, and this makes me cry, because I see people with arms raised up, and saying, "We wanted and needed your gifts."

My final message is this: empty that ship before you exit. Weed out the people who don't encourage you, or who stop you from living your potential and your dream. Weeding is a very important aspect of gardening. Sometimes we have to say, "I love you, but I have to move on."

# Paul Ditscheit

Paul Ditscheit is an experienced practitioner in the area of transformational attunement. His work is directed toward people who are interested in connecting to soul and the awareness that is soul. The result is a change in the person, and in how that person views the world. Paul conducts private sessions and many workshops both in Wisconsin and in other states. He has been a guest speaker and teacher at many events. Paul has a master of science, and has practiced guidance work for over twenty years. He is in private practice in Madison, Wisconsin.

**Contact information**
Paul Ditscheit, M.S.
Transformational Attunement
6320 Monona Drive, Suite 303
Monona, WI  53716
**Phone:**  608-226-0750

**What mystical arts do you practice today?**

I work in the area of what I call transformational attunement. It is really soul-directed work. Many definitions of the soul exist, but when I refer to the soul, I refer to Ralph Waldo Emerson's commentary on the soul from his essay titled *The OverSoul*. He tells us, "We live in succession, in division, in parts and particles. Meantime within us is the soul of the whole, the wise silence...." Emerson further describes the soul as "the background of our being...an immensity not possessed and cannot be possessed."

My work focuses on helping people connect with that soul, with that immensity, with that incredible power that is our true nature. The work deals with awakening potential within, and allowing that potential to transform from the inside out.

For most people, but not for everyone, the beginning work is to look at what is obstructing that awaken—the *baggage* of which we have a lot. Usually, I find that we have gotten ourselves into quite a state. We're tied up in knots and really disconnected from what I consider our true self — that immensity which is the soul and the great power.

**How do you go about untangling it all?**

What I do with clients in the beginning is that I try to psychically tune into their energy field and find where things are not in flow, where things are out of alignment, and then we talk about that. Soul is simply awareness, and so we analyze and become aware of the energies that are stuck and blocking. You ask how do I tune into this. I see it, I hear it, I smell it sometimes, and I even taste it. Through all of these senses, I become aware, and then I help the client get to that same awareness and experience the energies for him or herself.

**How does a person do this?**

Most people do this by feeling. It's the simplest way, because we do it all the time. People even talk about it unknowingly. We have all kinds of phrases. A person may say, "I feel heavy hearted." Well, is their heart any heavier than any other day? Likely not, but they *are sensing* something. The feeling is that something is "sitting" on the heart. If you could clairvoyantly see what is there, you would see a heavy energy in that area. Some people may say, "I feel all tied up in knots today." Seeing clairvoyantly again, we can observe the twisted, knotted, bunched up energy. We use numerous descriptions that speak to what is going on in our energy field. So people are already experiencing it, they just don't realize it. These fixed energies are usually very tight and very holding and dense in some way. When a person starts to hold the energies in awareness, the density and tightness starts to open up and relax, and that is the *beginning* of healing.

**What is the process from that point? Sounds like this could be difficult.**

Usually what I see at first is the surface of it all, as in how it's playing out in a person's life right now. A much deeper more complex route to tracking it emerges, and this is where I go. I track it with the awareness in feeling, seeing, hearing, and sometimes tasting (not my favorite). The core of the energy is deep within a person's consciousness and it is holding on intensely. What happens is the energy lets go, takes a deep breath, sighs, and says, "Whew, I don't have to do that anymore!" It's been trying to help you in some way or another, but it has usually overstayed its welcome. At the moment of letting go, the energy allows that person's soul to do the healing. The soul is always ready and on alert, but it won't go where the will opposes it. Usually, we are talking about an unconscious will.

People feel a shift in consciousness, and after awhile, they begin to notice they are doing things differently in their lives. They are not reacting in the same way as they had been in certain situations. They feel more of a freedom and more of a flow. Their struggle is beginning to shift. Each piece that one addresses is permanent. However, we have multiple "energy holdings" to address. I am amazed at how wound up people get, but I've done it myself, so I know how it is.

**How quickly does this change happen and how would a person know?**

It is a process. Some people quickly go through an initial

clearing to where their soul is really active and working for them. Other people have themselves so knotted up, that it takes awhile. There really is quite a range and variation. What are the changes experienced? The direction this takes people is that they become more centered, living more in the moment, feeling a flow in life as opposed to a struggle with challenges. It really depends on what the person's issues are. Some may have low self-esteem or self-concept. This work has opened people's hearts more to a point where they can feel it—not just as a mental concept, but physically feel it more towards others and towards themselves. They respond differently to people and aren't caught up in the whole struggle of life as before, however they continue with their activities, but in a different light. Many coincidences, interestingly, begin to happen. You start drawing to you, the things that are in alignment with your soul. Look at the word "coincidence" and pick it apart. "Co-incident" is essentially, what you get, and this really is a fitting word for what's happening.

**What's your answer to the skeptic?**

Oh boy, I'll tell you that I just spoke with a whole group of skeptics. I was speaking to a group in Chicago that I've never worked with before. A friend of mine invited me to work with a group of psychologists, and believe me they were skeptical. They were not afraid to voice their opinions either. They were all very "rational," as if psychology itself is always rational. Anyway, over four days' time, people started experiencing shifts and things started happening for them that they couldn't deny. As these "openings" occurred, people started connecting with what I define as soul. I would have these individuals speak in front of the class to describe what was happening, and what we'd hear is descriptions of radiant transformation.

**Is meditation involved in this procedure?**

Yes, one tends to go into a meditative state to do this. Meditation is really about helping one to begin to live it. It is not just about going into a quiet state and only having experiences while in that state. The process is about carrying this state forward so that you can go out into the world and live from that vantage point. The work transcends the mind, and it is difficult to put into words.

### Your thoughts on reincarnation?

Reincarnation is obvious to me. We are a work in progress. As I mentioned earlier, we have gotten ourselves into a quagmire of a state, and we are working ourselves out of it right now. It is a process to come back to who we are. Once one starts engaging in it, the process takes off! People can go through various connections, with their soul coming in very strong at times. It is a spiritual initiation. We clear the space and set the intention. Awareness and intention are the two biggest elements in spiritual transformation in any lifetime.

### Is there power in prayer?

Prayer can be very powerful. There is no doubt about it. Prayer is intention. A person coming to see me is an intention. Some come to me because they are in pain right now and they want to rid themselves of it. Many people see me because they want greater connection and depth. These are all intentions and there is action occurring, just as there can be with prayer. There are a lot of ways, including prayer, of going about helping people get to places. When we see various methods work, I believe it is because the person has ultimately engaged the Soul.

### Is there anything unique about practicing in Wisconsin?

People are open to my work here, especially in Madison. I don't have any problems keeping a very full practice. I also work by phone with people from other areas of the country. One thing I like about Wisconsin is that not as many people here are on the "glamour" side of it. It's more meat and potatoes for them. When I talk about "glamour", I think about California for example. What I've found there, is that they really don't want to dive in deeply. It seems to be more of a phase or a fad for them. They want to stay a bit more on the surface. It is an interesting phenomenon. Right now however, I think that things are changing all over the country. I teach in a school of energy and healing and our students are from various parts of the country. We have a branch of the school in Madison, Chicago, and Vancouver, Canada.

### Do you have a belief in a structured religion?

I gave that up at the age of 12. I grew up as a Catholic. Catholicism was presented to me as a compartmentalized system, and this was not me and it was not enough. I knew there was something different and something more, but I didn't know what it was.

### Do dreams have significance?

Sure, they are significant sometimes. People tell me dreams, but this is not my focus. I believe that in working with people my own senses are entering more directly. Dreams that are important to people can be helpful to me, but that usually is not the route we take with this work.

### When you are out and about are your abilities on hold?

I don't purposefully tune into people when I'm out. I do that all day here in my office. However, there are people whose energies are coming at me, and I can't help but notice. I don't feel drawn to saying things to people about this. Perhaps if I felt there was a need to say something, I would.

### Do world events affect your abilities?

Certainly, the events of September 11, 2001, affected people. In my clients, I felt a profound sense of shock in their energy systems and we really had to address that first before we could move forward. I would say that for a month after September 11, I think people were barely aware of the amount of shock present. I don't notice it as much these days, but I'd have to say the shock was extreme.

### Have you worked on police or investigative cases?

I have not worked investigative cases, but I have police officers that come to me as clients. Some of them have been dealing with post-traumatic stress disorder. They've tried other therapies without much satisfaction, and in a sense they were "desperate" enough to come to me as a "last resort" you might say. We go to work on the problem.

### What do friends and family think about your work?

This is my calling and I do this work full time. My family is very Catholic, and they don't quite understand what I do, but they are not negative about it. They just don't care to get involved and are not interested. Most of my friends know my work very well, and I have many friends in the community.

### What is your definition of a mystic?

A mystic is someone who is aware of other dimensions and is not only aware, but is comfortable in those places. Sometimes, to the inexperienced, it can become overwhelming when other dimensions or realms start opening for them and they don't know how to handle it. They are not grounded enough and they don't know how to hold that energy. I would not consider this person a mystic unless the person is able to accomplish grounding, and at the same time, move about in other dimensions, including the dimensions of self.

### What do you think about the psychic hot lines advertised on television?

I don't know much about them, and they don't hold my interest. I know some seers who have validity in what they say, but I think these things can be a bit tricky. At times, I believe people are in a clear channel where information is coming through, but this is not always the case. There has to be awareness that sometimes ego or shadow side brings things forth, even to the clearest of them. I try to discriminate carefully with this.

### Is there a Dark Side and do you point this out to people?

Absolutely. The shadow side is the dark side of an individual. However, other dark energies can actually inhabit people and are at play in the world. Dark energies are a common thing. I deal with dark energies the same way I deal with a person by helping the person to raise his or her vibration. Yes, I do point this out to the client. I say, "There is something here that does not belong, and it needs to go. It has darkness to it and we have to clear it out of the field." I don't put a lot of energy into it, however. I take that darkness and hold it in awareness of the soul energy where it eventually raises its vibration and goes into the light. It changes; I don't really drag it out of a person. I don't try to expel it; that's the hard way to do things. Energies can be much entangled in people, so it takes awhile to unravel this.

Some dark energies tend to run in families. There are all kinds of things. Actually, there are dark energies involved in substance abuse — that's the running in families thing again. It's interesting, because a person is born, and there it is—the dark energy. Some people seem to resist it, and have immunity to it. The darkness is there, but it can't get in, and if it does get in, it is not able to control the person.

### Do people ever describe "walls" to you?

Every day. I have the person describe the wall to me and describe the energy surrounding the wall. Of course, a wall is a defense system, and there are layers. We hold each layer in awareness and allow the soul to begin transforming each layer. It's not like you have to do the work yourself. This is difficult for people to believe that the soul can do the work. Start feeling and noticing it, and then the soul takes over and does the work.

### Do you think people should observe the soul as a "companion?"

The soul is one's true *self.* It's not hard to begin to experience it, but most people don't know how because they don't pay attention. They are scurrying here and there, living in the future, and living in the past, and very seldom do people come into the moment. Come into the moment — I mean really into the moment — then the soul starts to show up. People come to me with that strong intention, and they are ready to start.

We can be drawn to this and it creates a momentum in the world. My mission is to create that momentum, but the only way to do that is one soul at a time. Even in teaching, I am doing that one soul at a time.

**Do you have any cautions for people who seek this type of experience?**

What I always suggest to people is that they really listen to themselves and listen to their own heart. Don't be evasive — I mean *really listen*. People have trouble with that because they want answers immediately. We don't know where the answers will come from. Don't go in with all kinds of preconceptions of what the answer will be, and what it will look like, and where it will arise from. Sometimes it's difficult for a person to trust in himself or herself.

**What is your answer to hardcore science?**

I don't spend a lot of effort convincing people, because it is a waste of my time. If someone is coming in with that situation, that person is usually using reasoning as a distraction. They are unconscious of it, but it really is just a form of domination. I'm not saying everybody does this, but it is common among the hyper-rational.

**Do you have any final comments?**

My message is one of realization of our true nature — the soul — that immensity that is not separate from us. As humans, we are in the process of unwinding what has been wound up for a long time. Anybody who is interested in shifting, even though there may be a lot of "baggage" around them, is ready because that person has gotten a taste of it.

Clients arrive here who have never done anything like this before. Several have an incredible readiness in them, and it is actually greater than some people who have been "on the path" and doing all their "stuff" and trying to be spiritual. It is not about that. My point is that it does not need to be hard work if you let it happen from the soul. The soul knows what healing needs to happen and you don't have to figure it out. Just become aware and spend time doing that. Most people don't, and it's a loss. Take note of the soul of the wise silence.

# Caryn DePauw

Caryn Lea Arnold DePauw works primarily in the field of dowsing. She has also worked with Tarot cards. Caryn has facilitated several workshops on dowsing technique and works individually with clients. Her classes focus on self-empowerment as the key to success in most areas of life. Caryn feels a connection to the Lakota and the geographical openness and archeological richness of South Dakota where she lived as a young child. She is also a practitioner of Swedish massage that emphasizes lymphatic system work, cranial-sacral work, and the use of essential oils. Trips to Egypt have encouraged her study of perfume oils and the symbolism used in Egyptian jewelry.

<u>Contact information</u>
Caryn DePauw
Light Touch Therapies
125 Rickel Road
Sun Prairie, WI 53590
**Phone:** 608-837-3122
**E mail:** *caryn11@mer.com*
**Web site:** *www.merr.com/users/iafy*

**What mystical arts do you practice today?**

I am mainly involved in dowsing. I study and teach the many applications that come along with the art. Most of the time I use a pendulum to do this. A pendulum can be as simple as a bead tied to a piece of yarn. Contrary to belief, dowsing is more than just finding water with rods, or a forked stick. With dowsing, we can take our senses and use them to find insight into many questions or situations that come up. In every day matters, I often use dowsing to spark my intuitive abilities. As a "backup" you might say, I use various forms of Tarot cards, and find these too are an inspirational tool for intuitive divination. Mainly, I like to assist people in balancing what I consider to be imprints that influence people negatively.

**How did you develop this?**

I came into my life looking for this! I laugh because my sister says that when I was born, I was always trying to lean forward and get up and look around, and then look around again. I guess it was a constant habit of mine. My family attended various churches when I was a young child. Especially then, I was so curious about everything, and visually absorbed whatever I could in those churches. That habit is still with me, and sometimes I am stuck in one place too long, and finally have to move on. My older sister helped me become aware of this. It is interesting, in one of my toddler pictures, there is a "haze" surrounding me. I had the picture enlarged, and could not decipher any details, but I have a feeling it is some sort of energy that has been with me all the while. In fact, I tend to see a similar haze when I'm in a meditative state. I was born on December 11, and I weighed eleven pounds. Eleven is a unique number in numerology, and maybe it has significance for me.

My grandfather was a country doctor whom I believed used a great deal of intuition. Several readers have "seen" him standing behind me and have given a description of him. My mother's family was open and in tune with the other side. I think both of these factors influence me from day to day as I work on my life's journey. I'll probably haul this intuition along to the next life too—can't possibly use all your intuition up in one lifetime.

**How did you fine-tune these abilities?**

I probably got my feet wet when I went to Bernard Gherhard, an 86-year-young man for reflexology treatment on my back. The pain was greatly relieved, and I was on my way to discovering alternative therapies. While running my busy salon, I took a number of classes to keep myself sane, including obtaining a license as a registered massage therapist. Then I discovered a dowser in Arkansas by the name of Harold McCoy. He was speaking and teaching at workshops, and I followed his trail. There were several other people who had been students of his, including a retired FBI agent, who had an influence on my studies. This group of people also practiced remote or non-local healing.

Along came Anneliese Hagemann to the Seven Continent Dowsers Convention. The next thing I knew, I was taking training from her, and she was actually my mentor in dowsing. I believe that reading for friends and enemies, and attending psychic fairs has opened doors for me too. Of course, there is the matter of actually practicing and striving for accuracy that really has to have serious consideration if one is to use this for more than a game. Fine-tuning also came with studying the Course in Miracles. It is a good mind training exercise. Using tools to develop and refine intuition is important to me.

Animals have played a significant part in my development also. Living in Rapid City, South Dakota, I was influenced by the vast open spaces of land. The long-awaited pony appeared when I was a teen. Animals have more of a function than we realize, and it is believed that a pet can and does take on the characteristics of an illness the owner may have. Animals have messages and we must have reverence for this. A good resource for this is the book *When Animals Speak* by Penelope Smith, and the James Herriot books. I'd have to say that people, animals, and experiences put me where I am.

**Do you find there is a common thread among those who practice mystical arts?**

The common thread among us is the seeking of mystical knowledge. Those who truly take on mystical endeavors are not afraid to proclaim they are spiritual beings and on a path of growth. They consider their mission is to help people raise consciousness and advance. As spiritualists, they will say, "Welcome to the clan." I've noticed that another commonality is that at some point in life, usually in high school or even in middle grades, these people had a feeling of "not fitting in" as well as others.

### What is your answer to the skeptic?

I think I'm just getting to the point where I'm finally learning to deal with my feelings on this. It's been difficult. I used to be defensive, but now I use more reasoning in my own mind, and say nothing. With the help of those who have taught me, I don't engage in discussion in this area. I believe that many admitted skeptics, and perhaps non-admitted skeptics, have a fear of spirituality when it gets to the bottom line—it is an unknown. The belligerent skeptic is especially prone to fear, and almost panic. If the skeptic could recognize the fear for what it is, this would ease some of it. It's part of my journey, but not my mission, to see what I can do with the fear factor. I am always on the look out for validating occurrences to strengthen my understanding and my position.

### What are the criticisms that you hear?

Receiving money; not being Christian; being anti-Christian, fear of devil take-over. A friend of mine was in Salem, Massachusetts visiting a shop to have a reading from a person that advertised as an "angel reader." She thought this would be a safe place to have a reading, probably because it would not necessarily be associated with the Occult. So once, again, fear pokes it head through the doorway. Why she was in Salem, Massachusetts, city of several historic witchcraft trials, if she is afraid of such things, I'll never know. Getting back to the criticisms, some people will say, "I just don't want to know." Fear surfaces repeatedly in any discussion about skepticism and criticism. If a person criticizes my beliefs and my practices, I would probably suggest to that person to do some personal research. I am self-empowered, and with that comes a resistance to criticism and defensiveness.

### Is there anything unique about practicing in Wisconsin?

Wisconsin is the heartland, a balanced area of the country. However, it seems a little closed. But there are jewels out there that are undiscovered for the most part. People practicing in Wisconsin take their missions seriously. I do think it is time to break open the Midwest and get "out of the closet."

### Do world events affect your abilities?

They actually heighten my sensitivity. Everything changes the consciousness, no matter how heinous the actions are. I develop a deeper understanding from clients when I hear about the struggles they are going through. People can become so distressed. World events such as September 11, 2001, become stepping-stones, horrific as they are. The heart of the world opens up. It makes us all more aware. We need to hold that awareness forever.

### Do you practice a structured religion?

No, I currently am not associated with a structured religion. During my childhood, I attended the Methodist, Presbyterian, and Catholic churches. I learned a lot about the born-again and the Charismatic. The born-again helped me quite a bit when my mother died. The enchanting thing about the Catholic Church was the burning of candles and incense, and I like the ritualistic mysticism of that church. I've heard it said that we shouldn't get stuck too long in any one place or journey—that's how I view religion. It's in our lives for a purpose for a time, but not a place to settle. Religion can be a springboard and at the same time, a foundation for many of us.

### When you are out and about do you turn your abilities on and off like a switch?

I'm learning to turn them off. I don't like to intrude or manipulate. I have to sense how receptive a person is rather than coming on like gangbusters. Things that I contemplate saying are underlying and below the surface, and I usually try to keep them there.

**Are there any specific situations or readings you want to discuss?**

Recently, a friend of my son was at my house and I did a clearing for him because of his allergies. I didn't think I'd hear any more from the friend, and then about a month later I heard from my son that his friend had used very few allergy medications because it had been "his best year yet." The friend attributed his sense of wellness to the clearing. Then I had a second client where a clearing and a massage was done and she reported that her unbearable allergy symptoms had decreased significantly during the worst seasonal time for allergy problems. With the dowsing, this particular client found that she was able to dig up buried emotional stress from an unhealthy previous relationship, and clear it out. She stated that she felt strongly the dowsing played a part in relief of her stress, which in return played a role in the reduction of allergy symptoms.

Teaching people is one of the keys in helping them realize that they can change the vibration of things to fit their needs. When I think of vibrations and energy, I sometimes think of Kirlian photography. In the recording of this electromagnetic energy of certain fruits, very little energy shows up. However, once the fruits have been blessed, the light energy is increased and there is photographic evidence of this. Another easy example to illustrate vibrations is to think about a soprano singing at an intensity that shatters glass. These are sound wave vibrations. So, once again, things can and do change, often times in unexplainable ways.

**What is your view on charging for services?**

I've struggled with that a long time. Now I think of clear light, which is discussed in a *Course in Miracles* and in the *Tibetan Book of Living and Dying*. An acquaintance of mine said, "Oh I can't charge for using clear light visualization." So, I asked her if it cost her anything to study, go to trainings, and go to workshops. She said, "Yes, it costs quite a bit." People who engage in reading and other practices also have a life to support. I believe a high quality service or reading deserves an exchange, whether monetary or other.

**What is your take on psychic hot lines advertised on television?**

They give a bad rap to people who are doing readings outside of that mode. It is prostituting in a way. Personally, I would not contact any of these networks. What it does, however, is create awareness, and indirectly gives advertising of less desirable quality, to all readers on and off the networks. There may be some good readers on those lines, but they take such advantage of clients.

**What does your family and what do your friends think about your work?**

My daughter supports me 100% and my son 75%. My husband is…well, really thinking it over. At a family reunion, I taught some of the younger kids how to do dowsing with a bead on a string. One of the young boys went outside with the string and bead pendulum, came back into the house, and excitedly announced, "You know what? This thing works better when I'm outside by myself without all of these noisy people around me." He just took it for granted that this was a regular every day skill that he needed some practice with—what a refreshing response from this child with no preconceived notions.

I've noticed that many younger minds and older folks are more open. The people who are struggling, going to work every day, taking care of families, and things like that are less likely to take notice, participate, or examine the possibilities. I think a lot of it has to do with amount of time. People busy themselves today in almost as many activities as they can possibly fit into a twenty-four-hour day, and then what is left over is exhaustion. My grandmother once told me that when you are younger, count on physical strength, but when you get older, count on spiritual strength. My friends are incredible and are a great support system. I also find that by talking with somebody one on one, there is almost always some commonality to tap into.

**Do you have any advice for those with children who are showing abilities?**

Nurture the abilities! Teachers need to pay attention to this too. I believe there are spirits around children. In fact, it has been observed by a number of people that the room temperature in a baby's room usually seems a little cooler than the rest of the house. Whether this has anything to do with spirits or not, I don't know; it is just an observation that seems unexplainable.

The role a parent takes on is important. My parents were inspiring without being inspired, you might say. When I think of them, I think of butterflies — inspiring but not controlling. Freedom to think for myself has always been a corner stone of my relationship with them. Just be aware that children are really not miniature adults. They have a unique and fresh spirituality about them that is not characteristic of an adult. Every question a child asks is saying, give me reason, give me more information, and give me a basis to believe. They are reaching out to say, "Tell me more."

**Working in a salon, you must have had clients who came in loaded with lore.**

That's an understatement! They came in with things that they claimed to have never told anybody before. I think people keep things to themselves out of fear of reprisal or even downright disbelief. One of my clients told a story of when he was a small child. He conked out on the sidewalk, and when he came to, he asked his parents where George was. George was the neighbor's deceased husband, whom the kid had never met or heard about. The widow of George nearly dropped dead herself when this question was asked.

Time after time, I heard so many stories. Every once in awhile I'd hear a near-death-experience story, and the person would say they had never revealed it to anyone. It's important to be a listener, but the other important factor is the timing. There is a time and place to tell a story, and likewise, to keep a story.

**Is there power in prayer?**

Well, it depends. If people are asking for something from the outside to accomplish things, that's wishful thinking. But if one goes deep inside, he or she can tap into profound areas, meditative areas. I believe the power in prayer consists of vibrations and thoughts that can manifest for the spiritually minded. There is a source to tap into—a God source. Through choices, we determine what we end up with in the end. I want to stress the importance of meditation. You have a gift and a spiritual epiphany. Spend time in meditation, in nature, and listen to that small little voice that most people tend to ignore.

### Do you believe in reincarnation?

I have a strong belief in this. Think about children who have a recollection of previous lives. They know detailed history, they know places, and they know strange languages as well as recognizable foreign language. Where does the 5-year-old child get that? The major religions in the world believe in reincarnation — that's quite a chunk to argue with.

### How does information come through to you?

Mostly it is feeling and intuition. The best time is when I'm driving in my car because I feel so free. I felt it when I was riding my horse and when I was skiing because I was alone at those times.

Intuition and dowsing go hand in hand, only dowsing is more like Dumbo's feather. Dumbo the elephant thought he needed the single feather in order to fly, but actually he didn't need the feather at all. Dowsing is a tool for intuition, but that's all it is—merely a tool, and not absolutely necessary.

### What's your definition of mysticism or mystic?

I'll give you one of my "driving in the car" definitions. Mysticism is being aware of oneself on a journey to knowing God. Another way to say it would be, to know God is to know the mystery, but the only path is through knowing of self. A mystic goes to the edge to share what they can to help themselves and other people. Poets are mystics, and I find a lot of information in poetry. Philosophy and information is recycled from one person to the next, and this is a good thing. It keeps the knowledge alive. Carolyn Myss would say we are "modern mystics without monasteries."

**What do you think about coincidence?**

I've noticed that when I have a client who cancels an appointment, there invariably is something else that comes up for me that is more pressing than meeting with a client. Is that coincidence? It might be. Something happened to me very recently that I would consider a synchronistic event. For about a week, a nagging and uncomfortable thought had been occurring to me as I was driving. I kept asking myself, "What would I do if the brakes went out?" Would I head for the ditch, would the car roll, would I try to get to the shoulder of the road and coast to a stop? The following week I was driving to Milwaukee from Sun Prairie and I decided to take the Highway 83 exit to hit the fast food places because I was hungry for popcorn. Sure enough, my brakes went out. I put my foot to the floor and just barely stopped in front of a convenience store.

It was a fiasco, but in the middle of it all, I found eleven pennies on the pavement, and that's my master number. I think it was an indication telling me I had been fortunate, but I really should have been paying attention to my thoughts of a week ago. Another strange thing that happened was that the *left* side of my headphones went out, and it was the *left* brake that was so worn. After repair of the brakes, the headset worked again, too. Is that an indication that I wasn't listening to myself? There are subtle connections here. Listen and pay attention to yourself.

# S. Mir'iam Connelly

S. Mir'iam Connelly practices as a psycho-spiritual consultant and an energy practitioner offering "spiritual quickening." The Masters and Angelic Realm have guided Mir'iam since 1972. As a Reiki master-teacher, or an activator, she prompts others to connect in joy to their own personal missions. Mir'iam has co-authored personal growth programs and presented inner healing retreats throughout the United States and Canada. Her education includes a three-year spiritual guidance program, a three-year program in transpersonal development, and a program with Don Campbell in healing with color and sound. Mir'iam is an inter-faith ordained minister and offers ritual and ceremony as a component of her work. She conducts workshops, teaches small groups, retreats, charka classes, and works with various priests who are interested in her skills and intuitive abilities. Mir'iam lives in Belleville, Wisconsin.

**Contact information**

S. Mir'iam Connelly
57 Karl Avenue
Belleville, WI    53508
**Phone:**  608-424-1922
**E-mail:**  *radiatory1@hotmail.com*
　　　　*rumella@mhtc.net*

### What mystical arts do you practice today?

Who indeed is a mystic? I consider meditation a practice that leads one into the mystery of spirit. The activity of meditation has taken me into a place of transpersonal self where I can set aside ego issues. Really, we are never quite finished with that. When I think of mystical arts, I look at anything from clairvoyance, to meditation, to a way of life. I've tried to incorporate what I've learned on my journey as a means of allowing my gifts to come forth. However, I am cautious, because if we are hung up on looking at the gifts, then we lose the mystical element to the ego.

I have to give all my credit to the Divine Source or Spirit. A lot of the things I do have just come to me and I am directed to teachers or books later, as a confirmation of what I am doing. I've been intuitive since I was a child, and I prefer to call myself an intuitive. I use the label "psychic" with caution, despite my abilities to tap into information. A psychic enters the realm of the astral plane where there are dangers in the form of entities that seek to attach to the energy field of an unsuspecting person. Indeed, some of my work has been in the field of exorcism of such entities.

It seems like these confused and misdirected entities look for life energy to cling to, and some entities are strong negative thought forms of the living. People with psychic abilities who often enter an astral plane need to be cautious of being drawn into a dark side. This is visible to me in some people. It's wise to ask yourself about how am I directing my life and what are the consequences. Am I seeking only the Light? On the other hand, am I too eager to find information, and not very fussy about how it comes to me. Some people are caught up in the glamour of a mysterious place and seeking esoteric information, and this takes away from the domain of the mystic. The glamour is one of the things that ego likes to play with, and we all go there sometimes. Exposing yourself to a dark side is dangerous. I recognize these people, and their energy field holds heaviness, almost like a depression per se.

### How did you develop these abilities?

My abilities unfolded and had a life of their own. Initially, I was a trained spiritual director. I noticed that people carried their bodies in certain ways when they discussed particular issues. Later, while working as a massage therapist, I would place my hands on the client and could feel heat and vibrations in certain areas. During meditation one day, I received instruction to go to a bookstore, look on the third shelf, and locate a blue book that had an illustration of hands on the cover, and then read the book. Well, I thought this was silly, and I dilly-dallied around that day and finally made the trip to the bookstore. I located a blue book on Reiki that told me all the things I had already been doing. I then took instruction for certification in Reiki. That's an example of how something happens in my life, and then it is verified in some other way.

In the 1970's I started singing or speaking in a different language. At first, I was frightened of this. A friend awakened me at 2 a.m. the same night this happened and informed me that she had been told to pray for me. I thanked her, and said I was going through quite an ordeal. She asked me, "Do you know about singing or speaking in other tongues?" I had connected with our parish priest the next day to see what was going on, and he affirmed the situation. This is another example of the kinds of things that unfold for me. I have learned there are several ways to look at this phenomenon. A language of the Spirit speaks in prayer to God, or to whom we see as God. Another explanation is that it is soul language, or soul song, that can touch other souls, and bring healing. More recently, I have learned it is the voice of the ancient ones. Everything develops if you allow it to, and are discerning in the process.

**Have you studied other areas of mysticism?**

I was a child who really loved nature and saw all of creation as being part of me and me a part of it. When I was married, I took the religion of my husband as my own, and I loved it. Eventually grew out of it because I wasn't fitting into structures of formal religion. Then I started to study Buddhism and other religions to expand myself and get a feel for what my spiritual pathway was. The only thing I practice from that experience is meditation. Sometimes I love it, and sometimes I struggle with it. Meditation can really shift you into your body or into your pain and emotions. It can take you to a place that shows you how to heal, but sometimes it is not fun. Meditation is my attempt to live from soul rather than ego.

**Meditation seems to have a grip on you.**

Yes, it is a link, and it can be practiced without a dogma surrounding it. I encourage people to learn meditation and be persistent in it. People make a mistake in thinking they want to give it up. That's usually a critical time and it is at a juncture where the most improvement is about to be made. We often times are judging ourselves and judging our meditation. If we persist, instead of abandoning it, we can refine and move forward. Always be open to find the intuitive parts. This is possible for everyone.

**Do you find there is a common thread in people who practice mystical arts?**

Yes, the sense of surrender is the common thread. A person can avoid using gifts or practicing the arts out of fear. To take the power from fear and move forward, there has to be a surrender of the fear. Awareness of fear and releasing it in faith is what I use to dispel it.

**What is your answer to the skeptic?**

I think everyone has to experience something phenomenal before that person actually starts to believe. It has to be some kind of personal incident that delivers the message there is something greater I actually don't know about, and want to investigate. Many times, this opportunity comes in the form of a crisis. Believing will take root, if that personal experience is honored.

**Are there any criticisms that come along with the territory?**

There was a major person in my life who criticized the "unusual," so that was my "growth person." Now I consider the person to have been a gift who assisted my process. He prompted me to stand my own ground, and I am grateful for this.

**Is there anything unique about practicing in Wisconsin?**
Madison is quite open. In the smaller communities there seems to be more black-and-white thinking and fundamentalism. When I come up against that, I change my language and speak from a place where the people can understand. It's almost a bilingual situation. I am careful about introducing my thoughts on "energy body" for example. To the fundamentalists, the healer in their lives is Jesus, so when I speak of Jesus leaving the Spirit as an advocate, right away they connect to that because it is part of their faith and background. I continue to say that when Jesus left the advocate (Holy Spirit), that means there is a stirring within us, which allows us to open to our intuition (which is the gift of Spirit). We can then continue from there into energy training.

**Do world events affect your abilities?**
What is happening cosmically is the important thing. World events are energy, but we can apply our energy of love to manifest as much power as we can as individuals to help. When September 11, 2001, happened, a small group of us headed for the East Coast. An assortment of energy workers had done the same. When there is such a loss of life and such drama to the situation, it is an initiation for humanity.

This year there have been more cosmic flares, which are actually electromagnetic energy, than there have been in hundreds of years. This tires me and some days I could just drop from fatigue. I went through an interesting, although very frustrating time, when my electromagnetic energy field was fragmented. My small electrical appliances were figuratively and sometimes literally, "blowing up." I lost my microwave. I lost my coffee pot, a coffee grinder, a toaster, and the hard drive on my computer! I didn't know what to do! My lights were even flickering.

**Obviously, your Midas touch was acting out of sorts... so what did you do?**
I went to a practitioner whom I know, and he told me my electromagnetic field was looking for energy. He said this happens when the field is fragmented. The body looks for some-

thing electrical to bring the pieces back together. The practitioner worked on me and I haven't had any electrical instances happen since that time.

**Were there any more "fragmenting" events?**

In 1973 I was hospitalized on Christmas Eve in Dayton, Ohio, with a very serious illness. The surrounding situation in my emotional life was especially complex also. I had to undergo surgery, and at the time, I prayed that if I could live a life that was fulfilling and give credit to my Creator and assist humanity, then I wanted to live, otherwise I wanted to leave. The next thing I remember was that I was on the ceiling looking down at my gray and lifeless body. I did not remember anything until two days later. Seven days after the surgery, I was recovered and working, and had gained new energy and thought forms. The doctor said it was an unusual recovery after such a major procedure. I was understanding scripture with a new depth that lead me to easily see into situations. I didn't know me and neither did my husband.

Three years ago, a clairvoyant friend said to me, "Have you ever thought that perhaps you came from another place? Possibly a difference essence of your soul took the place of the old essence." She defined it as a "walk-in" which is a soul exchange where one soul is wanting out and another has been waiting to come in with particular information and gifts. I understand that it's possible to have an out-of-body experience and re-enter with another part of one's "oversoul." Whether or not I have a different soul at this point, or facet of my oversoul — well, who knows? When you talk about part of your essence being from a different place, most people don't understand this. When changes were occurring, I realized I was not going crazy and was still a normal person. I continued to be level-headed and those were good signs! Discovering this fragmented part of myself and choosing to anchor it, was mystical.

**Do you belong to a structured religion or take a universal approach?**

A structured religion is appropriate for anyone who is in that place and I do not judge it. I feel I have moved to a place where dogma and hierarchical structures no longer fit me. I can enjoy the structure and ceremony with someone else, but I can't stay in that structure because it goes against my truth.

**When you are out and about, are your abilities on hold or is there an on-off switch?**

Yes, I can temper and turn off my abilities. Really, it is an invasion to other people to gather information energetically without permission. It's a matter of spiritual law and ethics.

**What are your views on charging?**

There has to be an energy exchange, and that is not necessarily monetary. It can be a labor exchange, or food, or whatever the person has. If you begin giving away gifts you have, people start thinking of them as unimportant or of lesser value. They also tend to give away their own sense of power, making you the guru or the healer. Realistically, they are the healer or the Wise One, and I am merely the facilitator.

**What about psychic hot lines advertised on television?**

It's fluff.

**What is the opinion of your family and friends regarding your work?**

My older sons think I am a little weird. They don't like to talk about alternative medicine or anything else I may do...but they might call a 900 psychic hotline...just kidding. Part of it is that they are all gifted, but they deny it and have some fear regarding abilities. My daughter is interested in the work and freely talks about it. I've never had any problems with friends, and they are very accepting people. I think we draw to ourselves some of the character that we are, and we draw to ourselves those who need and accept what we have to offer. I honor beliefs of others, and accept that not all will see things as I do.

**Do you think there is power in prayer or wishful thinking?**

Yes, there is certainly power in prayer. I have seen it work many times. Instead of wishful thinking, I would use the term "intention." A directed intention has a power too. It's my belief that God or Godess will honor a prayer no matter what; however, it may be more complicated than one might think, and the answer may not come as we perceive it "should." The Franciscan nuns in La Crosse, Wisconsin, who have lived long and hard lives, pray for people, and miracles have happened. Collective prayer is especially powerful. We must be careful not to direct a prayer, as we would will it, but to direct it to the best interest. We may think we know what that is, but often times we don't because we're emotionally attached to the outcome and can't be objective.

In the past, I have seen people who are passionate about their faith who can't get past the superficial. Some will seek the "great high" or "touch of God" all the time, and that is impossible to achieve. A number of people try so very hard, while others just allow, and there is a big difference. I think one thing that hinders prayer is an attitude that there is only one correct way to enter into a dialogue with the Divine. Maybe answers to prayers take this into consideration.

**If a person comes back through reincarnation, is that person gone from the other side? Not that I'm trying to be difficult here, but the question suddenly popped up.**

The soul is not disconnected, you might say. You are always connected to the essence of that soul wherever it may be — past, present, or future — and that soul may be in many places. The collectiveness of the soul is called the oversoul. The Keys of Enoch and various ancient holy writings, including the Holy Scripture, which was not allowed to be part of the Bible, give some indication to this belief. A teacher of the divine told me there are 144,000 essences of any master, such as the divine Mother Mary, which are continuously on the planet. Let's say you are sitting here and a part of your essence is of Mary Magdalene, and I carry the essence of Mary or whomever. My whole essence is not Mary nor is your whole essence Mary Magdalene. A part of you that is the essence of Mary Magdalene, however, will live in the here-and-now from that sense of history and accumulated knowledge that you have in your soul. We may have some mysterious recognition of each other when meeting for the first time. When a person leaves this life, the essence that person carries moves to another individual for collective humanity. Since given this information, I have seen it in other sources.

I have a belief that one of my grandchildren carries the essence of my mother. She talks of a grandmother who was deceased before she was born, and she does some of the same motions with her hands that my mother used to do. If we have these multiple essences in our oversoul, the person who has crossed over can send part of the essence here to be honored and anchored again to learn more. I believe the child will not have that one particular essence exclusively. She will have multiple soul essences as we all do. Who really knows if that is the soul truth? With everything we discover, we find more questions that arise.

### On the topic of children with abilities, what do you say?

Children need to be encouraged and affirmed in what they see, what they hear, and what they feel is true. Don't underestimate this. The children coming in are a means to change old ways and structures that are no longer working…governmental, medical, educational, spiritual, you name it. We shall likely see that their intelligence is greater than our own, and as parents and teachers, our frustrations may mount. Think of the pain they may incur when they have an inner knowing that surpasses the elders around them. Our task is to *listen* to the children and *learn*.

### How do messages come through to you — images, scents, feelings, symbols?

All of this occurs. Instant thoughts where I "just know" happen a lot. Sometimes I experience scents. I visited Holy Hill near Milwaukee with a friend once. She looked at me somewhat strangely and whispered, "Do you smell anything?" I told her that I smelled roses, and since there were no flowers present, this was Divine Mother Mary and our experience was one of a visitation. It was a long stretch for my friend because she is very fundamental. We have to pay attention to all of our senses.

One tough test that has followed me is that of having only

enough information to get me from one step to the next. When I act upon or speak of the information, then I can move forward, but not until I've completed what is required in that first step. I call this "co-creation."

**Your definition of mysticism is...?**

I don't know if I have an adequate definition of the mystic. I don't think I can put myself even in the category of "ordinary mystic" because I feel like one must have years and years of spiritual voyaging. Perhaps mysticism is an element of the unexplainable in knowing that there is something greater than you are, that is operating in your life. I do believe I have had some mystical experiences and that Spirit constantly offers opportunity to strengthen our connection to other realities. I accept this with gratitude.

**Do you have any cautions for those who seek a reader?**

Go with your gut feeling. If you feel nervous, agitated, heavy, and are aware of your senses, listen to them. Beware of negative things. Remember that a prediction is merely something that is possible. If we poison someone's mind with negative predictions, then we help draw that energy nearer, and that's not a good thing. What we think of only grows larger because we also pull power in around it.

**Do you have an explanation for coincidence or synchronicity?**

Both happen. I see coincidence as "god-happenings" and synchronicity as Spirit keeping us on the right track at the right time. I don't like to key-hole experiences, however. Sometimes people read things as "signs" of something else because it makes sense to them. It is important not to read something as having a particular meaning because we *want* it to happen that way. We have as many means to why and how spirituality and the soul unfold, as there are people. There is always a *process* occurring. I have a friend who has gone to various practitioners, and it doesn't matter what kind whether they are traditional or alternative, psychic or other, she always gives total credit for her journey to the practitioner of the day. Unfortunately, she is dismissing the entire rich history of how *she* worked, and *she* accepted, and *she* progressed. There is a process to it all, not just a lone experience that got us to where we are. Being in the right place at the right time is an assist, and Divine timing does happen!

### Do you have any messages, goals, or final comments?

I was invited to my class reunion in Minnesota, but was unable to attend, so wrote a letter to the class. To my surprise, I received a very long letter in return with comments from people at the reunion. It was an awakening for me, because what came out in the letter was that my classmates remember me as always listening and interested in things. I had taken this for granted, and did not realize this years ago. Although, I do remember my mother yelling at me as a child to get down off the roof of the barn...so, I can't say I was exactly listening all the time. My goal is to continue with listening and having an interest in assisting people to be empowered no matter what it takes—energy work, a reading, whatever. I want to allow gifts to unfold.

The root of achieving anything is to have trust in oneself. Sometimes we have been wounded to the point where it is difficult to find that battered trust, but it's still there. Once you have trust in yourself, and once you accept the body that you have, you are on your way. Things will unfold more and more. As I mentioned before, there is a process, and it is not necessarily a mad passionate love affair right away. For the world, I would wish that we unearth some unity within humanity. We are fighting whom? And what is it are we fighting about? We are just fighting ourselves. We are all one, and I think we've lost sight of that. My prayer is that we bring peace and compassion to this planet as we enter these new times.

# Ken-Adi Ring

Ken-Adi Ring is the founding director of Tri-Unity Wellife, LLC, which is a Madison-based wellness and education center since 1975. A registered massage therapist and Reiki master, among his specialties are Swedish Esalen massage-body work, neuromuscular therapy, shiatsu, and acupressure. He is a certified instructor in the yoga sciences for health and self-realization. Ken is a clairvoyant practicing in the art of Tarot (Voyager) reading, graphology, runes, and the *I-Ching* (Chinese oracle). He is well known throughout Wisconsin for bringing speakers, authors, and other talents to Madison on a grand scale. He has arranged such engagements for Dan Millman, Joan Borysenko M.D., Wayne Dyer PhD., Bernie Siegel M.D., Deepak Chopra M.D., and many others. On a local Madison level, Ken organizes and presents intuitive arts exhibits and metaphysical fairs several times a year. His wife, Sally R. Ring, events manager for Tri-Unity Wellife, is an integral and essential component of the Tri-Unity Wellife LLC organization.

## Contact information

Ken-Adi Ring
Tri-Unity Wellife, LLC
1605 Monroe Street, Suite B1
Madison, WI 53711
**Phone:** 608-256-0080
**Fax:** 608-256-0082
**E mail:** *karing@wellife.org*
**Web site:** *www.wellife.org*

**What brought you into the realm of mystical arts?**

The first thing that I remember about being inspired — and that's how it is — it is a "calling," or somehow being chosen by something outside of myself, I felt "different." From about the age of 6 or 7, I sensed that I was unusual, but back then we called it weird. At times, I even felt persecuted. Curious, I was asking questions such as, "What about reincarnation, Dad?" He informed me there was no such thing and I should not talk about it. Although my parents are wonderful, they were Catholic, so things like that were out of bounds.

I spent some time daydreaming while growing up on the farm, and I was amazed at all of nature. I wanted to express myself and experience it all. I took it to the nth degree and then sort of lost it for a while. At age 19, I had an out-of-body experience related to extensive burns from a horrendous car accident that I barely survived. From then on, I took life much more seriously. Massage therapy that I received while recovering in the hospital contributed significantly to my healing, and it inspired me. After those experiences, I studied meditation and yoga in a pursuit for "answers." Sometimes we don't like life's lessons, but they happen anyway. Serious burns, physical trauma, the healing journey, and a search for answers led me to establish a wellness center that has served Madison for over twenty-five years.

**Tri-Unity Wellife Center?**

The Tri-Unity Wellife Center originally evolved from massage work and the teaching of yoga sciences. Today, it has expanded. It affords an opportunity to bring people together under a multicultural roof to strive for an evolution of consciousness. The Center is magnanimous in that respect. Bringing in well-known speakers, production of the Wellife Exp, meditation classes, psychic and metaphysical events all assist people in helping and healing themselves. We are a healing organization that focuses on a unification of body, mind, and spirit. Three levels of Christian Deity and three levels that are a part of Hinduism, influence the title Tri-Unity. Wellife was coined from well plus life. The motto is *Harmonious Integration of Body, Mind, and Spirit.*

The mighty and the little struggles in life were compassion builders for me. You might say this evolved through my dealings with pain. People learn by pain, although pain is not necessary for learning. Yes, pain does teach you — *it really does teach you*. It grabs your attention as a wake-up call. The first premise in Buddhism is "there is suffering." It is how one relates to the struggle and suffering in life, that teaches. As I grow in middle years, I am aware there is a lot of learning left to do. I need to continually get out and nurture others, as I learn myself. The way I do it is under the umbrella of Tri-Unity Life. A number of volunteers and part time people assist in the organization. Somehow, we all bring forth great things. I couldn't do it alone. We create five to ten events per year. It is a great opportunity for me to grow as well as to give.

**What does your own practice consist of?**
I am a massage therapist/healer and yoga instructor. I have done this professionally since 1975. I'm currently offering classes for the "chronologically gifted" (the elderly) and physically challenged people. Because of my physical limitations, due to recent knee surgery, I am catering to that group. I have worked in the area of handwriting analysis (graphology) and Tarot card reading for many years as well. I have been practicing *I Ching* for about thirty years and was formally trained by a visiting Chinese professor, Dr. Richard Ho, who later became my mentor and friend.

Gestalt therapy, neurolinguistic programming, EST training, also known as Erhard Seminars Training that works in personal development traditions drawing from Buddhism to Scientology, contributed to a transforming growth process. I decided I wanted to bring this kind of awareness to people. My first endeavor was to create a festival in a naturescape, rather than a closed-in hotel convention room. So, the first Mother Earth Festival was born in 1978 at Black Hawk Ridge, Wisconsin. The weekend event consisted of Native American ritual, yoga, tai chi, relationship workshops, other kinds of work, and vegetarian meals. It was a very health environment to bring people into for three days. As we drove out to the sight for the very first festival, it was raining, which was not the greatest weather for a naturescape event. When we arrived however, the rain stopped, the sun appeared, and a rainbow spread across the sky. I believed this indeed was an auspicious sign. Since the first one, we produced eighteen annual festivals. We are considering bringing it back for a 20th year, and have been getting inquiries and requests to do so. People felt transformed and rejuvenated from the experience.

**Your brush with the illustrious is a rather unique activity. How do you manage that?**

I have met world famous speakers, authors, and cutting edge teachers by attending their seminars and lectures, and book signings. After my flashy smile and frequent connections with them, they started recognizing me and I simply said, "Would you like to come to Wisconsin to speak?" Eventually I asked enough times for them to take notice and then they gave me contact numbers. Most famous people are very authentic and nice to be around, but I can't say they are all that way. Maybe so much attention has jaded some of them. I don't know, but I think they get tired sometimes. Generally, I love bringing these innovative celebrities to town and associating with interesting people.

The first best selling author Tri-Unity Wellife brought to town was Dan Millman, author of *Way of the Peaceful Warrior.* We had a modest audience of 200 people at the Barrymore Theater in Madison and it was a wonderful event. People loved it. Being a nationally renowned gymnast originally, he even lifted to a handstand off the side of the table. Mr. Millman was a marvelous person to visit with, and a teacher who "walks his talk." The next speaker we brought in was Dr. Joan Borysenko, former director of the Mind-Body Clinic at Harvard Medical School. The way I managed to bring Dr. Borysenko to Madison was rather bold. I traveled to Boulder (no pun intended), Colorado, drove right up to her house, and knocked on the door. Wouldn't you know it, she wasn't home, so I talked to her office manager and we set up some dates. It was an amazing event, and over six hundred people attended. We were off and running; following this with the Mystical Arts of Tibet, an entourage of twelve Tibetan Monks who performed sacred and cultural dance and overtone chanting.

When I attend various expos and events, I take the opportunity to see and feel what it is these talented people do, and how the audience reacts and responds to them. I scope it out. When in the role of producer, I tend to see it from my eyes, and I enjoy seeing it from the eyes of the audience too. If I am impressed, I try to make use of that impression. Madison is a small to medium-sized city, and most of these high profile speakers tend to go to the big cities such as Chicago, San Francisco, or New York. I decided the Madison community has a lively and vibrant audience for this, and banked on it. The large attendance at events has proven a good indicator. Wayne Dyer, Deepak Chopra, and Neale Donald Walsch were all great. I was especially impressed by Dr. Chopra with his quiet reservation, yet strong sincere presence.

**Compared to a few years ago, what changes have you seen in mystical interests?**

Since September 11, 2001, something quite different is happening. Such apparent and visible turmoil is not just affecting the "other guys." We are seriously affected by it. We are scrambling to do something about it, and it is a wake-up call for world consciousness. Since that devastating tragedy, speakers such as Deepak Chopra, have spoken to this terrible event with hope. I believe we are all seeing a more serious, careful, and studied work as to where we park our mind, where we spend our time, and where we put our energy. Yet Spirit or mystic mind is as alive now as it ever has been. It seems challenged, yet it is quite alive. There is resurgence. We are bringing ourselves to wakefulness and it's about time. Unfortunately, we learn by a kick in the butt—we learn through pain, and that was the pain of September 11. Our whole civilization and its cultures are feeling the fallout of that pain. I truly am a team player when it comes to encouraging the world to listen to itself and find a positive way of response.

**Do you believe there is a common thread in the universe?**

Yes. I believe there is a common thread throughout the universe. The Deepak Chopras of the world are the large waves in the ocean, but everything trickles down to the droplets—the individuals. We can all aspire to be larger waves, yet we are part of the same ocean. We are touched by, and evolving out of the God Force. It doesn't matter whether you believe it or not. It's there. The books *Listen Humanity,* and *God Speaks* by Meher Baba, and *The Taboo Against Knowing Who You Really Are*, by Allan Watts, are "giant waves" that really influenced me in my world, mystic view. Awe-inspiring.

### Definition of a mystic?

Anyone who practices, feels, believes, and senses the eloquence of Spirit running through him or her. The mystic considers him or herself an intimate part of the universe and is able to harmonize with it for the benefit of self and others. The mystic is one who knows and feels the entire world is a living entity. Negative sides exist, because we are creative beings, and we believe there is darkness, and we want to play with this. It's an illusion. The ego, playing with a mystical experience, says, "Wow, this is coming from me—I'm strong and powerful and can manipulate this." Be careful for yourself and others. Remember that to help someone where there is not permission or need, can push someone further into illusion. Many experiences are mystical and uplifting when you experience them, including pain. Ask who is experiencing this. And from where is the experience coming? You'll find the answer is the same. I paraphrase an old Buddhist saying, "before enlightenment chop wood, carry water; after enlightenment, carry water, chop wood."

### Where do the notoriously "evil" people fit into the menagerie?

It's all about the ways people have applied their egotistic perceptions of grandeur. The pain, and the challenge of pain, filtered through misconceptions, somehow leads to charismatic power that glows in the dark. In the process of overcoming the challenges, darkness catches up with them, and the perception of power becomes them. They run with this when they aren't ready to do so. The result can be unbelievably widespread harm. They view their deeds as approved and hand stamped by God or Allah or whomever. Yet, they are blind and cold to the pain and tragedy they cause. Duality is the thing — it is a perception of separateness. Limited awareness is used and abused. Evil wants to create an effect, but it's usually "my effect is better than your effect." It is a big lie. Look at the Crusades or the Holocaust. It's happened throughout history and it's still happening today! Chain links of history are connected and there are lessons to learn.

### Do you have an answer for the skeptic?

It's healthy to be a skeptic, and not simply to believe because someone says it is so. I'm skeptical of about half of what people say they can do or have done. If the skill is demonstrated clearly enough and I get a good feeling from it, I can then support it. That's how I bring psychics to my fairs. I do interviews by receiving a reading from them to see how authentic they are, and how much they know about the subject, and to determine if I can sense an internal sensitivity in them that will listen to people. I can usually tell this when I meet a person. It may be a subtle warm feeling, or it may be a feeling of dislike. First impressions almost always resonate for me in further meetings with the person. We all have to beware of error, however, because what might be triggered is some of our own personal background linked to others in our history. More often than not, your feelings are right-on though. I've made a couple of mistakes in screening psychics and have let go of a few who did not meet my standards.

The Amazing Randi is a guy who's out to prove *everything* outside of the realm of the senses is hocus-pocus. He is beyond skeptic. He is a non-believer and close-minded. If we knew it all, nobody, including reputable scientists, would be researching and seeking. For whatever reason, the non-believer has dire memories of childhood, or strong indoctrinated training from their religion of origin. Skepticism is a healthy thing. Just as in buying a pair of shoes, you really need to try them on, before you take them home. Be open to possibilities, however.

Equally as dangerous is the religious fundamentalist. The dangerousness there could be comparable to what we see in the terrorist. A fundamentalist in *any* direction, whether we're talking about a non-believer fundamentalist, or a Bible or Korantoting fundamentalist, is dangerous to all other paths. There's a pathology and sociopathic flavor about them. The mystic favors a compassion for openness and a passion to seek it.

**Anything unique about practicing in Wisconsin?**

Wisconsin has the ambiance, and wonderful magical mysticism of Celtic Ireland. The four seasons speak in equal messages. Not one of them gives us too much calamity such as drought or flooding or forest fires. Everything seems to have a balance, especially in the southern areas of Wisconsin—not too much snow or cold, but enough to appreciate it. Mystically, Wisconsin is a fairyland. Spring has an expression of yearning and growth. Summer brings richness and vibrancy. In the fall, things become seasoned, and the winter brings us those misty soft snowfalls — a time to go within. It is just a magical place. Nature, for me, gives it full expression. If you can't live within the bounty of nature, you cannot call yourself a mystic. Wisconsin thrives in mysticism.

**What would you advise clients be aware of when seeking a reader?**

Listen to your own intuitive revelations about what is being said to you. Pay attention to your feelings about the reader or healer. It's okay not to jump or bolt at the first impression because of what you might perceive as negative, or lacking, or less than, or not touching base, yet take caution. Be patient, spend time, and give some feedback so there is an energy generating in the reading. It's more than body language. It's the energy and light that you have. When all is said and done, a person should be the true guide to himself or herself. Be cautious of any out-and-out negative statement about yourself or your future. No one can confirm that because there are so many variables. You *are* in charge of your life and you are the center of your universe. All a psychic can do is open the door for you to let yourself in. Some psychics are more gifted than others are. It's best if they come from a deep spiritual place.

**What's your opinion about the psychic hot lines?**

I think they are all scams, really. Maybe some talented

psychics are hired, but the largest share of the money goes to the promoters. Many people are suckered into it, because there is such need and wonderment about it. I would not advise calling these lines. It's best if you can meet the practitioner and have a good strong referral from a friend or someone you trust. Treat it as carefully as hiring a counselor.

### Comments about the hardcore scientific minded?

The scientific minded are brilliant people. A number of the so-called hardcore scientific, must portray themselves as such, but believe me, they are exploring too. They aspire to the empirical, hard truth, litmus paper test about what's really going on in the world. Sometimes they're struck by unexplainable enlightening in the process. They run head-on into synchronicity, scratch their heads, and ponder how in the world did that happen. A number of scientists are developing into cosmic pioneers and unveiling an exploration into the unknown. Black hole phenomenon is as psychic and psychotic as anything is...and what in the world (or out of the world) is it...Star Trek, Star Wars? The macrocosm and microcosm are where the pioneer's quest is.

### Excuse the redundancy, but... what are your thoughts on thoughts?

Thoughts we create exist somewhere in this unbelievably vast universe. They exist in some dimension, even if it's not in the dimension in which we live. A mystic's calling is to be open in thought to the close-mindedness of other people. Paths of restriction are as authentic as the mystic's path. Narrow mindedness of any breed fundamentalist kills all other paths and all other possibilities, when indeed all paths lead back to the source.

### Do you have a goal or mission?

I have a mission to serve life and wellness to every Soul on the planet including myself. Love is always the backdrop. You must be ultimately Selfish with a capital "S." "Selfish" means knowing you are an intimate part of every thing. By intimate, I mean knowing that your well-being is affected by everything else in the Universe that is unhappy, not satisfied, or not nurtured. Take care of yourself emotionally, spiritually, and physically so that you can represent yourself as the best you can be to the world. Make a rippling effect in the universe.

### Do you have any final thoughts you want to manifest?

Love is all there is. It's as simple as that. We are all connected. Taking care of ourselves is an act of love to another person. The more we accept love, the more we can express it. Know that by hugging a tree, you're not necessarily a liberal democrat. Ha! In hugging a tree, one feels the tree, and the tree feels you...that's a mystic. A saying among the Native Americans— *Mitakuye Oyasin*—we are all related.

# Resources

# Epilogue

## The Balance of Science and Spirituality

In preparation for writing this book, I examined numerous publications related to mysticism and spirituality, theories of the mind and consciousness, physics, philosophy, psychic phenomena, and mediumship. When I scrutinize this complex alchemy, what I see is a reserved, but *exciting* interlocking. Scientific pieces of a universal jigsaw puzzle frame themselves with mystery. Even though this is an old battlefront of sorts, opposing sides are beginning to call a cautious but bonding truce. Polarity is lessening, and respect is tiptoeing into the picture. Science does not disappear, but neither do mystical events that are subtle, but difficult to dismiss as rational wisdom gone awry.

Let's examine some illustrations of *combination* and *balance* in science and spirituality. In 1981, four years after the death of his 14-year-old son Aaron, Rabbi Harold S. Kushner wrote the book, *When Bad Things Happen to Good People*. He left us with this message:

> I think of Aaron and all that his life taught me, and I realize how much I have lost and how much I have gained. Yesterday seems less painful and I am not afraid of tomorrow.

This speaks of balance. In Aaron's short life, the advances of science were unable to save him. At the same time, prayers of compassion and hope were unable to keep him with us. Aaron was diagnosed with a condition at the age of 3 that would not permit him to live far into his teenage years. The gifts and teachings left by this young Soul for his family and friends were far stronger than science and prayer combined. Aaron's death was both a physical medical event and a metaphysical event. Rabbi Kushner and his family painfully experienced the dual

flames of science and spirituality in a candle burning at both
ends. In the end, they accepted them both.

Combination and balance of science and mysticism is discussed in Norman Friedman's book, *Bridging Science and Spirit.*[1]
In his discussion, he says:

> A determinist would say that if all the information for the
> entire universe, were available, then the laws of physics would
> be perfectly accurate. That would be closing the spectrum on
> one end. Bohr[2] closes the spectrum on the other end, by
> saying there is a final ambiguity (randomness) that can never
> be made orderly by more information — in effect, a kind of
> quantum randomness. The essence of Bohm's[3] view is that
> the information spectrum is infinite on both ends of the con-
> tinuum. A physical system never contains *all* the information
> necessary for a complete and detailed description.

Friedman offers an analogy, and suggests viewing this as if
we are climbing a mountain (of information) that is infinitely
high. On each plateau, a broader vista is available (i.e. there is
more information), but we can never see everything (information is never complete). He says, "We might say that the mystic
is on a higher plateau, that the mystic's view is broader, but not
as detailed as the physicist's view from a lower plateau. But the
mystic's information is also incomplete, because that level of
order is also a subset of a greater truth."

So, we have the physicist on the lower plateau deciphering
detail by doing the math. At the same time, we have the mystic
on the high end, looking at the broader and qualitative scope of
esoteric knowledge. Yet neither has complete information because they are both subsets of a greater truth. I tend to look at
this as the mystic saying to the physicist, "I can see what's ahead
out there, but I can't see all of it. If you do the math to tell me
where I am, both of us can continue climbing up the mountain." If this is the case, the physicist, in a way, uses the mystic
as the pioneering lookout, while the mystic uses the physicist to
confirm the compass coordinates, Both depend on each other
— combination and balance once again.

The mystic tells us that accidents do not happen; everything is connected. Author Craig S. Bell did a study of connections in his book, *Comprehending Coincidence.* He tells us that

in his view, "any experience that is very unusual and unexpected should be considered a potential coincidence. If something could have happened hundreds or thousands of times before, but did not and then on one particular occasion it does happen, this is a potential coincidence."

Bell goes on to assert that "the more intelligent behavior is to treat something as potentially meaningful—which may later be discarded if meaning cannot be established—rather than dismissing it in the first place as not worthy of consideration."

Bell identifies two basic types of coincidences. One type, *mirror coincidence*, is always associated with and is a reflection of a heightened concern, interest, or desire of the individual. He goes on to tell us that although the ability to identify mirror coincidences gives us greater capacity to understand the meaning of important events in our lives, that type of coincidence does not provide us with guidance on how to conduct our lives. On the other hand, *directional coincidences* do occur to guide us on our personal paths toward becoming richer, more evolved human beings. Mr. Bell's true-life examples of directional coincidences illustrate that they are often subtle, rather than sensational. But he notes that if we are open and receptive to them, they will occur when needed to assist us on our life's journey. And, in fact, as I revealed in my prologue, that was my experience in relation to how this work became a reality.

Mr. Bell tells us that in considering a metaphysical basis for the existence of meaning in coincidence, answers are provided from a combination of modern physics of the West and metaphysical perceptions of the East, particularly India.[4] Again, we find a meeting and analyzing of science and spirituality—combination and balance that really does not tip the scales heavily toward any one side.

**\*\*\*\*\*\*\*\*\*\*\***

Let's look at the three illustrations I just presented. One comes from Rabbi Kushner whose *questioning* into the realms of mysticism made a universal contribution to the world when his book was translated into many languages. One comes from two renowned scientists of the 20th century, Niels Bohr, and David Bohm, as discussed in Norman Friedman's account. The physicists did not discount opening up to new paradigms that take into account explanations of the unknown. The last comes from Philosopher-Psychologist Craig Bell, who *literally* put "two and two together" and dissected patterns and incidents that were not easily explained away by chance. He asked himself the question, "If not chance, then what have we?"

What these three people have in common is that each of them recognized a duality not in parallel, but in a process of assimilation. They studied, they questioned, they theorized, and they struggled. The scientist became the spiritualist, and the spiritualist became the scientist. In their own ways, they all become the mystic who strives to see the big picture or the greater truth.

Maybe you are reading this book because spiritual answers or confirmations are lost in a black hole for you. Maybe the undecided scientific dabbler in you is just plain curious. Perhaps you merely grabbed this book on a whim, as I did when I bought *Comprehending Coincidence*. Why you're reading this book is relatively unimportant, and maybe there is no outstanding reason. The fact is, you own this book for the moment, and somehow and in some way, it will have significance for you. Again, the Mystic would tell you there are no accidents. What do you think? Be open and be aware.

### Madison, Wisconsin

It is the end of September 2002. I feel like I have been on such a grand adventure — challenging, alluring, energizing, and sometimes tiring. The people most patient with me were those whom I interviewed, and generous editors who provided critique. Patience seemed to be in their nature. Memorable moments, and even coincidences, continue to follow me.

As Kathleen Schneider, the psychic reader who predicted I would be writing this book in the year 2002, said to me a few years ago, "You have the final say." Therefore, I will take that liberty. Going into this project, I put on my dubious rabbit ears. Life to me is a hugely complex science project and we are all involved in it, some would even say, trapped in it. For my own benefit, I needed a "statistics boost," and I turned to some famous research work by J.B. Rhine of Duke University. He offered statistically significant evidence in support of precognition over the course of thirty-three experiments involving approximately a million trials. His work was successfully replicated in independent labs. I don't know if precognition is a mystical phenomenon, or a scientific event. Maybe it's somewhere in the balance. In any case, it exists.

I think I wanted to decide what was important to me, and I felt compelled to do further research. What I came to realize, and what I'd like to stress as essential, at least in my opinion, is *to have an open mind, but not necessarily an accepting mind.* Acceptance comes after scrutiny. I think the person who illustrates this best is Dr. Gary Schwartz. He was formerly the Director of Yale Psychophysiology Center, and is now Director of Human Systems Laboratory at the University of Arizona, and author of the book, *The Afterlife Experiments.* He took on the project of investigating the possibility of consciousness after death using a group of five well-known mediums. Dr. Schwartz clearly laid his reputation on the line, knowing this kind of research was as popular as Galileo's suggestion that the earth was not the center of the Universe. Schwartz mapped out his hypotheses, employed double blind experiments on mediumship, and even brought on what he termed the "Devil's Advocate Committee" to keep him on track and help him retain scientific detachment.

Results of three years of experiments were astounding, and supportive of the authenticity of mediumship. So compelling was the evidence that Schwartz *struggled* with the observations even in his own mind. He remarked that to dismiss this data would be committing the ultimate scientific sin of not accepting the responsibility of respecting the *reality of the facts.* Schwartz admitted that he was experiencing "a growing personal and professional fear." His fear was that when he summarized the results and integrated the observations, "I might be forced to conclude that — at least concerning the specific research mediums we worked with — the skeptics were completely wrong."[5] Dr. Schwartz astutely addresses the skeptic:

> It's one thing to be skeptical — open to alternative hypotheses. It's another to be *devoutly* skeptical — always 'knowing' that cheating, lying, fraud, and deception are the explanations for any not-yet-explainable phenomenon. What does it mean when a person

concludes that an event 'must be due to fraud' no matter how strong the data are? At what point does the instinct to dismiss data reflect a bias so strong that it begins to border on the pathological? Simply put, when does skepticism become skeptimania? When does skeptimania become so strong that a person will engage in double deception rather than report the facts as they actually occurred?

Although this was a carefully constructed scientific endeavor, there seemed to be a degree of soul-searching, for lack of a better term, in Dr. Schwartz's conclusions. I have the feeling he wasn't planning to go on that picnic. But, well... we know things don't happen by accident.

I suppose we could say this was my own flirtation with the notion of skepticism, in which case I really have to give my interviewees enormous credit. The people I met and interviewed have better things to do than dwell on the mind-set of the skeptic, and that seems to be a *freedom* they have strived for and earned through the years. For some people, this book will be an interesting diversion, for others it will be of help and comfort. Maybe the book will see its place in your garage sale waiting for the next curious soul to find it. But I do hope it turns out that you are the curious one. Perhaps the balance between science and mystical arts will meet you at a junction in your life where you could use a dash of both. In any case, thank you for accompanying me through these pages of mystery, wisdom, and common sense. I hope they did more than just stimulate your curiosity and raise a few questions.

\*\*\*\*\*\*\*\*\*\*

[1] Friedman, Norman, *Bridging Science and Spirit,* 1990, The Woodbridge Group.

[2] Niels Bohr (1885-1962) was best known for investigation of atomic structure and his work on radiation. He received the Nobel Prize in Physics in 1922. His three famous papers *On the quantum theory of spectra* were written between 1918 and 1922.

[3] David Bohm (1917-1992) worked on the Manhattan project in 1943 and became a Professor of Theoretical Physics at Princeton University, and Bristol University in London. In 1951, he wrote the classic text *Quantum Physics,* which gave a clear account of the Copenhagen interpretation of quantum physics formulated by Niels Bohr and Werner Heisenberg in the 1920's.

[4] Bell, Craig S., *Comprehending Coincidence Synchronicity and Personal Transformation, 2000,* Chrysalis Books.

[5] Schwartz, Gary E., *The Afterlife Experiments,* 2001, Simon and Schuster.

# Reading List

These books were recommended by interviewees. The list is not inclusive.

Andrews, Ted. *Animals-Speak: The Spiritual and Magical Powers of Animals Great and Small.*

Andrews, Ted. *Psychic Protection: Beginnings.*

Baba, Meher. *God Speaks.*

Baba, Meher. *Listen, Humanity.*

Bell, Craig S. *Comprehending Coincidence—Synchronicity and Personal Transformation.*

Browne, Sylvia. *Adventures of a Psychic.*

Chopra, Deepak. *Seven Spiritual Laws of Success.*

Crow Dog, Leonard, et.al. *Crow Dog: Four Generations of Sioux Medicine Men.*

Cunningham, Donna. *How to Read Your Astrological Chart—Aspects of the Cosmic Puzzle.*

Diamant, Anita. *The Red Tent.*

Edward, John. *Crossing Over.*

Elliot, William. *Tying Rocks to Clouds: Meetings and Conversations with Wise and Spiritual People.*

Emerson, Ralph Waldo. *The Essential Writings of Ralph Waldo Emerson [Essay: The Over-Soul].*

Ferguson, Marilyn. *The Aquarian Conspiracy.*

Forrest, Steven. *The Inner Sky.*

Fox, Matthew. *One River, Many Wells: Wisdom Springing From Global Faiths.*

Hall, Judy. *Way of Psychic Protection.*

Hanaker-Condag, Karen. *Foundations of Personality.*

Harner, Michael J. *Way of the Shaman.*

Hatch-Hanon, Geraldine. *Sacred Space—A Feminist Vision of Astrology.*

Hayes, Louise. (any titles)

Ingram, Julia, et.al. *The Messengers: A True Story of Angelic Presence.*

Lee, Scout Cloud. *The Circle is Sacred: A Medicine Book for Women.*

Mailes, Thomas. *Fools Crow: Wisdom and Power.*

McGaa, Ed. *Eagle Vision: Return of the Hoop.*

McGaa, Ed. *Native Wisdom: Perceptions of the Natural Way.*

Millman, Dan. *The Life You Were Born to Live.*

Millman, Dan. *The Way of the Peaceful Warrior.*

Myss, Caroline. *Anatomy of the Spirit: The Seven Stages of Power and Healing.*

Norman, Michael. *Haunted Wisconsin.*

Peck, M. Scott. *People of the Lie.*

Pert, Candace and Chopra, Deepak. *Molecules of Emotion.*

Redfield, James. *The Celestine Prophecy.*

Reed, Henry. *Edgar Cayce On Channeling the Higher Self.*

Rudhyar, Dane. (many titles on astrology).

Ruiz, Don Miguel. *The Four Agreements: A Practical Guide to Personal Freedom.*

Saraydarian, Torkom. *Battling Dark Forces—A Guide of Psychic Self Defense.*

Sarydarian, Torkom. *Obsession and Possession.*

Sarydarian, Torkom. *The Ageless Wisdom.*

Sogyal. *The Tibetan Book of Living and Dying.*

Sugrue, Thomas. *Story of Edgar Cayce There is a River.*

Tall Tree, Robert. *Legend of Spinoza: The Bear Who Speaks from the Heart.*

Tanner, Wilda. *Mystical Magical Marvelous World of Dreams.*

Tolle, Eckhart. *The Power of Now: A Guide to Spiritual Enlightenment.*

Transformation.

Van Praagh, James. *Reaching Heaven.*

Van Praagh, James. *Talking to Heaven: A Medium's Message of Life After Death.*

Vanzant, Iyanla. *One Day My Soul Just Opened Up.*

Vaughn, Frances. *Selections from a Course in Miracles.*

Walsch, Neale Donald. *Conversations With God: An Uncommon Dialogue (Book 1).*

Williamson, Marianne. *Healing the Soul of America.*

Wilson, Colin. *Afterlife.*

Wolf , Stacey. *Get Psychic!: Discover Your Hidden Powers.*

Work, Rich and Groth, Ann Marie. *Awaken to the Healer Within.*

Work, Rich and Groth, Ann Marie. *Proclamations of the Soul.*

Yaconelli, Michael. *Messy Spirituality: God's Annoying Love for Imperfect People.*

Zukav, Gary and Francis, Linda. *Heart of the Soul.*

Zukav, Gary. *Seat of the Soul.*

### Audio List
C.D.'s and cassette tapes recommended by interviewees

Cooper, David. *The Mystical Kabbalah Tapes.* (phone 1-800-333-9185)

Edward, John. *Understanding Your Angels and Meeting Your Guides.* (meditation)

Nakai, R. Carlos. Native American flutes.

Walsch, Neale Donald. *Communion With God.* ("It's just great; it's a stitch.")

### Books, Other Writings, and CD's by the Interviewees
Bright-Green, Sylvia. *The Making of a Mystic.* (book)

Hagemann, Anneliese and Hagemann, Doris. *Using the Inner Art of Dowsing in the    Search for My Spiritual Enlightenment.* (workbook)

Hagemann, Anneliese and Hagemann, Doris. *To Our Health.* (workbook)

Hagemann, Anneliese. *A Quick Guide to Body, Mind, Spirit Wellness.* (workbook)

Hagemann, Anneliese. *Dowsing/Divining.* (workbook)

Kay, Beverly. *The Blueprint of Your Soul.* (in progress)

Phoenix. *The Shield of Wrath—The Phoenix Speaks.* (book)

Smoker, Debbie. *Joy of Jamaica.* (book)

Smoker, Debbie. *Turn on Your Magic Eyes.* (book)

St. Germain. *Mantras for Ascension.* (CD)

St. Germain. *Meditation to the Angels.* (CD)

# Bibliography

Bell, Craig S. *Comprehending Coincidence—Synchronicity and Personal Transformation.* West Chester, Pennsylvania: Chrysalis Books, 2000.

Craze, Richard. *Graphology.* London: Headway, Hodder, and Stoughton. 1999

Crescimbene, Simonetta. *Egypt.* Cairo, Egypt: Ark, 1996.

Friedman, Norman. *Bridging Science and Spirit.* Eugene, Oregon: The Woodbridge Group, 1990.

Holzer, Hans. *Psychic—True Paranormal Experiences.* New York: Smithmark Publishing, 1999.

Kushner, Harold. *When Bad Things Happen to Good People.* New York: Avon Books, 1981.

North, Anthony. *The Supernatural—A Guide to Mysticism and the Occult.* London: MPG Books, 1998.

Pierson, George. *What's in a Number?* New York: Abbeville Press, 1996.

Pollack, Rachel. *The Complete Illustrated Guide to Tarot.* Boston: Element Books, 1999.

Schwartz, Gary E. *The Afterlife Experiments.* New York: Simon and Schuster, 2002.

### Audios

Listed are a few CD's that kept me sane on this project.

*Adiemus—Songs of Sanctuary.* Caroline Records, Inc. New York.

*Enya—The Memory of Trees.* Warner Records. UK.

*Evita—Music from the Motion Picture.* Warner Brothers. US.

*Santana.* Sony Records. New York.

*Titanic—Music from the Motion Picture.* Sony Music. Hollywood, CA.

# Glossary

**art**: skill acquired by experience, study, or observation; a branch of learning.

**astrology**: the study of the supposed influences of the stars and planets on human affairs and terrestrial events by their positions and aspects; study of the heavenly bodies (Greek meaning), "as above, so below." Astrology is seen as a form of guidance through life, and offers indications, not defined predictions.

**aura photography**: photographing of a distinctive atmosphere, or luminous radiation surrounding a given source; based on principles of Semyon Kirlian, a Russian electrician.

**BCE and CE**: comparable to B.C. and A.D., Before the Common Era, and Common Era.

BCE and CE are references commonly found in Jewish texts.

**channel**: a conduit for contacting the deceased. Channeling is thought to involve "possession" of the channeler by other entities when the channeler is in a trance state.

**clairaudience**: the power or faculty of hearing something not present to the ear but regarded as having objective reality.

**clairsentience**: responsive to, or conscious of sense impressions; aware, knowing.

**clairvoyance**: the power or faculty of discerning objects not present to the senses; ability to perceive matters beyond the range of ordinary perception.

**coincidence**: "a surprising concurrence of events, perceived as meaningfully related, with no apparent causal connection."

**divination**: the art or practice that seeks to foresee or foretell future events or discover hidden knowledge usually by the interpretation of omens or by the aid of supernatural powers; unusual insight; intuitive perception.

**dowse or dowsing**: refers to bodily reactions observed when using a dowsing instrument such as rods or a pendulum. Many times indicated by increased blood pressure or higher pulse rates over a reaction zone (force fields of an unknown nature); refers to the response of plants, animals, and the human body in relation to these force fields. The art of dowsing traditionally was used to find water and lost objects. Today it is also used to tune into a "higher consciousness" to ask questions and receive responses through the dowser's heightened senses.

**Feng Shui:** ancient Chinese art of creating harmony and balance in the home and business environment through the physical surroundings (furniture, décor, etc.). The words literally mean "wind and water." Feng Shui is practiced throughout the world today and is thought to attract prosperity and success for those who employ it.

**graphology:** the study of handwriting, especially for the purpose of character analysis.

*I Ching:* the Chinese *Book of Changes* that formed the very center of spirituality in China. It is one of the fundamental books of Confucianism, and is over 3,000 years old. The symbols used in divination are thought to be 5,000 years old. The *I Ching* is the most spiritual resource and oracle in Asia. Popularity has spread to Europe and the Americas.

**intuition:** immediate apprehension or cognition; the power or faculty of attaining to direct knowledge or cognition without evident rational thought and inference.

**Kabbalah:** the most influential stream of Jewish mysticism; also: Cabala, Cabbala(h), Qabala.

**karma:** the force generated by a person's actions; a belief held in Hinduism and Buddhism to perpetuate transmigration and its ethical consequences to determine his or her destiny in the person's next existence.

**medicine wheel:** large stone circles. The term was first applied to the Big Horn Medicine Wheel in Wyoming. The formation is a central cairn (rock pile) surrounded by a circle of stones. Lines of cobbles link the central cairn. The structure resembles a wagon wheel. The "medicine" part of the name refers to its religious significance to the Native Peoples.

**meditate:** to engage in contemplation or reflection; to plan or project in the mind.

**medium:** a go-between or intermediary for communication between the earthly world and the world of spirits.

**mysticism:** the experience of mystical union or direct communion with the ultimate reality reported by mystics. The belief that direct knowledge of God, spiritual truth, or ultimate reality can be obtained through subjective experiences such as intuition or insight.

**numerology:** the study of the occult (hidden) significance of numbers.

**Ouija** (trademark): used for a board with the alphabet and other signs on it. The board is used with a planchette to seek spiritualistic or telepathic messages.

**palmistry:** the art or practice of reading a person's character or future from the markings on his or her palm.

**paranormal:** not scientifically explainable: supernatural.

**past life regression:** also known as PLR and refers to journeying into one's past lives while under hypnosis.

**psychic:** sensitive to nonphysical or supernatural influences and forces: marked by extraordinary or mysterious sensitivity, perception, or understanding.

**psychometry:** divination of facts concerning an object or its owner through contact with or proximity to the object.

**Reiki** (ray-key): Universal Life Energy. Laying-on-of-hands technique that addresses body, mind, and spirit to bring about balance and wholeness. Reiki is of ancient Buddhist origins, but is not a religion. It was rediscovered by the monk Mikao Usui in Japan in the 1800's.

**reincarnation:** a rebirth of a soul in a new human body.

**religion:** a personal set or institutionalized system of religious attitudes, beliefs, and practices.

**Rider-Waite:** the world's most popular and recognized Tarot deck, designed by Arthur Edward Waite and painted by Pamela Coleman Smith. The name "Rider" comes from its original publisher, and was initially published in 1910.

**rune stones:** comes from the word *runa* meaning "secret discussion" (ca. 1685). Rune stones depict any of the characters of several alphabets used by the Germanic peoples from about the 3rd to 13th centuries, and are often associated with mystery and magic.

**science:** a knowledge covering general truths or the operation of general laws especially as obtained through scientific method; systematized knowledge as an object of study.

**Seven Rays:** refers to the divine qualities of the absolute, or the fundamental Divine energies behind life in the universe. The concept originated in the ancient Vedic literature of India and was introduced to the West by Madame Blavatsky.

**skepticism:** the doctrine that true knowledge or knowledge in a particular area is uncertain; a method of suspended judgment, systematic doubt, or criticism characteristic of skeptics.

**Soul:** the immaterial essence, animating principle, or actuating cause of an individual life, the spiritual principle embodied in human beings, all rational and spiritual beings, or the universe.

**spiritualism:** the view that spirit is a prime element of reality; sensitivity or attachment to religious values, or relating to supernatural beings or phenomena.

**synchronic:** synchronicity; derived from the word *synchronous,* meaning happening, existing, or arising at the same time; chronological arrangement of historical events and personages to indicate coincidence or coexistence.

**Tarot:** refers to the art and practice of Tarot reading which uses a deck of 78 cards for the purpose of divination, and uncovering understanding. The deck is believed to have first appeared in the 15th century in Italy and was known as the *tarocchi.* The European cards may have been influenced from similar Islamic cards brought to Europe by the Crusaders from Palestine. As the cards became popular, they attracted condemnation from the church, and were banned. They contained an element of heresy because the cards taught that a person can find truth and salvation through that person's own efforts rather than through help of a priesthood or church. Edicts against the cards also banned board games, dice, and chess. Tarot and chess were two games associated with the nobility.

# About the Author

Hannah Heidi Levy is a graduate of the University of Wisconsin-Madison, and the University of Wisconsin-Oshkosh. She is a licensed clinical social worker and practices in the field of addictions in Madison, Wisconsin. Prior to this work, she worked as a clinical microbiologist for eighteen years and a blood bank supervisor for three years. She has published fiction and nonfiction for various publications, written a weekly newspaper column, and lectured on creative writing at area schools. Her other interests are art, anthropology, antiques, and Greek mythology. She has two sons and two cats, uses her intuition, and tries not to whine.

**Contact information:**
www.hannah-heidi.com
hannah-heidi@att.net

## About the Office Assistant

Albert immigrated to my home in March of 2002 from the Dane County Humane Society along with his cat friend Bebe. He is 3 years old. His assistance in sitting on every stray page, open book, and pile of papers in my office is noteworthy. His skill in catching bugs on warm summer nights that  somehow got through the window screen...well, let's just say he tried.